THE BOOK OF ALL TERRIERS

The Terrier, from an engraving by Sydenham Edwards, *circa* 1800, and appearing in his *Cynographia Britannica*.

THE BOOK OF
All Terriers

by JOHN T. MARVIN

1964 HOWELL BOOK HOUSE

845 THIRD AVENUE, NEW YORK, N.Y. • 10022

Badger digging with Basset Hounds, *circa* 1560.

To Valerie, my
daughter

Boidheach, a favorite Westie of Colonel E. D. Malcolm. From a painting about 1905.

Acknowledgment

THE preparation of this book has been made even more interesting and enjoyable as a result of the help given me by my many friends in the fancy. I wish especially to thank The American Kennel Club, Mr. John Neff, its Executive Vice-President, and Mr. Arthur Frederick Jones, Editor of *Pure-Bred Dogs—American Kennel Gazette;* Mrs. Frances Wells for material concerning working Sealyham Terriers; Dr. Josephine Duebler for material on the Dandie Dinmont; Mrs. Harry Webb for photographs and background information on the Shelburne and Border Terriers; Mrs. Milton Fox for her work in connection with the chapter on Australian Terriers; Mr. George Pugh for his suggestions as well as for the use of his fine library of books on sporting dogs; Mrs. George Hanning who has been so helpful with the sections on Kerry Blues and Norwich Terriers, and many others who have assisted with information and photographs.

My especial gratitude, and apologies also are due my dear wife who has stood patiently by while I have long been delving into the vagaries of the past. And my debt is hereby acknowledged to David Cook, that young and ardent Terrier enthusiast for his help in typing and re-typing this manuscript.

Contents

Scotch Terriers with cropped ears as depicted by W. R. Smith in 1835.

THE BOOK OF ALL TERRIERS

1

An Introduction
to the Terrier

THE Terriers are among the finest of all our dogs.
They are strong, alert, inquisitive and courageous, friendly and
playful but withal excellent workers. They are endowed with a
degree of hardiness seldom encountered in dogs of other kinds, and
they have a surprising ability to withstand disease. Asleep or awake,
they are alert to unusual sounds and commendably suspicious of
strangers. Their inherent curiosity bespeaks their intelligence, and
their naturally happy temperament denotes their very joy in liv
ing. They are adaptable, too, in fact, they fit into almost any kind
of life and, if properly chosen as to breed, they usually fill the bill.
   Though the many Terrier breeds stem from a common origin,
they do exhibit certain differences. The Scotch and English Terriers, for instance, are as different as Scotsmen are from English-
men. The former are steady and strong albeit perhaps a trifle
dour while the latter are easier to meet but as enduring as their
cousins. Those hailing from Ireland are as Irish as any lad from
County Cork, ready to fight at the drop of a hat, ever ready to
play and to prove their affection.
   It is hoped that this book will explain to fancier and casual
reader alike the Terrier's original background, the course of his
development through many years, and the important role he plays

1

in the congregation of modern purebred dogs. Much has been written about the dog in general and about specific breeds. Early books have stressed the importance of the Sporting dogs and the Hounds. Few have elaborated upon the Terrier. In fact, none of those early literary efforts has mentioned the important part Terriers have played in the development of all breeds and the popularity they enjoy nowadays.

This seems strange since the Terrier is a dog bred for a purpose. The distinct breeds of this day were evolved by crossing various known strains in order to establish the characteristics desired by 19th and 20th century sportsmen who were mainly responsible for their evolution.

This book will attempt to fill the void in canine literature by giving full attention to the Terrier; by scanning the past for first mentions of the strain; by survey of the arts for obvious representations of Terriers, and by documenting available literature so that students of modern breeds may trace their background back to the ever dimming past.

Herein also will be given a detailed study of each of the Terrier breeds together with their derivation and standards of perfection. Changes in standards through the years will be reviewed where relevant to give the newcomer a better understanding for evaluating a given breed today. Authority for much we have written goes to the many authors and students from whose works I have borrowed. In every case credit is given where credit is due so as to enable the reader to authenticate statements and to find the sources readily. Due to the bibliographical nature of certain sections of the treatise the student may follow the pattern I have drawn and delve even more deeply into the interesting composition of the subject.

Naturally, a book written in the 20th century cannot speak with authority about what happened one hundred or more years ago without reference to the works of others. However, every effort has been made to deduce logical conclusions from the mass of accumulated data. Such conclusions may not always conform with those of other authors nor with the conclusions of readers who may have sufficient information to draw their own.

A delineation of the background of Terriers in general and individual breeds in particular is important if we are to keep the several breeds distinct and capable of doing the work for which they were originally bred. Some faddists would change the standards of the breeds because "they are not being used for work any more." While this may be so in most cases, it is not a sufficient reason for modifying or changing completely characteristics that required years to breed true.

It would appear that every Terrier breed was evolved carefully by our knowledgeable forefathers and that the consequent development required years of study and effort. If we consider that the basic factors of individual breeds are of no importance, we will tend to tear down what took centuries to build. For example, a Terrier must have good feet, good teeth and a punishing jaw. He must also possess the attributes required for his particular type of work, namely, proper size, hindquarters, coat quality and temperament. If, to appease the ego of a breeder more interested in beauty than in work, we disregard these in any breed, we do that breed a grave injustice. And if we follow such a course for long without getting back to fundamentals, we will lose the very attributes that have brought admiration.

This book will stress the features that were important a century or more ago and the reasons why they often meant life or death to the dog. We trust that this background will instill in all who read the urge to hold the line and breed for soundness and utility first and beauty second. Without soundness and utility no breed can long hold the high regard of the fancy and the general public.

The unearthing of a fox, 14th century.

2

The Dog of Old

THE dog is the starting point for this book since the dog as an animal of course preceded the Terrier. The dog can be traced as far back as records have been kept. George Louis Buffon (1707–1788) credited the shepherd's dog as the one most nearly approaching the primitive race and shows the Terrier to be descended from the Hound. Buffon's *History of Quadrupeds* was one of his best known works and his geneological table of the different races of dogs influenced many early writers to agree that all dogs were descended from the shepherd dog. His theories have been largely discredited but his proposition that the Hound was the starting point of the Terrier is still sound.

According to *The Complete Dog Book* (1951), the dog is mentioned some forty times in the Old Testament of the Bible which certainly lends antiquity to our canine friend. Ancient and medieval history gave the dog an important and generally esteemed place in the plan of human life.

Representations of dogs have been found carved on slate tablets dating back to 4000 B.C. while excavations have unearthed rock paintings of the Paleolithic Age more than 10,000 years ago. These earliest paintings depicted scenes of the chase in which hunters were accompanied by dogs.

The Egyptians held the dog in great veneration and canine figures carved in relief adorned their temples and tombs. The Romans also treated the dog with great respect and the words *Cave Canem* were frequently engraved above the doors of their abodes warning "Beware of the dog" and indicating beyond doubt that the dog was domesticated at the time. Ancient kings and princes offered dogs as highly prized gifts to their contemporaries in other states. In fact as recorded by W. Youatt in his book, *The Dog* (1845) only the early Israelites, Mohammedans and Hindus did not hold the dog in veneration—these peoples considered dogs unclean and seldom permitted them in their homes. As time progressed, however, even this aversion disappeared and today we find the dog beloved by all.

Specific writings which mention the dog with a purpose go back many centuries. The Bible depicts the dog as a watch animal (Isaiah 56:10) and as a shepherd's helper in guarding the flocks (Job 30:1). Early books on sports mention in detail the dogs used in the chase since the sport of hunting was always the pleasure of kings. Two such early writings are *La Chace du Cerf*, (*circa* 1250), and Twici's *Art de Venerie*, (*circa* 1320).

Allegorical history is full of dog stories and Aesop, famous for has fables, used the dog freely as the central figure in many of his tales. *The Dog and His Shadow* is one of the most famous of these. Heroic literature is also replete with complimentary references to dogs. Homer's *Odyssey* describes the return of Ulysses with emphasis on the fidelity and peculiar ability of the dog Argus, which recognized his master after many years of absence.

With such a background, it is small wonder that the canine and human races have such strong ties. Dog and man have always been inseparable companions with reciprocal affection that exists between no other animal and man. Lord Byron said it in a few words:

> *The poor dog: in life the firmest friend,*
> *The first to welcome, foremost to defend;*
> *Whose honest heart is still his master's own;*
> *Who labours, fights, lives, breathes for him alone.*

Sir Walter Scott offered a more elaborate, if no more touching, eulogy when he wrote: "The Almighty, who gave the dog to be the companion of our pleasures and our toils, hath invested him with a nature noble and incapable of deceit. He forgets neither friend nor foe, remembers, with accuracy, both benefit and injury. He hath a share of man's intelligence, but no share of man's falsehood. You may bribe an assassin to slay a man, or a witness to take his life by false accusation, but you cannot make a dog tear his benefactor. He is the friend of man, save when man justly incurs his enmity."

These are but two of innumerable quotations that pay homage to the dog.

To obtain a better insight into the canine race, the zoological ranking and biological background of the animal are of interest. The dog belongs to that division of quadrupeds termed *Vertebrata* and it ranks in the class *Mammalia* because the female suckles her young. It is of the tribe *Unguiculata* since it is armed with non-retractile nails or claws, and is of the order of *Digitigrades* because it walks on its toes. The dog is of the genus *Canis* in view of its tooth arrangement, and belongs to the sub-genus *Familiaris* due to the round shape of the eye pupil which distinguishes the dog from the wolf, fox and jackal.

Members of the genus *Canis* are basically carnivorous animals. The dog is equipped for a meat diet with an excellent set of forty-two teeth, including twelve incisors (small front teeth) adapted for cutting and seizing; four canines (the long, pointed tusks or fangs) which are for tearing, stabbing, or "fixing" the struggling prey, and twenty-six premolars and molars (the broader, heavier back teeth which have generally flat, complex crowns) used as grinders for crushing food. The milk or puppy teeth are fewer in number since certain of the molars and premolars have no predecessors. In general, the permanent teeth begin to replace the puppy teeth at about four months of age.

The dog tears food and often bolts large pieces which the stomach is capable of digesting. The intestines are of medium length between the short ones of the true carnivores and the long ones of graminivorous animals. Thus, the dog can digest diverse foods, including grains and vegetables, in addition to meat and, therefore, can thrive on mixed diets.

The dog's use to man has been enhanced by man's own ingenuity. The first printed listing of dog types or breeds catalogs fourteen different kinds. These were used mostly for hunting,

Early type bull-and-terrier dog, from a painting, *Low Life*, by H. S. Beckwith after Landseer, 1829.

herding and related activities. This number increased slowly as man found additional functions in which the dog proved useful. By 1873 some forty breeds were on the schedule, while in 1929 the American Kennel Club indexed ninty-three breeds.

Today, the AKC recognizes 115 distinct and separate breeds. This tremendous increase in types or breeds of dogs demonstrates the usefulness of the animal.

The increased number of breeds has been caused in part by the greater specialization required of dogs and by the fact that breeders wanted to produce specimens true to a fixed type. For example, whereas a single Spaniel was known in the 14th century, dogs of this strain varied widely in size and speed. As time progressed and the need arose, sportsmen began to breed large ones and small ones specifically to fill their needs and when the type was set after many years, a new breed was born.

The same was true of Terriers. In early times Terriers were all classed as a single breed and came in a wide variety of sizes, coats and colors. Then sportsmen began to show greater preference for the special abilities of certain dogs. Different strains were evolved slowly for use under different conditions of prey and terrain. Such strains, which became distinct breeds after many years of effort, frequently bore the name of their habitat, work or breeder.

Darwin explained the derivation of breeds lucidly and his words bear repetition. He said, "A breed, like a dialect of language, can hardly be said to have a distinct origin. A man preserves and breeds from an individual with some slight deviation of structure, or takes more care than usual in mating his best animals and thus improves them, and the improved animals slowly spread in the immediate neighborhood. But they will as yet hardly have a distinct name, and from being slightly valued, their history will have been disregarded. When further improved by the same slow and gradual process, they will be spread more widely and will be recognized as something distinct and valuable, and will then probably first receive a provincial name. In semi-civilized countries with little free communication, the spreading of a new sub-breed would be a slow process. As soon as the points of value are once acknowledged, the principle, as I have called it, of unconscious selection will always tend—perhaps more at one period than at another according to the state of civilization of the inhabitants—slowly to add to the characteristic features of the breed, whatever it may be. But the chances will be infinitely small of any record having been preserved of such slow, varying and insensible changes."

This excerpt offers a plausible explanation of the many reasons why the background of most breeds is obscure and why the many claims of the more enthusiastic and uninformed proponents thereof are often misleading and unsupported by the few and hazy facts available.

This is the basic background of the dog. No detailed history has been offered since this may be found in other books that are accurate and complete. This work is directed to the Terrier and this branch of the canine family will be examined critically in the chapters to follow.

3

Terriers Through the 18th Century

THE Terrier is a dog that goes to ground. The name comes from the Latin, *terra*, meaning earth; the dog is therefore an earth dog that digs and hunts beneath the ground. Little reference to the Terrier can be found in early writings on sporting efforts. Probably the medieval sportsmen had dogs for the purpose but failed to give credit because the early Terriers were probably classed as small Hounds that went to ground.

An early reference to what might have been a Terrier will be found in Oppian's poems of the second century. Here a dog, referred to as a Hound, was described as "small, rough and crooked-legged." Since Terriers were originally classified as Hounds it is possible that the reference was to Terriers. In all fairness, however, it is pointed out that the Basset Hound of various sizes was also known at the time and the reference may have been directed to a rough-coated Basset Hound.

One of the very first mentions of the Terrier strain is found in Gace de la Vigne's *Poème Sur la Chasse* (*circa* 1359):

> *Le va querir dedans terre*
> *Avec ses bons chiens terriers*
> *Que on met dedans le terrier.*

This may be translated literally as follows:

9

He goes to seek in the earth
With the good terrier dogs
That they put in the burrow.

This translation substitutes "burrow" for "terrier" in the last line since, in early English "terrier," borrowed from the French, also meant "the burrow of an earth animal" such as a badger, fox, etc.

Early works of art offer some interesting conjectural background. One of the earliest of them is a carving found on an ancient Egyptian monument, a copy of which is depicted in George Rawlinson's *History of Ancient Egypt* (1881). Here a kind of fox dog is shown. The dog has small, upright ears very similar to those of a Terrier and a relatively short tail carried well up. The dog looks more like a Terrier than a Hound.

Another even more pertinent reference is an engraving entitled *The Unearthing of a Fox,* found in a manuscript in the Royal Library. This piece dates back to the early 14th century and is the first known representation of Terrier work. It shows smooth-coated dogs, not unlike Greyhounds in make, with three men engaged in unearthing a fox depicted as running from the scene. The reproduction pictured here was found in Joseph Strutt's *The Sports and Pastimes of the People of England* (1801). Blaine's *An Encyclopedia of Rural Sports* (1840) shows a similar picture but the author has converted the dogs to wire-haired or long-coated varieties.

Since basically the Terrier is of British origin a mass of early data concerning the strain is contained in English literature dealing with sports. Thus the first known listing of different breeds or strains of dog that embrace the Terrier is found in the *Boke of St. Albans* printed in 1486 and originally credited to Dame Juliana Berners although the second edition in 1496 included much of the work of Wynkyn de Worde. The listing reads:

Firft ther is a Grehownde, a Baftard, a Mengrell, a Maftyfe, a Lemor, a Spanyell. Rachys, Kenettys. Teroures. Bocheris houndes. Muddyng dogges. Tryndeltayles and Prikherid curris and fmale ladies popis that beere a Way the flees and dyue ris fmale fawlis.

Hubbard, in his *Introduction to the Literature of British Dogs* (1949) says that "Tryndeltayles were probably long-tailed sheepdogs similar to Collies or Welsh sheepdogs." Mongrels and other uncomplimentary names denote dogs of casual lineage.

Many of the breeds noted are still recognized such as the Greyhound, Mastiff, Spaniel and Terrier. This catalog of breeds became a well known classification and was used by Shakespeare when he introduced dogs into his *King Lear* in 1606. In this play (Act III, Scene VI, 1.71) the Bard sets forth "Mastiff, greyhound, mongrel grim, Hound or spaniel, brach or lym; or bobtail tike or trundle tail."

In 1570, Dr. Johannes Caius gave to the world one of the first books devoted solely to dogs. Printed in Latin, this was a relatively short treatise entitled *De Canibus Britannicis*. The contents resulted from research done by Caius for his friend Conrad Gesner, the naturalist who published much of it as a part of his monumental work *Historia Animalium* in 1553.

De Canibus Britannicis contains a great deal of information about British dogs of the day. Caius was an extremely well educated man, for many years chief physician to three British monarchs, the last being Queen Elizabeth. His research was so well done and thorough that the statements in his book carry a degree of authority. Caius was the first to classify the several known breeds or strains into groupings according to their temperament and use. In the 1570 edition of his work, the following is found:

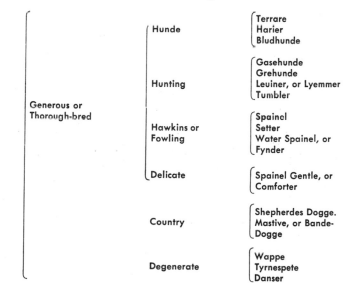

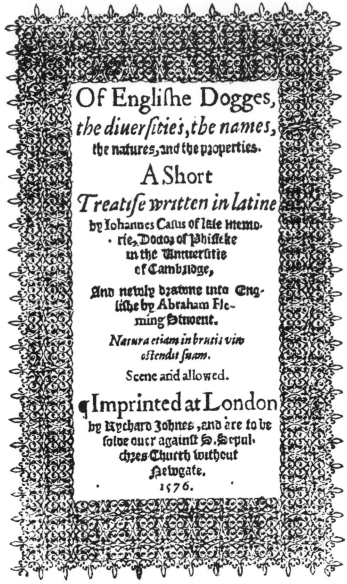

Of Englishe Dogges,
the diuersitie's, the names,
the natures, and the properties.

A Short
Treatise written in latine
by Iohannes Caius of late memo-
rie, Doctor of Phisicke
in the Vniuersitie
of Cambridge,

And newly drawne into Englishe by Abraham Fle-
ming Student.

Natura etiam in brutis vim
ostendit suam.

Seene and allowed.

¶ Imprinted at London
by Rychard Iohnes, and are to be
solde ouer against S. Sepul-
chres Church without
Newgate.
1576.

Of Englishe Dogges. Title page of the first book devoted
to dogs, as printed in English in 1576.

Caius went on to describe the various dogs he had listed. He thought very little of the "country" and "degenerate" kind since these dogs were not valued by gentle folk, being used mainly by tradespeople, farmers and peasants. Caius' description of the Terrier is the first we have which delineates the special abilities of the strain. He classes the dog as a "Fox or Badger Hound," called Terrarii and offers some slight description of the work done beneath the ground by these game dogs.

De Canibus Britannicis was translated and expanded in 1576 by Abraham Fleming, a student and an admirer of Caius. Fleming entitled his book *Of Englishe Dogges* and the enlarged version of the earlier Caius effort became probably the first book devoted exclusively to dogs to be printed in English. In this work, which is still available in reprint form from Howell Book House, the dogs are broadly classified in three groupings as follows:

All Englisfhe Dogges be eyther of,	A gentle kinde, seruing the game,
	A homely kind apt for sundry necessary vses.
	A currishe kinde, meete for many toyes.

Fleming elaborates further upon the "gentle kinde" which, according to his classification, were dogs "seruing y' pastime of hunting beastes." The book reads as follows:

| Dogges seruing y' pastime of hunting beastes. | are divided into | Hariers Terrars Bloudhounds Gasehounds Grehounds Leulners or Lyemmers Tumblers Stealers | In Latine called Venatici |

The homely kind include the "country dogs" leaving the "currishe kinde" to the ill-fated Turnspits, Wapps and Dancers. The adjectives "gentle," "homely" and "currishe" were used to separate the breeds into stations of association and, as in the case of Caius, indicated the caste of the owner who would have or use such a dog.

The Fleming book was an important milestone in the literature dealing with dogs. It included most of the meat of Caius' original

13

work with a great deal of additional material. Furthermore, the book was printed in English which made it more easily digested and left a greater impact upon English-speaking people.

Fleming's treatise offered additional information on the Terriers. He classed them among the "perfect smelling group" and the smallest of the Hounds. Fleming follows Caius with the statement that the Terrier is a Fox or Badger Hound only and, like Caius, he fails to give any detailed description of the appearance of the dog. Fleming followed exactly Caius' description of the work of a Terrier with this very excellent passage:

Of the Dogge Called a Terrar

"Another sorte there is which hunteth the Foxe and the Badger or Greye onely, whom we call Terrars, because they (after the manner and custome of ferrets in searching for Connyes (rabbits), creepe into the grounde, and by that meanes make afrayde, nyppe, and byte the Foxe and the Badger in such sort, that eyther they teare them to peeces with theyr teeth beyng in the bosome of the earth, or else hayle and pull them perforce out of their lurking angles, darke dongeons, and close caves, or at least through conceaved feare, drive them out of their hollow harbours, in so much that they are compelled to prepare speedy flight, and being desirous of the next (albeit not safest) refuge, are otherwise taken and intrapped with snares and nettes layde over holes to the same purpose. But these be the least in that kynde called 'Sagax'."

This description fits well the Terrier of today for any of the many distinct breeds now known. In fact, the Terrier, being basically a dog that goes to ground, was well described almost four centuries ago.

Contemporaneous with *Of Englishe Dogges* was George Turbeville's offering entitled *The Noble Arte of Venerie or Hunting,* published in 1575 but sometimes said to have been published in 1576. Turbeville (1540–1610)—also spelled Turbevile—was an English poet who spent several years of his life in the diplomatic service as secretary in the British Embassy in Russia. He was not well known as a sportsman and, while there is some dispute concerning the originality of portions of his book, it nevertheless enhances our early background material on the Terrier by the following description of the strain. Here is Turbeville's version of hunting for the fox and badger:

Of the Huntinge of the Foxe and Badgerd

"Now to speake of Foxe houndes and Terryers, and how you should enter them to take the Foxe, the Badgerd, and suche like vermine: you muste understand that there are sundrie sortes of Terriers, whereof wee hold opinion that one sorte came out of Flaunders or the low Countries, as Artoys and thereabouts, and they have crooked legges, and are shorte heared moste commonly. Another sorte there is which are shagged and streight legged: those with the crooked legges will take earth better than the other, and are better for the Badgerd, bycause they will lye longer at a vermine: but the others with streyght legges do serve for two purposes, for they wyll Hunte above grounde as well as other houndes, and enter the earthe with more furie than the others: but they will not abide so long, bycause they are too eagre in fight, and therefore are constreyned to come out to take the ayre: there are both good and badde of bothe sortes."

Much of Turbeville's writting in *The Noble Arte of Venerie and Hunting* was based upon an earlier work by Jacques du Fouilloux, a French author who wrote *La Venerie* (*circa* 1560). Some say that Turbeville's book was merely a free translation of the Fouilloux effort while at least one editor, Richard Blome, in *The Gentleman's Recreation* (1686) indicated the Turbeville work as being "stuft with more Errors than Truths." Whatever the truth about the book, it must be admitted that it offers some very interesting thoughts about the Terrier not previously advanced.

Turbeville's description of the Terrier was of considerable moment for several reasons, the most important of which was the notice that "there are sundrie sortes of Terriers." This statement was elaborated upon by the descriptions of two "sortes," a long-legged and a more desirable "crooked legged" kind. These two types of Terriers were generally short- and long-haired varieties respectively. Turbeville displayed common sense when he concluded the description by stating "there are both good and badde of both sortes."

Since Caius had already classed the Terrier with the Hound, it is

15

easy to reason that the crooked-legged, generally smooth-coated Terrier of Turbeville had consanguinity with the progenitors of the present-day Basset and Dachshund. This reasoning is well supported by a woodcut reproduced in Jacques du Fouilloux's book which shows dogs and men digging the badger. These dogs resemble the Basset Hound more closely than the Terrier since they have heavy, large and pendulous ears and they must have lacked voice since they are wearing collars with bells to note their progress in the earth. Du Fouilloux describes them as crooked-legged with short coats and also mentions a second variety with straight legs and heavy coats like the Barbet, a small Poodle type. He liked the crooked-legged variety better because of its staying power although mention is made that the straight-legged kind ran better with the Hounds as would be expected. He also concludes "There are good and bad ones of both species."

Undoubtedly, these ground-going Bassets were crossed with dogs of Terrier blood which explains the heavy, low-set ears of the Dandie Dinmont and Bedlington Terriers. Croxton Smith, in his article on Basset Hounds found in *Drury's British Dogs* (3rd ed., 1903), states unequivocally that, "One *cannot* breed Hounds from Terriers, whereas one *can* breed Terriers from Hounds." He further brings the small Basset into close relationship with the Dachhund Terrier. The only explanation of the infusion of the Basset or Dachshund blood into the Terrier breeds is by the invasion of the French and German breeds that were companions of itinerant gypsies who went back and forth between the countries. This hypothesis is supported by Stonehenge and Gray in later works of authority.

Turbeville and du Fouilloux both offered interesting and explicit instructions of considerable similarity for the training of the earth dogs. Turbeville's teachings, which follow and are a bit gory for today's consumption, offer insight into the temper of the times. Many later authors have used substantially the same words for a like purpose:

"And bycause it is a good pastime, and brave fight, without great payne or travayle to the huntesman, therefore I have thought good to set downe here some preceptes for the entryng of Terryers, and for the better fleshyng and encouragyng of them.

"You shall beginne to enter them as soone as they be eyght or tenne moneths old: for if you enter not a Terryer before he be a yeare old, you hardly ever make him take the earth. And you must take good heede that you encourage them."

This "entering" was best accomplished as follows:

> And whin you have taken the old Foxes or Bagerds,
> And that there is nothing left in the earth but the young cubbes,
> Take out all your old Terryers and encourage them, crying,
> 'To him, to him, to him': and if they take any young cubbe
> Lette them take theyre pleasure of him,
> and kill him within the grounde;
> And beware that the earth fall not downe upon them and smother them.
> That done, take all the rest of the cubbes and Bagerd pigges home
> With you, and frie theyre livers and theyre bloud with cheese
> And some of theyre own greace,
> And thereof make your Terryers a rewarde,
> Shewyng them alwayes the heads and skynnes to encourage them.

This description of training was well supported by a later author, Nicholas Cox, in his *Gentleman's Recreation* (1677) where he stated, "There are two sorts of Terriers—one with legs more or less crooked and with short coats while the other are straighter in leg and have long jackets. . . ." Cox was also an advocate of different types of Hounds for every chase. This indicated that there was a deficiency in the abilities of available stock and that one type could work better than another for a given purpose. It carried the implication that Terriers also had their shortcomings and thus heralded the separation of the strain into several and distinct breeds each with a purposeful duty and ability.

The *Sportsman's Dictionary or The Country Gentleman's Companion* (London 1735) included a more concise but equally broad generalization on the Terrier and the training of Terriers with the following:

Dandie Dinmont and his Terriers, after a painting by Gourlay Steele, *circa* 1865.

"Terrier, a kind of hound used only, or chiefly for hunting the fox or badger; so-called, because he creeps into the ground, as the ferrets do in the coney burrows (rabbit warrens), and there nips and bites the fox and badger either tearing them in pieces with his teeth, or else hauling and pulling them by force out of their lurking holes; or at least driving them out of their hollow harbours, to be taken by net, or otherwise. The Huntsmen have commonly a couple of terriers, to the end they may put in a fresh one, as occasion serves, to relieve the other."

This description which reads somewhat like a condensation of the original Caius effort varies only in the definite statement that the Terrier is a kind of Hound thereby offering some possible clarification of Turbeville's alternate use of the terms: Foxhounds and Terriers. In other words, the Foxhound at that time probably meant a Terrier that went to ground for fox.

In 1774, Oliver Goldsmith added the desirability of "voice" to the Terrier attributes. He wrote:

18

"The terrier is a small kind of hound, with rough hair, made use of to force the fox and badger out of their holes; or rather to give notice *by their barking* in what part of their kennel the fox or badger resides, when the sportsmen intend to dig them out."

Goldsmith recognized that a Terrier without tongue was no Terrier at all. He was the first since Fleming to appreciate that Terriers do not always make a kill. Fleming mentioned that the Terrier may drive the prey out of the hole whence it can be taken in a net, and Goldsmith added to this the use of voice to tell the sportsman in what part of the burrow the predator was holed up. Barking was here recognized as a very important adjunct of a Terrier's equipment and this reference was the first to set forth specifically that Terriers can be used to hold the prey at bay within the burrow while the hunters dig him out.

Buffon added to this meagre background by his rather terse definition of the Terrier. It read, "A small thickset hound, of which there are two varieties, the one with short legs, long back, and commonly of a black or yellowish colour, mingled with white; the other more sprightly in appearance, with a shorter body, and the colour reddish brown or black. It has a most acute sense of smelling, and an inveterate enmity to all kinds of vermin. Nor is it excelled by any Dog in quality of courage. It will encounter even the badger with the utmost bravery, though it often receives severe wounds in the contest, which however, it bears with unshrinking fortitude. As it is very expert in forcing foxes and other game out of their coverts, and is particularly hostile to the fox, it is generally an attendant on every pack of hounds; in which case the choice of the huntsman is not directed by the size of the animal, but by its strength and power of endurance."

This writing gives two interesting facts to consider. It offers a rather good description of black-and-tan Terriers and also the old Scotch Terrier, and it mentions the use of the Terrier with a Foxhound wherein size is of no great moment to the author. Since this was written during the latter part of the 18th century, it adds useful information to the facts surrounding the Terrier and its evolution into separate breeds.

This was the background of the Terrier prior to 1800. A composite and general picture of the dog as described by the many authors and artists brings us a small sort of Hound with either smooth or rough coat of many colors, with straight or crooked legs and good voice. Above everything the Terrier should have courage and persistence. The size of the dog must be sufficiently small to enable him to crawl into either a fox or badger den.

No statement or suggestion can be found in any of these early treatises of any definite breed. In fact, the background of the Terriers was quite varied and included the blood of many kinds of dogs according to the desires of the breeder. One point stands out, however: the Terrier was known before the first mention of the strain in the previously noted Gace de la Vigne's *Poème Sur la Chasse*, about 1359, a long, long time ago.

Out of this rather confused picture, it is not difficult to see a definite plan of breeding beginning to emerge. The short-coated, straight-legged dogs of reddish brown or black color were undoubtedly the forerunner of the Manchester Terrier, while the white ones with smooth and heavy coats and shorter backs have the requirements of the Old English White Terrier, a precursor of the Fox Terrier's two varieties. The Scotch branch of the Terrier family can be recognized in the crooked-legged, generally long-backed, little dogs that had such fine staying power. As noted in later chapters, the various strains or breeds began to stabilize because of the desires of the sportsmen. These trends have an interesting history.

> *Body and limb go cold,*
> *Both foot and hand go bare;*
> *God send teroures, so bold, so bold,*
> *Heart will harbour no care.*

Dr. Still—1543

Fox dog, from Rawlinson's *History of Ancient Egypt.*

4

Emergence of the Breeds

DESPITE claims made by writers who champion the antiquity of several of today's Terrier breeds, years of careful research have failed to disclose a single reference to any reproducible breed prior to 1800. In fact, the only deviations from the earliest descriptions are variations noted as to coat, size and legs.

Gerald Massey, one of the greatest living authorities on canine literature, has made a similar observation. Mr. Massey's highly respected articles on various phases of dog art and literature are fully documented. And so let those of us who are truly interested in any Terrier breed realize that the strain, bred for a purpose, may be hundreds of years old, but that no given breed can lay claim to these early beginnings in preference to any other.

The 19th century brought a new approach to the art of breeding dogs. Fanciers and sportsmen were more aware of the special abilities of certain strains and, in an effort to perpetuate them and improve the abilities of individuals, they began to use great care in their breeding programs. This resulted in the emergence of separate and distinct breeds among the Terrier strains to replace the hitherto hit-or-miss type of breeding. This development did not occur quickly. The trend, however, was apparent after the turn of the century as gradually more and more strains became reproducible.

Possibly one of the most important books published during the early years of the 19th century was the *Cynographia Britannica* by Sydenham Edwards. It consisted of colored engravings of the different dog breeds existing in Great Britain, drawn from life with observations on their properties and uses. The book was published in parts scheduled to appear every three months, but unfortunately it was never fully completed. Today it is one of the rarest and most important of all early dog books.

The title page states: "Dogs have always been the ready and affectionate servants of men, are excellent companions when human society is wanting, and are the faithful and incorruptible guardians of their master's person and property. Dogs are honest creatures, they never fawn on those they love not, and I'm a friend to dogs."

Published in London in 1800, this was the first illustrated English dog book and only the second printed in the English language to be devoted entirely to dogs. Other writings, mentioned heretofore were books of a sporting nature dealing with sundry subjects and including passing reference to the dog. Edwards was a contemporary and competitor of William Taplin whose *Sportsman's Cabinet* was published as a monthly magazine. Possibly this was one reason why Edwards' effort did not reach its full promise.

Since Edwards was a talented artist, the colored plates in his work are invaluable as guides of the times. His section on the Terrier is interesting, and instructive also because of the engraving showing five Terriers. One, the Manchester, was recognizable as a purebred specimen and, according to Massey, this plate was the first to show a definite variety of Terrier. The other four probably depicted the now extinct White English Terrier, a Bedlington, a Scotch Terrier of Skye or Cairn type and a working-type Fox Terrier that looked more like a Jack Russell Terrier than anything else. This book is very useful to present-day researchers. It is indeed a pity that it is so scarce and that no one has republished the work for the benefit of fancier, student and sportsman.

Following closely on the heels of the *Cynographia Britannica* came the Rev. William B. Daniel's rather large work *Rural Sports* (1801–1813). This writing covered the whole field of sporting subjects including their legal phases. The portions covering dogs were varied in character and those covering Hounds were quite useful. The Terrier portions were not scholarly and did not reflect what

22

Scotch Terrier about 1840.

Scotch Terrier, Vixen, 1821.

Skye Terrier, about 1840.

Dandie Dinmont Terrier, 1842.

English working Terriers, 1803, from the Sportsman's Cabinet.

was known of the strain at that time. This statement is supported by the works of Edwards and Taplin which had their beginning about the same time and which showed a greater knowledge and more sympathetic approach to the subject.

Daniel implied that the Terrier of the day lacked voice by the suggestion that "a collar of bells" be hung around the Terrier's neck to help trace his progress within the earth. Such equipment which have been a nuisance and a deterrent to any Terrier worthy of the name harks back to the Bassets of du Fouilloux. *Rural Sports* suggested that Terriers were a motley assortment of dogs of various sizes with preference expressed for large dogs to run with the Hounds, although Daniel expressed some understandable concern that these larger dogs would not be of much use underground. He was somewhat sensitive to color and preferred the black or red-and-white dogs since those of "reddish color" were often mistaken for a fox by "awkward people." The Daniel description of a Terrier is interesting if not enlightening and certainly not indicative of any substantial progress, so far as Daniel was concerned.

"The breed of Terriers was recommended to be from a Beagle and Mongrel Mastiff or from any small thick-skinned dog that had courage, which two articles of Coat and Courage proceeded from the Cur, and giving mouth from the Beagle . . ." He then goes on to give suggestions for training young Terriers which appear to have been adapted from Turbeville or du Fouilloux.

The next work of importance and one with some authority was the aforementioned *Sportsman's Cabinet* (1803–04). Here was another large work on sporting subjects with some emphasis on the dog. Taplin offered the best written description of the Terrier to that date. His delineation included many physical attributes not heretofore suggested by other writers and thus helped set the stage for the many breeds to follow. He said:

"Terriers of the best blood, and most determined ferocity, are now, by the prevalence of fashion, bred of all colours, red, black (with tanned faces, flanks, feet, and legs), and brindled sandy; some few brown, pied, white pied, and pure white; as well as one sort rough and wire-haired, the other soft, smooth and delicate, the latter not much inferior in courage to the former, but the rough wire-haired breed is the most severe biter of the two. And this breed

24

has been enlarged, and repeatedly crossed in-and-in with the bull-dog for the favourite sport of badger-baiting with the lower classes, that they are increased in size, strength, and stimulus for that particular purpose, since the more inhuman practise of bull-baiting has been on the decline.

"The genuine and lesser breed of terrier is still preserved uncon-taminated amongst the superior order of sportsmen, and con-stantly employed in a business to which his name, his size, his forti-tude, perservering strength, and invincible ardour all become so characteristically and truly subservient, that he may justly be said 'to labour cheerfully in his vocation.' This is in his emulous and exulting attendance upon the fox-hounds, where like the most dignified and distinguished personage in a public profession, though *last*, he is not the *least* in consequence. Since the truly ecstatic and exhilarating sport of fox-hunting is so deservedly and universally popular in every country where it can be enjoyed, these sagacious, faithful, courageous little animals have become so high in estimation, that few stables of the independent are to be seen without them."

Taplin goes on to relate that Terriers for fox hunting are of a very particular kind, well-bred and superior in their qualifications. "Size is not so indispensable as strength, but invincible fortitude must be equal to both. The black, and black-tanned, or rough wire-haired pied are preferred, as those of a reddish colour are some-times—halloo'd off as a fox." Foxhunting is the major sport for the Terrier according to Taplin but "In addition to their superior and more dignified office with the hounds, they become eminently use-ful in the inferior, but entertaining sports of badger-hunting, badger-baiting, rat-catching, vermin-killing, and other pursuits in which their owners are frequently employed."

From this portion of the *Sportsman's Cabinet* it is apparent that the Terrier had progressed quite a way from the dog mentioned by Daniel as a cross between a "Beagle and a Mongrel Mastiff." Even though these two books were almost contemporary, Taplin appre-ciated breeding and stressed that sportsmen bred with care to gain the attributes they desired. His description of the "genuine" Ter-rier is a beautiful tribute to the dog and its abilities.

The description of the Terrier offered some sound information on the early development of different breeds. Here we have rough-and smooth-coated dogs of various colors and textures of coat. Since the book is English in background and stressed the English varieties of Terrier, it is not difficult to envisage the beginnings of the Fox Terrier, Manchester, Bull Terrier, etc.

In spite of the definitive work of Edwards and Taplin, identification of the several breeds by name was not forthcoming for several years. Possibly this was because no book devoted entirely to dogs was published during the period. Sporting authors, who included chapters on dogs in their frequent works, very likely copied from their predecessors with minor variations, sometimes more harmful than helpful. A few books appeared indicating complete ignorance on the part of the authors that Terrier varieties had progressed at all and some went way back to Caius' description for their definition.

First mention of a definite breed of Terrier did not come until about 1815. This was when Sir Walter Scott drew attention to Dandie Dinmont in his novel *Guy Mannering,* second of the Waverly series and published about 1815. In this book Dandie Dinmont of Charlieshope is introduced as owner of several small and distinctive Terriers by the names of "Auld Pepper," "Auld Mustard," "Young Pepper," "Young Mustard," "Little Pepper" and "Little Mustard." These Terriers, which he had "a' regularly entered, first wi'rottens, then wi'stots or weasels," he said, "fear naething that ever cm' wi'a hairy skin on't."

Dandie Dinmont was said to be in real life a Mr. James Davidson of Hindlee who was known to own Terriers of the stamp noted. There is some controversy regarding this point. Some say Scott never met Davidson until some time after *Guy Mannering* was written. Charles Cook intimates the opposite. Whatever the facts, it is admitted by most historians that Dandie Dinmont bore a strong resemblance to the Hindlee store-farmer and that the dogs were accurately described. Thus, although Scott did not name the breed precisely, he called it Dandie Dinmont's Terriers, and the name eventually rubbed off onto the breed. For this reason it is difficult to say that the Dandie is the first breed to carry a distinct name, but it is certainly a fact that dogs of the Dandie type were known and well established at the time.

In 1822, Pierce Egan in his *Annals of Sporting* alluded to a specific dog as a "Bullterrier." This general type of Terrier had been known for many years as a fighting dog; it was previously referred to as a "Bull and Terrier" dog, a name suggested by the breeding technique used to produce the strain. The use by Egan of the term "Bullterrier" was accepted by others almost immediately and it thus became the first breed name known today to be widely used in the early days of the 19th century.

Thomas Brown in 1829 brought out his excellent work, *Biographical Sketches and Authentic Anecdotes of Dogs,* the first dog book to be published in Scotland. This book, by its Terrier definition, initiated another development in the chain of events that helped to identify the several Terrier breeds by name according to their type. Brown's definition was of great value since it included a breakdown of the general term Terrier into Scotch and English branches of the family. Each of these broad categories had been noted by previous authors as nameless varieties of the breed class of Terriers but no one had deemed it expedient to name the species according to habitat and land of origin. Brown further divided the Scotch branch into three additional varieties whereby four well defined species or breeds were named. His definitions were so important that they bear verbatim repetition as follows:

"It is now impossible to trace the origin of the terrier, but from the many characteristics peculiar to itself, we would almost be induced to consider it a primitive race. Certain it is, that this dog has been for many ages assiduously cultivated and trained to the particular sports to which nature seems to have so well adapted him. To the fox, hare, rabbit, badger, polecat, weasel, rat, mouse, and all other kinds of vermin, he is a most implacable enemy; he has also a strong natural antipathy to the domestic cat.

"The name terrier seems to be derived from the avidity with which he takes the earth in pursuit of all those animals which burrow.

"There are two kinds of terriers: the rough haired Scotch and the smooth English. The Scotch terrier is certainly the purest in point of breed, and the English seems to have been produced by a cross from him.

"The Scotch terrier (*Canis terrarius*, variety A.) is generally low in stature, seldom more than twelve or fourteen inches in height, with a strong muscular body and short and stout legs; his ears small and half pricked; his head is rather large in proportion to the size of his body, and the muzzle considerably pointed; his scent is extremely acute; so that he can trace the footsteps of all other animals with certainty; he is generally of a sand colour or black; dogs of these colours are certainly the most hardy, and more to be depended upon; when white or pied, it is a sure mark of the impurity of the breed. The hair of the terrier is long, matted, and hard over almost every part of his body. His bite is extremely keen.

"There are three distinct varieties of the Scotch terrier, *viz.*, the one above described; another about the same size as the former, but with the hair much longer and somewhat flowing, which gives his legs the appearance of being very short. This is the prevailing breed of the western islands of Scotland. The third variety is much larger than the former two, being generally from fifteen to eighteen inches in height, with the hair very hard and wiry, and much shorter than that of the others. It is from this breed that the best bull-terriers have been produced.

"This dog, the wire-haired Scotch terrier, is indispensably necessary to a pack of foxhounds, for the purpose of unearthing the game. From the greater length of leg, from his general lightness, and the elegant construction of his body, he is more adapted for running, and of course better enabled to keep up with the pack than the Scotch terrier.

"The terrier, amongst the higher order of sportsmen, is preserved in its greatest purity, and with the most assiduous attention; and it seems of the utmost importance not to increase its size, which would render him unsuitable for the purpose in which he is employed, that of entering the earth to drive out other animals from their burrows, for which his make, strength, and invincible ardour, peculiarly fit him. On this account he is the universal attendant upon a pack of fox hounds, and though last in the pursuit he is not the least in value.

"Indeed a brace of these dogs is considered indispensable in a complete fox-hunting establishment, and they are generally of different sizes, so that the smallest may enter an earth which will not admit the other. As soon as the hounds are thrown into covert,

Terriers as depicted by Alken, 1820. Note the Bull Terrier, Manchester and Scottish Terrier.

Bear baiting, 1821. By H. Alken.

the terrier becomes the busiest in the field when endeavouring to find the fox; whenever the game is started, and the hounds running breast high, and at their utmost speed, this active little animal is seldom far behind, and is sure to be up at the first check. It is when the fox is supposed to have earthed, that the services of the terrier are most essentially required; he enters with the utmost eagerness, and soon informs the ear of the sportsman whether or not he is in, and at what distance from the mouth, when he is speedily dug out.

"The principal objection to the reddish coloured terrier in a pack is, that by juvenile sportsmen, in the glamour of the chase, they are frequently hallooed off for a fox.

"The English Terrier (*Canis terrarius,* variety B.). This is a handsome sprightly dog, and generally black on the back, sides, and upper part of the head, neck, and tail; the belly and the throat are of a very bright reddish brown with a spot of the same colour over each eye. The hair is short and somewhat glossy; the tail rather truncated, and carried slightly upwards; the ears are small, somewhat erect, and reflected at the tips; the head is little in proportion to the size of the body, and the snout is moderately elongated. This dog, though but small, is very resolute, and is a determined enemy to all kinds of game and vermin, in the pursuit and destruction of which he evinces an extraordinary and untaught alacrity. Some of the larger English terriers will even draw a badger from his hole. He varies considerably in size and strength, and is to be met with from ten to eighteen inches in height."

From the first variety of Scotch Terrier mentioned, it is easy to identify the progenitors of the West Highland White, Cairn and Scottish Terriers of today. The second variety is surely the early Skye Terrier with its flowing coat and coming from the western islands of Scotland. The third variety was the so-called "wire-haired Scotch Terrier" whose terminology caused much confusion among less knowledgeable writers for many years to follow. In fact, some identify the wire-haired Fox Terrier as a Scotch breed because of this early definition. Of course, the Fox Terrier as we know him today was not derived from the Scotch branch of the Terrier family, but is instead of English origin.

John Lesley in his *History of Scotland* (1830) gave another facet of Terrier character particularly with respect to the Scotch branch. He said: "There is also another kind of scenting dogs, of low height, indeed, but of bulkier body; which creeping into subterranean burrows, routs out foxes, badgers, martins, and wildcats from their lurking places and dens. He, if he at any time finds the passage too narrow, opens himself a way with his feet, and with so great labour that he frequently perishes through his own exertions." This excerpt is of interest stressing as it does the digging ability and determination of the short-legged Scotch Terrier.

The English variety is equally recognizable as the present-day black and tan or Manchester Terrier. The heights offered even suggest the toy and standard varieties, although specific figures are not in line with today's requirements. However, the markings, colors, coat texture, etc., all match their modern counterparts.

Rawdon Lee in his book *Modern Dogs* (Terriers, 1893) says the Scotch branch is "undoubtedly older" than the English. Foundation for this statement is not known—Brown is the only authority suggested. What Brown actually says is that the Scotch is of "purer blood" than the English. This does not give first blood to either branch nor is the statement clear since all Terriers admittedly came from the Hound with generous infusions of foreign blood to obtain desired characteristics.

The general breakdown given by Brown was well received as evidenced by the works of several later authors who copied or substantially copied the definition. In 1833 the exact definition was used by Effingham Wilson in his *Field Book* while Charles Hamilton Smith in Volume 2 of his excellent *Natural History of Dogs* (1840) uses a somewhat similar description including the English branches of the family. This book offers another interesting addition to the breed classification in the form of a plate depicting "An Isle of Skye Terrier." Resembling very closely a prick-eared Skye of today, this is the first mention known of this breed.

Smith's *Natural History of Dogs* was issued in two volumes. The first in 1839 was confined to wild dogs while the second in 1840 was for domesticated dogs. All plates in both volumes are engraved by Lizars after Charles Hamilton Smith and are hand-colored to make this the third dog book with color plates. These two volumes are also identical with Volumes 9 and 10, respectively, of the *Naturalist's Library* of the Jardine series.

Youatt in his important work *The Dog* (1845) quotes Brown almost verbatim for his Terrier description indicating that nothing of great importance had transpired since 1833 to suggest any deviation from Brown's definition.

Thus we come to the year 1845 with specific names having been used in connection with the Dandie Dinmont Terrier, the Bull Terrier, the Isle of Skye Terrier and the broad classes of Scotch and English Terriers.

In spite of the absence of names for the several breeds it is undeniable that they did exist long before this and were surely reproducible. This is proved by works of art which show the dogs in easily recognizable forms. In addition to Edwards' colored engraving already described, we have the rather excellent print by Alken, dated 1820, which shows seven different Terriers that may be recognized as a Black and Tan (Manchester), a Bull Terrier, a Scotch Terrier and a White English Terrier. The remaining three dogs, more difficult to name, undoubtedly depict deviations from the other breeds. Henry Thomas Alken (1785–1851) was one of the greatest English artists of sporting subjects including dogs.

In 1839 Landseer painted *Dignity and Impudence* which shows a West Highland White Terrier. This one would fall into the broad category of "Scotch Terrier" at the time. Smith's 1840 engraving depicts two Scotch Terriers with trimmed ears as was customary to keep them from being mutilated during work and supposedly to improve hearing. It is interesting to note that, through the more than one hundred years to follow, most of the breeds derived from this progenitor have been bred selectively to obtain a natural prick ear so that cropping is no longer necessary.

Little of constructive nature took place during the next ten to fifteen years. The books that did appear seem to have been shamelessly copied from their predecessors, often with no attempt to give credit, and in some instances they even misquoted the earlier authors. In any event, several breeds had already arrived and many more were developed, awaiting only a name to bring them identity. The next few years were indeed important to the development of the Terrier tribe.

5

Terriers According to Stonehenge

B<small>Y</small> popular knowledge "Stonehenge" is a notable example of ancient stone circles situated in the Salisbury Plain about two miles from the town of Amesbury, England. These great stone pillars date to between 2000 and 1500 B.C. While these historical facts have nothing whatever to do with dogs, or with Terriers in particular, the name has an important connotation for it was the pseudonym chosen and used by John Henry Walsh (1810–1888). Although a member of the Royal College of Surgeons, Walsh appeared to have greater interest in sports than in surgery and in 1857 became editor of *The Field*. He wrote many books on sports, veterinary pursuits and dogs and in 1856 published the first edition of his *Manual of Rural Sports* which was so popular that it ran through sixteen editions and is considered authoritative even today.

Shortly after this book appeared, Walsh was asked to write an "up-to-date" book on the dog and he set about the task with diligence. The first edition which came out in 1859 included the natural history of the dog, descriptions of the several breeds known at that time, methods for breaking and managing the dog, and a rather lengthy treatise on dog diseases and their remedies. Stonehenge admitted that Youatt's book *The Dog* was consulted freely and firsthand information on various breeds was obtained from active breeders of the day.

This book, entitled *The Dog in Health and Disease* (1859–1887) was destined for great success. It ran through four editions which in many cases were concurrent with a later book, edited and compiled by him, entitled *Dogs of the British Islands*. This was first published in 1867, and re-published in expanded form through five editions. Stonehenge may be considered the foremost authority on dogs during the period from 1859 until his death in 1888. Since he borrowed from Youatt, it may be assumed that his writings brought up to date many of the latter's concepts and often clarified statements made by him which might have been otherwise misleading. Stonehenge's works were an important marker in dog development and the literature pertaining to it. Without these books the history of several breeds would be difficult to trace.

Publication of the first edition of *The Dog in Health and Disease* coincided with the beginning of dog shows during the same year. Thus dog shows, which were the greatest single influence upon the improvement of quality and stabilization of type had a strong bearing upon the Stonehenge series which recognized new breeds as they appeared in the ring.

The first dog show was held at Newcastle-on-Tyne in 1859 with J. H. Walsh (Stonehenge) officiating as one of the five judges of some sixty Pointers and Setters. Terriers did not appear on the dog-show agenda until 1860 when the Birmingham show included classification for "Scotch Terriers." Records show that the winner was a "White Skye." (Stonehenge did not list the Skye with Scotch but as a separate breed in his 1859 edition.) The dog in question was probably closer to a West Highland White than to a Skye, a supposition supported by a statement found in Webb's *Books of Dogs* (1872) which mentions two types of Terriers known on the Isle of Skye. One, termed the "long-haired variety" undoubtedly refers to the presently known Skye Terrier and the other "an extraordinary strain—a small white Terrier with light yellow ears." Since yellow or tannish ears are still found in some West Highland strains, probably the "small white Terrier" was an early Westie and the "White Skye" winner at Birmingham the same.

34

Mr. Carrick's Otter Hound, Lottery (left) and Mr. Knight's Airedale, Thunder. From Shaw's *Book of the Dog*, 1881.

Waiting, by Webb after Landseer, 1839, showing a Deerhound, Foxhound, Bloodhound, Greyhound and Highland Terrier.

In the first edition of *The Dog in Health and Disease* (1859) we find the Terrier classed with the Hounds including the Beagle, Harrier, Foxhound, Otter Hound and Dachshund. The Terrier is described as a "strong useful little dog with great endurance and courage, and with nearly as good a nose as the Beagle or Harrier.

From his superior courage when crossed with the Bulldog, as most vermin Terriers are, he has generally been kept for killing vermin whose bite would deter the spaniel or the beagle but would only render the terrier more determined in his pursuit of them."

Stonehenge offers the following classification for Terriers of different scope than any heretofore found: "Terriers are now usually divided into four kinds—1st, the Old English Terrier; 2nd, the Scotch, including the Dandie Dinmont; 3rd, the Skye, and 4th, the modern toy dog."

This is the first reference to the Dandie Dinmont *as a breed* although Scott gave birth to the name many years before. Stonehenge's descriptions of several Terrier breeds differ from previous ones in some cases, and they give evidence of additional breeds that have become reproducible through years of knowledgeable effort. The Bull Terrier was mentioned but classified as a cross-bred dog. This differs from Brown (1829) who said the Bull Terrier "has now assumed a fixed character."

The Fox Terrier was also classified under cross-breds. It is said that "the field fox-terrier used for bolting the fox when gone to ground" is of a Terrier and Bulldog cross wherein the Bulldog goes back to the third or fourth generation. The statement is made that "most of our smooth terriers are slightly crossed with the bull-dog in order to give courage to bear the bites of the vermin which they are meant to attack."

As to this oft repeated statement about the Terrier and Bulldog cross, the Rev. Jack Russell in his *memoir* (1878) explained the method of developing the modern Fox Terrier as follows: "They begin with a smooth bitch terrier; then to obtain a finer skin, an Italian greyhound is selected for her mate. But as the ears of the produce are an eyesore to the connoisseur, a beagle is resorted to, and then little is seen of that unsightly defect in the next generation. Lastly, to complete the mixture, the bulldog is now called on to give the necessary courage; and the composite animals thus elaborated, become, after due selection, the sires and dams of the fox terriers. This version of their origin I received from a man well qualified to speak on the subject."

Thus, the early use of the Bulldog as a cross with Terriers of the Scotch and English varieties is undoubtedly true. It did not permanently influence physical conformation since all structure of

36

the Bulldog was lost rather quickly when the progeny were bred back into the original line, according to Stonehenge who records an experiment to prove the premise. In this experiment a Greyhound was bred to a Bulldog, an offspring from the mating bred back to a Greyhound and the process repeated for three generations. At the end of this time no physical attribute of the Bulldog could be seen—the progeny appeared to be purebred Greyhounds. Bulldog courage, however, was still evident. A documented history of the above experiment, with photographs of the four generations mentioned will be found in Stonehenge's *The Dog in Health and Disease,* third edition, pages 257–264.

Walsh described the English Terrier as a smooth-haired dog weighing between six and twelve pounds, black and tan in color in the preferred state. The description fits the Manchester, while a plate showing Francis Redmond's bitch "Lady" leaves no doubt that this dog is the same type shown by Edwards in his terrier plate published in 1800. The weight given as a guide makes one think that this was the toy variety of the breed although later descriptions by Stonehenge include up to about 20 pounds.

The Scotch Terrier of Stonehenge differs from that of earlier authorities in that it "closely resembles the English dog in all but his coat, which is wiry and rough, and hence he is sometimes called the wire-haired terrier, a name perhaps better suited to a dog which has long been naturalized in England and whose origin is obscure enough." He goes on to suggest that, while the breed comes in various colors, "a pepper and salt appearance" was characteristic of the true Scotch Terrier. His description of the breed which differs widely from previous delineations is confusing to the student who finds it difficult to reconcile the discrepancies. Actually Walsh's description is the first of its kind and the dog "Peto" offered as an example of the Scotch Terrier does not fit the descriptions of earlier authors.

Where Walsh obtained his information is not known, although he must have been in error for in the fourth edition (1887) of the same work he admits that "Peto" was his own dog and goes to some length to clear up misconceptions that might have been gained from his previous writings. He also reproduces an engraving of a dog that more nearly resembles the Scotch Terrier as it was known by others. Generally his work was accurate and why he deviated in

37

Vero Shaw's White English Terriers, 1870.

English Terrier and Setter. By Lewis after Landseer.

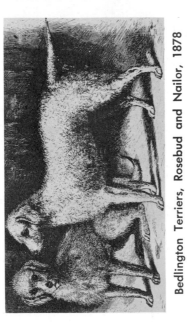

Bedlington Terriers, Rosebud and Nailor, 1878

Mr. Jamison's Irish Terrier, Souds, 1876.

38

this breed is not known. Perhaps he wanted to remain loyal to his dog that he claimed was a Scotch Terrier, though this explanation is difficult to believe in view of the general excellence of his work.

The Dandie Dinmont is classed as a breed variety of the Scottish branch of the Terrier family and the description which is similar in many respects to present-day requirements calls for "a heavy dog" weighing from 18 to 24 pounds. Walsh then makes a rather startling observation when he says, "It will be seen that the points differ a good deal from those usually ascribed to this breed in England, where Dandies have almost invariably prick ears, and are of smaller size, seldom exceeding 10 to 12 pounds." From a sketch of an "English Dandie" the breed appears similar except for the ears which were half-pricked and relatively small. This is the only reference to the English variety that can be found to this time and it is puzzling in its concepts, although the small ears are consistent with the ears shown in Landseer's portrait of Scott with his Dandies which exhibit ears much smaller than those of today's variety. This deviation in ear size led Stonehenge to suggest the Dachshund cross which observation first appeared in his third edition of *The Dog in Health and Disease* (1879).

The Skye Terrier is described by Stonehenge as having a long weasel-shaped body with short fin-like legs, a wide head, long neck and an exceedingly profuse coat. There were three varieties, one small with long soft hair, another larger with hard, wiry hair and a third between the two. The Stonehenge Skye had drop ears although prick eared varieties had been noted heretofore (*see* Charles Hamilton Smith's plate, 1840).

The toy Terrier appears to have been a cross between the English Terrier and an Italian Greyhound or with a King Charles Spaniel. Another cross between a Skye and a toy Spaniel was mentioned. In all cases the toy dogs did not weigh over 7 pounds and $3\frac{1}{2}$ to 4-pounders were the most prized, particularly when a pure black-and-tan of the small size could be obtained.

Passing to the second edition of *The Dog in Health and Disease* (1872) we find the statement, "Terriers are usually divided into eight kinds:—1st, the old English Terrier; 2nd, the Scotch; 3rd, the Dandie Dinmont; 4th, the Skye; 5th, the Fox Terrier; 6th, the Bedlington; 7th, the Halifax Blue Tan; and 8th, the modern Toy Terriers of various kinds."

This interesting classification is a decided expansion from "the four kinds" suggested in the 1859 edition of the same work. Added during the period of 13 years between the two editions was the Bedlington and the Halifax Blue Tan. The Dandie Dinmont had now reached a position of separate breed status, having been classified previously under the Scotch Terrier kind, and the Fox Terrier had progressed to a "kind" or breed from the ignominious classification of a "crossed-breed" dog which still included the ill-fated Bull Terrier.

Descriptions of the breeds common to both editions are quite similar. The old English Terrier is described as a true Black and Tan or Manchester with the typical pencilling on the toes, thumbprints over the eyes, etc. The weight was limited to from 6 to 10 pounds or less than the maximum of 12 pounds suggested in 1859 and does not agree with statements made in Stonehenge's earlier book *The Dogs of the British Islands* (1st ed., 1867). The Scotch Terrier was still at variance with descriptions offered by other writers while the Dandie remained about the same. The Skye Terrier was broken into three varieties and this suggested such related breeds as the Clydesdale and the Silky, or Fancy Skye. Also mentioned was a crossed Skye with Dandie blood and last a fancy London variety which came from a cross between the Skye and a Spaniel.

The Fox Terrier described was of the smooth variety weighing about 16 pounds; this was the first mention of the breed other than as a crossed breed in the first edition. From 1859 until 1863 no class had been assigned the breed at any of the shows. This was probably due to the fact that although the breed existed, its identity was not known beyond the confines of the many Foxhound kennels where Fox Terriers were raised and highly prized. Thus, until 1863, the Fox Terrier was a working Terrier first, last and always. In 1863 Mr. John Walker and Mr. Cornelius Tongue prevailed upon the Birmingham show committee that Fox Terriers merited a classification and thereafter the breed grew more rapidly than any other Terrier. By late in the century fully twenty-five per cent of all Terriers shown were Fox Terriers, a condition that also prevailed in America.

The newly classified Bedlington Terrier rated a very short description which noted the topknot, filbert-shaped ears and sandy, liver and blue colors with nose color deviations for the sandy and liver as permitted today.

The Halifax Blue Tan Terrier, otherwise known as the Yorkshire Blue and Tan, was a new breed resembling an Old English Terrier except in coat which was long and silky in texture and rich blue and tan in color. The dog came from a probable cross of the English Terrier with a Maltese and weighed from 10 to 18 pounds. Under toy dogs Stonehenge says, "The Halifax Blue Tan is a toy dog, whether the weight is 16 pounds or 3 pounds." This points to the Yorkshire type of Terrier known today. In any event the Halifax Blue Tan Terrier now does not seem important when viewing Terriers. The numerous other toy Terrier breeds included toy Scotch, the Skye and Spaniel cross and the toy English Terriers under 7 pounds and preferably from 3½ to 4 pounds. It is said that these small ones generally included crosses of Italian Greyhound or King Charles Spaniel.

Seven years later (1879) another edition of *The Dog in Health and Disease* appeared with several changes and additions. Meantime the English Kennel Club, formed in 1873, had had a stabilizing effect on dog shows. Undoubtedly this was one reason for the expanded descriptions offered by Walsh in his third edition.

The previously mentioned breeds or "kinds" are all mentioned except the Halifax Blue Tan which now has been renamed the Yorkshire Terrier. Stonehenge states, "I do not know why the prefix 'Halifax' was applied as both Huddersfield and Bradford have a greater claim to be considered the headquarters of the breed." He goes on to state, "According to my judgment, the whole tribe ought to be included among the 'toys,' since they are never used for any kind of terrier work; but the committees of our shows make two distinct classes for them, one being distinguished as for 'Yorkshire Terriers,' and the other for 'broken-haired toy terriers,' in which latter small Yorkshire Terriers always carry off the prizes."

The wire variety or "Rough Fox Terrier" was included in the greatly expanded chapter on Fox Terriers. In fact all chapters of the recognized breeds are fuller and more descriptive in the third edition than in any previous one. The Irish Terrier was the only added breed. This new breed differed from today's representative since the color then as now was a preferred red although yellow or gray was acceptable. Brindle colors suggested a Bulldog cross.

Weights from 17 to 25 pounds were allowed. The breed was said to be descended from the Scotch Terrier although it was alleged to have been bred pure in Ireland from about 1830 or thereabouts. Ears could be cut if desired.

Under English Terrier we find the name Manchester Terrier mentioned for the first time. This was used interchangeably with Black and Tan. In the same chapter the White English Terrier was mentioned as a breed that "has fallen into neglect" although resembling the Manchester in shape and judged on the same scale of points except for color.

Expanded descriptions of all other breeds are offered which are quite useful and which undoubtedly are the basis of present-day standards. As in past editions, the Bull Terrier remains classified as a crossbred.

The description of the Scotch Terrier is of interest herein for in this edition Stonehenge admits that his dog "Peto," used as a model for the breed in all past editions, leaves something to be desired as a Scotch Terrier, particularly with respect to color. He makes the interesting observation that classes for the breed were abandoned in 1875 because of lack of entry and poor quality, and that the breed for show purposes was all but extinct. This was probably the case since the Dandie and the Skye, two offshoots of the original Scotch Terrier, then had separate classifications and since varieties of the Skye possibly included some of the other strains.

In the final and fourth edition of *The Dog in Health and Disease* (1887) three new breeds were added.

Concurrent with publication of the fourth edition of the Stonehenge book in 1887, D. J. Thomson Gray (Whinstone) published Part I of *The Dogs of Scotland*. This paper-backed booklet of forty-eight pages is a rarity today since it was the first book directed exclusively to the Scottish Terrier. While the book goes into the history of the Scotch Terrier, its main purpose is to establish the Scottish Terrier as a distinct breed and to this end the author goes to some length. According to Gray, the first attempt to exhibit the breed was in 1877 when the Aberdeen Terrier was unsuccessfully introduced. Attempts continued until about 1880 when classes were sometimes provided for Hard-coated Terriers in which many of the Aberdeens were shown. The early titleholders such as Dundee, Ashley Charlie and Skittles were all shown between 1884 and 1886

42

Early Terriers, from *Dogs of the British Is.* 1865.

Scotties at work, 1835. A caricature by Robertson.

which indicates the breed came into being just before the publication of Stonehenge's fourth edition.

The first of the additions was the Airedale Terrier, a dog that differs "chiefly in color from the Irish" and one which is "much fancied by pitmen" of the north country. Walsh seemed to have little interest in the breed since he states, "Personally, I have no knowledge whatever of his characteristics." Be this as it may, the breed was established and became another of the Terrier family to add to the growing list.

In place of the Scotch Terrier a new breed termed the "Hard-haired Scotch Terrier" was substituted. The illustration depicts a dog more closely resembling the present-day Scottish Terrier than any previous illustrations. The gameness of the breed was stressed with the statement that in gameness the breed is not surpassed by any except the Bulldog and the Bull Terrier. Color had been stabilized over the "almost any color" of the old Scotch Terrier and reads, "steel or iron grey, brindle, black, red, wheaten, and even yellow or mustard color.—White markings are most objectionable." Ears were described as small, prick or semi-prick but never drop and the coat hard and wiry. In general the description and standard follow closely later requirements for the breed. Apologies for "Peto," which is still pictured, were again offered.

The final "new" breed was the Welsh Terrier. Here again the description is sketchy. It says that the breed resembles the Irish except in size and color which are usually 15 inches and black, or grizzled, and tan and free from penciling on the toes. The scale of points set forth in the book was approved by a committee meeting at Carnarvon on August 4, 1886.

So ends the Age of Stonehenge. The year after the publication of the fourth edition of *The Dog in Health and Disease* Walsh died (1888). Thus ended a full and illustrious career. His influence on the development of dogs was tremendous and his writings in books and in *The Field* had a strong and lasting influence on several breeds.

Recapitulating, we find that from the beginning of dog shows in 1859 through the fourth and final edition of Stonehenge in 1887 the following breeds had been classified and had gained recognition as reproducible breeds: The English Terrier (predecessor of the Black and Tan or Manchester Terrier); the Skye Terrier; Dandie

Dinmont Terrier; Fox Terrier (two coats, smooth and rough or Wire); Bedlington Terrier; Halifax Blue Tan Terrier (now known as the Yorkshire Terrier and no longer a member of the Terrier group); Irish Terrier; White English Terrier (now extinct); Airedale Terrier; Welsh Terrier; Hard-Coated Scotch Terrier (now known as the Scottish Terrier); the Bull Terrier, never accorded breed status by Stonehenge (unjustly to be sure); and the Toy Terriers of various kinds. In all, ten breeds known today were listed. The Halifax is no longer in the group nor are the Toy Terriers which include the Toy Manchester of today. Of the entire lot, only the White English Terrier is now extinct.

The accuracy of Stonehenge's observations is attested by contemporary authors of stature. Vero Shaw, in his *Illustrated Book of the Dog* (1881) offers an identical list for the Terrier tribe. G. O. Shields (Coquina) in *The American Book of the Dog* (1891) gives a rather similar set of observations although the Welsh Terrier was not mentioned and the book was published four years after the last effort of Stonehenge. *The American Book of the Dog* was the first extensive all-breed book published in America to include breed chapters by fanciers of experience. "Idstone" (Rev. T. Pearce), a contemporary writer who between 1872 and 1889 published a continuing series of books entitled *The Dog,* offered no more and in some cases less.

This was an important period for Terriers. It marked the early era of show dogs, and the breeds recognized through these years gained an undeniably high niche in the Terrier world. These were the leaders and these were the breeds that had the edge because of early recognition. In the chapters to follow we will find that some advanced, some declined, but none, as in the case of the White English Terrier, failed to maintain its position among its peers.

For students, no better time can be spent than to study the several editions of Walsh's works, *The Dog in Health and Disease* and the equally interesting, *The Dogs of the British Islands,* a compilation of articles written in *The Field* by various authorities which includes much discussion by knowledgeable persons of the times. These books offer authoritative information concerning dogs of the day and discussion by acknowledged experts of the problems existing at the time. This is recommended reading if you wish to have background knowledge which surpasses the excerpts offered.

6

From Stonehenge Onward

THE death of Walsh (Stonehenge) closed a classic era in the development of dogs in general and Terriers in particular. This period, from 1859 to 1888, coincided with the beginning and prime development of the dog show. During the same period the English Kennel Club, formed in April of 1873, was followed by the American Kennel Club in September of 1884, though dogs had been registered in America prior to then.

During Walsh's life many Terrier breeds became established sufficiently to gain a niche in the recognized Kennel Club records under separate and identifiable names. Ten of the breeds of his times (including two varieties of Fox Terriers) are still active members of the Terrier group. In the seventy-five years to follow ten additional breeds have been recognized that are still active and several of these were known in 1887 but had not yet reached breed status.

Many astute dog men were developed during the second half of the nineteenth century. In addition to Walsh there was the Rev. T. Pearce (Idstone), Vero Shaw, Dr. Gordon Stables, D. J. T. Gray (Whinstone), Hugh Dalziel, Harding Cox and Rawdon Lee, to name a few. Two of them were particularly important in the delineation of the Terrier's development and Lee, because of his excellent documentation of all breeds of dog during the waning days of the 19th century, merits particular mention.

Lee who followed Walsh as editor of *The Field* was an author of rare ability. His four editions of *The Fox Terrier*, first published in 1889, are today prized additions to the shelves of any library on Terriers. His greatest work was *Modern Dogs*, published in four volumes in 1894 and revised and enlarged in 1897. This important effort included an entire volume on Terriers which mentioned all of the breeds recited in the last edition of Stonehenge. In addition, Lee gave information on the Clydesdale or Paisley Terrier which was an offshoot of the Skye and resembled the Skye closely except in color and texture of coat. The Clydesdale had an attractive silky blue coat which pointed to the cross with the Halifax Blue-Tan or what is now known as the Yorkshire Terrier. The breed could work but was used mainly as a pet and according to at least one wag of the day, the dog was "neither fish, fowl, nor good red herring." Lee concurred that the wag was not far from wrong.

The Skye and the Clydesdale were never very well separated as evidenced by one of the specialty clubs, called the Skye and Clydesdale Terrier Club, which functioned for many years. Prior to 1887 both breeds were shown in the same classes and the Clydesdale won in many instances which outraged the Skye fanciers. In 1888 the Kennel Club gave the breed status although the Clydesdale

Chs. Longmynd Chamberlain and Enchantress, Welsh Terriers. Painted by Maud Earl, 1905.

Ch. Heworth Rascal, Scottish Terrier winner about 1900. By the artist, John Emms.

Terrier Club had been formed the year before. This club failed within a short time and was replaced by the Paisley Terrier Club. The breed was known in various sections by the names of "Glasgow Terrier," and "Fancy Skye Terrier." In spite of this apparent early interest, the breed slipped into oblivion early in the 20th century.

Modern Dogs offered interesting background for a breed in a chapter on "Other Terriers." This described dogs of special abilities found near Patterdale which were the early progenitors of today's Lakeland Terrier. Also noted were Terriers of the Sealyham strain, found at Mr. J. H. B. Cowley's of Callipers, that were said to be excellent hunters. Credit for this early strain was given to Captain Edwardes near Haverfordwest. The Border Terriers of Jacob Robson of Byrness were described at length and it was commented that these fine small dogs resembled the old Elterwater Terriers. In retrospect, several of the later recognized breeds were quite accurately described and even named. Fom Lee's efforts however only the Clydesdale Terrier could be added to the tribe of Stonehenge during the waning days of the 19th century as a recognized and distinct new breed.

As we move into the early 20th century, we find Major Harding Cox editing what is now known as a collector's item. This work was to have been published in four volumes and was entitled *Dogs, by Well Known Authorities*. Cox solicited the aid of many authorities to write breed chapters for his work. The Terrier volume was the first published in 1906. Unfortunately, after publication of the Hound volume in 1907 no further issues were forthcoming. The two volumes that were published are of folio size and beautifully printed with color illustrations by many top artists of the day. The works of Wardle, Earl, Emms and Binks among others grace the pages of the books and depict many of the famous winners of the times. Cox listed all the Terriers found in Stonehenge's final work with the exception of the Halifax Blue-Tan and the Toy Terriers. These included the Black and Tan, Skye, Dandie Dinmont, Fox Terriers (two coats), Bedlington, Irish, White English, Airedale, Welsh, Scottish and Bull Terrier. The Clydesdale had already slipped from view as had the Toy Terriers, and the Halifax Blue Tan was now properly classified among the toy dogs. One new breed, the West Highland White, was added. The breed had gained recognition in England about 1904.

Thereafter the nine remaining breeds in the Terrier group as presently recognized in Britain became known officially, though such recognition required about thirty-seven years for fulfillment. First in line was the Cairn Terrier. Probably the least modified of all the Scotch breeds this one more closely resembles the old Scotch Terrier than any of the others. It was not until 1909 at the Inverness show that classes were provided for the first bench appearance of the breed under its present name.

Following the Cairn closely came the Sealyham Terrier from the area around Pembrokeshire where it was propagated by Captain Edwardes whose estate of Sealyham eventually gave the breed its name. The dog was used on all types of vermin and was bred to the color of white so as to distinguish the dog from the fox. Known from about 1860 the breed carried a considerable mixture of blood combining, according to Captain Lucas a basic foundation of the Pembroke Welsh Corgi with a rough-coated Terrier. Added to this was a bit of Dandie Dinmont, an early cross of Bull Terrier and even a little West Highland White Terrier. In fact, in the early days of the century the breed seemed more closely related to the Fox Terrier than to any other and this was probably because of frequent crosses with that breed. Actually, the early Sealyham appeared much like a Jack Russell Terrier. As time progressed the legs were shortened and the conformation stabilized until we have the stylish dog of today.

The next breed to gain recognition was the Border Terrier in 1920. Why this required twenty-six years from the time Lee first wrote of the breed is not known. Both the Border and the Sealyham were first mentioned by him in *Modern Dogs* in 1894 and were described at some length.

The last breed to gain status during the twenties was the Kerry Blue Terrier, a product of Ireland. In 1922 the breed was first exhibited at Crufts. The Kerry had been known in both Ireland and England for many years, but recognition did not come as a separate and reproducible breed until the 1922 winter date.

The Lakeland Terrier is another late comer. This fine little Terrier was also mentioned by Lee as a likely sort bred around Patterdale in the Lake District but nothing came of it until the Lakeland Terrier Association was formed in 1928 to bring together fanciers of the breed. It was not until 1931 that breed recognition was attained by the group. The Norwich Terrier came into the spotlight with admission to the register in 1932 although the breed had been known for some time and quite a few "Jones" Terriers had been exported into the United States. "Jones" Terriers were similar to, if not the same breed as, the Norwich and carried the name of their breeder who was prominent as an exporter of the little dogs. The following year the Australian Terrier gained breed status though the breed had been known for many years in the land "down under."

Staffordshire Bull Terriers were recognized by the English Kennel Club in 1935. The breed was not a new one but fanciers of the dog had little interest in shows, preferring to fight the dogs in the pits. As public sentiment turned against this "sport" fanciers became interested in shows and the breed came of age. The Staffordshire Bull Terrier of England is not at all similar to the Staffordshire Terrier of the United States. It is true that both are descended from fighting dogs but the two breeds bear so little resemblance to each other that neither could win in the other's country. The English version of the Staffordshire came from the same basic Bull and Terrier cross upon which the Bull Terrier was founded and goes back to 1860 or 1870 for its beginnings. However, the Staffordshire resembles more closely the original cross than the Bull Terrier. It is generally a smaller dog seldom weighting more than from 34 to 38 pounds; the present strain came from the Cradley Heath area where short, thick muzzles were much prized.

After recognition by the Kennel Club the breed became extremely popular. The dog was always able to take care of himself in or out of the ring and made a good pet, or could offer a savage fight at the desire of his owner. Today the English Kennel Club benches offer a good cross section of the breed at most shows.

The last breed to join the Terrier tribe was the Soft-Coated Wheaten Terrier that has definite consanguinity with Kerry Blue and Irish Terriers and which, if the claims of enthusiasts are given credence, was the progenitor of both breeds. In any event the breed claimed a specialty club in Ireland in 1934 and was placed on the official list of that group in 1937. In England, recognition did not come until 1943. A dog with the colorful name of Cheerful Charlie made the first championship in Ireland and to him goes a great deal of the credit for the breed's popularity. The breed is gaining a following in the United States.

The Miniature Schnauzer, a member of the Terrier family in the United States, has never been recognized as a Terrier in Great Britain. Both the Miniature and the Standard Schnauzer have always been classified as members of the non-sporting group in Great Britain. Since the Miniature Schnauzer is of foreign origin, a short resume of its background will be of interest.

Both Schnauzers are of German ancestry. The two were originally varieties of the same breed though the Miniature was bred by crossing the Standard with an Affenpinscher and then selecting the size of progeny desired for future breeding plans. The breed is not basically Terrier in blood. It is said that there was a cross of Black and Tan Terrier in the background but this has never been proved conclusively. Basic blood of the Schnauzer was that of the German Black Poodle and the Grey Wolf Spitz with a dash of Pinscher and it was from this last cross that the British Terrier blood was supposed to have come. The Schnauzer was exhibited in Germany many years ago and the Miniature variety was said to have been shown first in its native land about 1899, so the breed is a relatively old one.

Thus closes the period of development of the presently recognized Terrier breeds. Since 1859, nineteen still active breeds have been granted registration by the English Kennel Club. Among these the Fox Terrier includes two coats, and the Bull Terrier offers two varieties, white and colored. During the period several other breeds were recognized that have since transferred to other groups or have been lost in oblivion due to lack of fancier interest. In the first category the Halifax Blue Tan, now known as the Yorkshire Terrier, is a member of the toy group. In the second class, the Clydesdale Terrier enjoyed only a few years of popularity before losing identity while the White English Terrier, basic blood for many of the Terrier breeds, is no longer known. Several other names mentioned during the tour through the years of development are no longer used but the breeds are still active under more sophisticated identifications.

What the future will bring is not known. It is doubtful if many additional Terrier breeds will be developed since Terrier work is of little present-day importance or interest. However, one new breed is being sponsored at the present time by the name of "Webster Terrier." This strain has been kept pure for more than a decade by Robert Webster of the Dorset District in England. The dogs measure about 8 inches at the withers with a body of twice that measurement. Reddish in color with shaggy coat and low set ears the dog resembles a Dandie Dinmont. Efforts are presently being made to gain official recognition.

There are few other breeds or strains which might have a chance of being taken into the official Terrier family of show dogs, but changes may come that will open the door. It will be interesting in ten, twenty or thirty years hence to view the scene.

The Intruder, by Beckwith after Landseer, 1819. A rough or wire-coated Terrier surprises a cat with a rat.

7

The Early Terrier Tribe
in America

THE development of Terrier breeds in America coincided with the history of dog shows. Americans admittedly followed the British in their tastes and efforts involving dogs of all breeds. A late addition to the public fancy, Terriers did not become of great importance for many years after dogs had become a fixture on the American scene. Possibly this was because colonial Americans led a more rugged existence than the British and most of the people in the New World did not have time to enjoy the hunt and related efforts that captivated the fancy of so many Britishers. Further, the country was more open and depredations of wildlife did not cause shortages in food which necessitated the hunt and the dig.

Americans were more interested in the sport of shooting and so the sporting breeds flourished. Pointers, Setters Retrievers and Spaniels were the dogs that caught the public fancy in early days. However, with the advent of dog shows in Britain, the sport of exhibition began to be noticed in America and some years after the first English dog show Americans started to exhibit as well as run dogs in the field. The first of such events took place in 1874, fifteen years after the first English effort. With this incentive, Terriers soon began to take hold and it was not long before Terrier entries soared and several breeds became popular.

Americans followed British tastes in Terriers and as new breeds came into focus in the Old World they were quickly acknowledged and soon imported into America where their presence created popular demand. Thus, the several early Terrier breeds came from Britain, were recognized and took their place in the dog-show scene.

Actually, no Terrier breed was developed in America until the Staffordshire Terrier was recognized in 1936. Even the "Staff" has a British background but it did not follow British lines too closely for a similarly named British breed. The Miniature Schnauzer and the Australian Terrier are the only others that did not come directly from Britain and in the case of the Australian, the basic blood was British. Thus, America owes a great debt to Britain for the metamorphosis of the Terrier tribe.

There were two other breeds in the Terrier group that were not British in origin but these are no longer considered Terriers, However, they will be discussed briefly to offer a proper survey of the overall subject. The first is the Lhasa Apsos, an oriental breed from faraway Tibet where it is known as the "Lion Dog." The breed was admitted to the Stud Book as a Terrier about 1935 and competed in the group until 1956 when it was transferred to the non-sporting group where it is now shown.

The second "ex-Terrier" is the Standard Schnauzer, a dog of German derivation. When the breed gained recognition in 1926 both Standard and Miniature Schnauzers competed as varieties of the same breed. In 1933 the varieties both gained breed status and competed under separate breed classifications in the Terrier group. This condition continued until the Standard Schnauzer was transferred to the working group (at specialty club request in 1946) where the Schnauzer breed originally competed.

To survey more closely the development of the Terrier scene we should study the early history of dog shows in the United States and the published records of their results. Probably the first records of any kind were printed in the *American Kennel and Sporting Field* published by Arnold Burges in 1876. This treatise included a record of all winners at bench shows from the first held in 1874 at Mineola, New York, through an event at Memphis, Tennessee, in October 1875. A show was held earlier at Chicago, June 2, 1874, but no awards were given, so the Mineola event was the first to offer awards. No Terriers were exhibited at any of these early affairs. A subsequent edition of the *American Kennel and Sporting Field,* published by Burges in 1883, included no show records because of the existence at the time of the National American Kennel Club which, Burges stated, "could give such a work a character no private individual could."

The National American Kennel Club was the first organized group in America whose efforts were directed entirely to dogs and the first to sponsor field trials and bench shows. This occurred in 1876 when the club was founded in St. Louis. The club formulated rules for existing shows and trials with minor changes for many years and its stud book, of which only two volumes were published, became the forerunner of the *American Kennel Club Stud Book.* Through the first four volumes of the published stud books there is some confusion because of the several publishers and the changing conditions involving several kennel clubs. Volume 1 of the *National American Kennel Club Stud Book* was published in 1879.

Volume 2 of the *National American Kennel Club Stud Book* was purportedly issued by the club but was actually published and copyrighted by Dr. N. Rowe. Dr. Rowe was editor and manager of *The Chicago Field,* now known as *The American Field,* from 1876 on for many years. Before this he was a free-lance writer of widely recognized ability and an authority for the sporting press over the *nom de plume,* "Mohawk." He was also responsible for Volume 3 of the stud book (1886) which was entitled *The American Kennel Stud Book.* The AKC took over these three volumes and in Volume 4 acknowledged the work of Dr. Rowe of *The American Field,* stating he gave them right of republication. In Volume 4 it was further stated, "The plan that they have adopted recognizes all registrations in either volume of *The American Kennel Stud Book* of which Dr. Rowe was owner and publisher." No mention is made of Volume 1 but recognition was accorded. Thus, the confusion in early stud books is apparent. Subsequent issues, starting with Volume 4 and entitled *The American Kennel Stud Book,* were chronological continuations of the earlier books.

The American Kennel Club was founded in Philadelphia on September 17, 1884. At that time the club included a number of Canadian members in spite of the existence of a rather loosely knit organization known as the Dominion of Canada Kennel Club which was active from about 1883. On September 27, 1888 the pres-

55

ently known Canadian Kennel Club was founded and many of the clubs previously included in the American group dropped their affiliation to become members of their national club.

The two national clubs worked well together and in 1889 signed a reciprocal agreement still in effect, honoring each other's records for registration purposes.

About five years after the start of the *National American Kennel Club Stud Book,* in 1883 *Field and Stream* commenced to publish an independent stud record known as *The American Kennel Register.* The American Kennel Club offered to take over the activities of this register at the same time a similar offer was made to the National American Kennel Club but the *Register* declined to cooperate. In 1888, the *Register* failed for lack of support after publication of only six volumes.

Some of the bench show rules prevailing at the first organized dog shows of the National American Kennel Club appear odd today. These deal with standards and champions, also restrictions on entering the various classes which were generally two in number, namely open and champion. Three of these rules read as follows:

Rule 7. Dogs are to be judged by the scale of points laid down in Stonehenge's 3rd edition of *Dogs of the British Islands.*

Rule 8. A dog having won two first prizes in the open classes or a champion prize at any bench show or shows in America shall be debarred from entering the open classes at future shows.

Rule 9. A dog which has not won two first prizes in the open classes or one champion prize at any bench show or shows, in America shall not be eligible to the champion classes at future shows.

Rule 7 is of interest since it demonstrates the tremendous influence that Stonehenge had upon the canine scene during the period of early development of dog shows.

Rule 8 infers that there were champion dogs in existence prior to the first National American Kennel Club show while Rule 9 requires that a dog qualify before entering the champion class. This is reminiscent of American Kennel Club's action in the 1940's.

Lhasa Apso, a breed no longer in the Terrier group.

Normack Kennels' Ch. Zeck v Egelsee, Standard
Schnauzer now classed as a working dog.

Volume 1 of *The National American Kennel Stud Book,*
published in 1879, covered shows from 1876 to 1878 inclusive.
These shows were Chicago, 1876; St. Louis, 1876; Baltimore
1876 and 1877 (a single show which continued for six days starting on
December 28th and continuing through January 3rd); New York
(Westminster) 1877, St. Louis 1877 and 1878, Boston 1878 and

Baltimore 1878. No Terriers were exhibited at any of these affairs. The classification included only Sporting dogs such as Pointers, Setters, Retrievers, Spaniels and Dachshunds which were first exhibited at Westminster in 1877.

Volume 2 of this stud book was published in 1885 with a different format that was probably due to Dr. Rowe's editorship. In this book the shows were not delineated. All dogs registered were listed by breeds with numbers and as much information as was available. After each dog's listing, show placements, if any, made during the period covered by the book were included. In this volume we find the first registration of Terriers. Fox Terriers lead the parade with 7 males and 10 females identified. The dog Cricket 3289, the first, was a Smooth by Vandad out of Mettle and owned by J. P. Stinson of Leavenworth, Kansas. The first Smooth bitch registered was Fashion 3297 owned by J. H. Whitman of Chicago and noted as having won first prize at St. Paul 1878.

The other Terrier breeds registered so few dogs that all were listed under "Miscellaneous." Here we find two Bull Terriers, two Scotch Terriers, two Irish Terriers and a Yorkshire Terrier. The Bull Terriers were Nellie II 3308, an American-bred whelped August 12, 1878, and Viper II 3312 by Teddy out of Nellie II whelped March 2, 1880, both owned by H. C. Tellman of Leesburg, Va.

The two Scotch Terriers, both owned by J. H. Naylor of Chicago, were Prince Charlie 3310, whelped April 1881 by Billy out of Lady and bred by D. O'Shea of London, Ontario, Canada, and Queen Lilly 3311 whelped in England January 20, 1881 by King out of Lady Blossom.

Aileen 3306, the first registered Irish Terrier, was owned by Dr. J. S. Niven of London, Ontario. The breeding was by Joe out of Norah. Norah, 3309 (registered later than Aileen), won first at both London, Ontario 1881 and Cleveland 1882.

It will be noted that all the listed Terriers bore closely related numbers indicating almost simultaneous registration. The effort was actually started in 1895 with Cricket 3289, the first Terrier of any breed to become registered in the stud book. The first two stud books and their predecessor by Burges also indicate that Terriers were not shown before 1878 when Fashion, the Fox Terrier, won at St. Paul. A dog named Spigot 3295 won second at Boston the same year—which won first is not known; it may have been an unregistered Fox Terrier. Spigot, owned by J. P. Stinson, was by Trounce out of Barmaid and was bred in England by J. A. Doyle.

Other notes of interest are the fragmentary data given on several dogs. Many did not have sires and dams listed; for others no breeder or whelping date was given. In other words, the requirements in 1885 were considerably less demanding than today.

In the second volume of the stud book, besides the Terrier breeds already noted and the Sporting breeds and Hounds mentioned in connection with Volume 1, Beagles, Bassets, Wolfhounds, Greyhounds, Collies, Mastiffs, St. Bernards and Pugs were added.

Volume 3, entitled *The American Kennel Stud Book* and published in 1886, showed increased interest in Terriers. Fox Terriers, Scotch Terriers, Dandie Dinmont Terriers, Bedlingtons and Bull Terriers were registered. The numbers were not large but addition of the Dandie and Bedlington breeds was encouraging. The first Dandie to gain a number was a pepper-colored dog named Bonnie Britton 4472 owned by Mrs. J. H. Naylor of Chicago. He was by Border Minstrel out of Wee Miss, whelped in February 1884 and bred by A. Steele of Scotland. The dog was shown at Cincinnati and Chicago in 1885. In bitches, Pansy 4473, a pepper whelped in February 1884 by Minstrel Boy out of Ch. Linnett and bred by A. Steele, was another winner owned by Mrs. Naylor. She won at New Orleans, Chicago and Cincinnati in 1885. Pride of Leader 4474 was another pepper owned by John H. Naylor.

The first Bedlington to be registered was Ananias 4475 owned by W. S. Jackson of Toronto. A blue bred by J. Hall of England, Ananias was by Quayside Lad out of Jean. Eight others gained consecutive numbers at the same time, all owned by Jackson. Of these, Elswick Jock 4476 was one of the most shown in America having been on the bench at Chicago, Toronto and Montreal in 1884 and Toronto in 1885. Senator 4478, by Tip out of Rose, had a big record in England and was a champion; he was not registered until after his death.

In addition to the breeds registered, bench records of such Terriers as Black and Tans, Rough-haired Terriers, Skye Terriers and Irish Terriers were listed. Several of these breeds had not yet gained registration but were being shown extensively.

Passing to Volume 4 we find a tremendous increase in registrations for Fox Terriers, indicating that the popularity of the breed was in the ascendency in 1887. During the year 159 were registered, bringing the breed into contention with many of the other Sporting breeds. (Fox Terriers were the only Terriers classified with Sporting dogs. All other Terriers were listed under Non-Sporting, the only other classification.) Two new breeds made their appearance in this issue when Lever 7585, a Black and Tan Terrier, and Romach 6184, a Skye Terrier, gained registration. Lever, owned by C. P. Lawshe of Philadelphia, bred by Edward Lever of the same city, was whelped October 11, 1886 by Ch. Vortigern out of Fortune. Vortigern was English-bred and Fortune was not registered. The Skye Terrier, Romach, a bitch owned by the Maizeland Kennels, was whelped July 1884 and bred by Lt. Col. H. Cornwall (England). She was listed as a blue by Ch. Kingston Roy out of Col. Legh's Zulu.

In connection with both newly registered breeds, bench-show records for a sizable number of Black and Tans and Skyes were published in Volume 3 of the stud book for winnings during 1885. Among the winners was Vortigern which won the champion class at Philadelphia. From these observations it is apparent that registration was not a prerequisite to exhibition and many fanciers did not register but showed with zeal.

Another first registration may be found in Volume 4, but this was for a Terrier breed no longer existent. Only one dog, Royal Diamond 6907, a White English Terrier owned by J. W. Newman of Boston and bred by J. F. Campbell of Montreal, was listed. He was whelped November 29, 1885 by Hornet II out of Lulu. The dog had a small brindle spot over one eye according to the record.

Returning to the popularity of the Fox Terrier we find that while 159 of the breed were in the 1887 stud book only forty-one other Terriers gained registration. This was reason enough why the Fox Terrier was becoming widely known on the dog show scene. Several reasons may be submitted for the high figures for the breed. First, the Fox Terrier had always been an attractive dog and in England as well as in America seemed to gain the eye of more fanciers than any other Terrier. Second and more important, Fox Terriers were blessed with two strong kennels that bred large num-

Arthur Wardle's famous painting, "The Totteridge Eleven" Smooth Fox Terriers of 1897.

bers of dogs and exhibited them at most of the shows. One of these was the Blemton Kennels owned by August Belmont, Jr., a powerful man in dogdom, president of the American Kennel Club, and second president of the American Fox Terrier Club. In Volume 4 alone Belmont registered twenty-five homebreds with many more imports. Among these were the famous Bacchanal 5452, English-bred by Ch. Belgravian out of Bedlamite; another import, Lucifer 5459 by Ch. Splinter out of Kohinoor, and the homebred Resolute 5465 by Result out of Diadam.

The second extensive Fox Terrier kennel was the Warren establishment owned by Lewis and Winthrop Rutherfurd. A great show threat for many years this kennel outlasted the Blemton Kennels in time and impact upon the breed. In fact, Ch. Warren Remedy owned by Winthrop Rutherfurd (Lewis died in 1901) won best in show at Westminster in 1907, the first year the official award was offered, and repeated the triumph in 1908 and 1909. Winthrop Rutherfurd was president of the American Fox Terrier Club for more than twenty-five years and as late as 1934. During this same period Fred Hoey, and W. R. Bingham (Toronto) had strong if somewhat smaller kennels and were competing in breeding and exhibition with the two "giants."

One other point of interest in Fox Terriers: the year 1887 brought out the first registration of the Wire-haired variety. This honor went to Broxton Virago 5479 owned by R. W. Dean of Oakville, Ontario. Bred in Canada by G. Whitaker she was whelped April 1885, by Pincher out of Squish. Inbreeding was practised then as now for Squish was by Pincher out of Venom.

Volume 5 of the stud book (1888) brought two more breeds into the registered class. These were Airedales and Welsh Terriers. The first Airedale was a dog named Pin 9087 owned by Prescott Lawrence of Groton, Massachusetts. Pin's particulars were unknown but he was good enough to win first prize at New York in both 1886 and 1887. Pin had a kennel-mate in Needle 9088, a bitch whose particulars were also unknown.

The first two Welsh Terriers to gain the register were also owned by Mr. Lawrence and they had the interesting names of Which and T'Other. T'Other, the dog, drew the earliest number 9171 while Which, the female, was identified as 9172.

Two other Terrier breeds bearing mention appeared in Volume 5. The first was Caesar 12050, a Russian Terrier, the second Harrison 12052, a Bob-tailed Terrier. No particulars were given for the Russian Terrier, but the Bob-tailed tyke was owner-bred and its full pedigree was listed.

All breeds in the Terrier group had improved their position by 1888 and the rising numbers indicated what was to come for Terriers gained the very pinnacle of canine popularity during the next few decades.

In 1888 the new American Kennel Club rule requiring registration for any dog entered in a show became effective—it was passed December 6, 1887. (See pages VII and following, Volume 5, Part 3 AKC Stud Book.) Registration costing fifty cents could be accomplished at time of entry if the show secretary forwarded a registration application to the AKC. Many other rules which improved the format of shows and similar to some now in force were passed at the same time. During 1888 the AKC registered the then record total of 4,456 dogs.

In 1889 stud book records divided the Smooth and Wire-haired varieties of the Fox Terrier. It also noted a drop in total registrations to 4,116 dogs, probably due to the 1888 requirement for registration prior to exhibition. In any event, the dog show still flourished though no new Terrier breeds came into recognized focus. One item of interest, however, was the registration of a White English Terrier Royal Diamond 12901. This was the same name used in 1887 for a White English Terrier number 6907. Oddly enough, comparison of the particulars of the two dogs reveals that they were one and the same. Both were by Hornet II out of Lulu, both were whelped August 21, 1885 and both were bred by J. F. Campbell, Canada. One difference was the owner, the later registration having been made by H. A. Harris of North Wilmington, Massachusetts. The other difference was that the second time Royal Diamond was registered, he had lost that brindle spot over the eye whether a case of integrity or bleach, I do not know. The situation is interesting since it demonstrates that records were not too accurate at the time.

For the year 1890 registrations had fallen to only 2865 but the Terriers were coming up. Smooth Fox Terriers registered 204, Wires another six, making a total of 210 in spite of a general decline. Among the new breeders listed were the Oriole Kennels of Youngstown, Ohio, Clarence Rathbone of Albany and John E. Thayer of Lancaster, Massachusetts.

Other Terrier breeds were also on the upsurge. Bull Terriers had gained almost threefold from their earlier efforts while Black and Tans, Scotch and Irish were also gaining. Dandies, Bedlingtons, White English and Skyes were stagnant while Airedales and Welsh Terriers failed to register a single dog.

One other book of records came upon the scene in 1892 when Major J. M. Taylor first president of the American Kennel Club, published his *Bench Show and Field Trial Records and Standards* which offered a partial listing of winnings from the beginning of dog shows. The most complete records covered field work and the only Terrier winnings, which were complete, were those for Fox Terriers. Interesting but incomplete the book failed to offer the more comprehensive background to be gleaned from the stud books. The book also listed approved judges, officers and members of the several specialty clubs that were AKC members at the time. The only Terrier Specialty group noted was the American Fox Terrier Club, first Terrier specialty club, also the first to become a member of the AKC.

The task of delineating the metamorphosis of the several Terrier breeds becomes increasingly difficult as time progresses. Registrations gained steadily through the years and the desire to own a purebred dog became increasingly strong. It took until 1935 for registrations to reach the million figure, but the trend had been established and the second million required only ten years. During the next decade an additional three million dogs gained the pages of the AKC Stud Book. Thus, the practice of registering a dog to assure the ancestry of the progeny has really taken hold.

The Terrier breeds continued to become recognized through registration. Following the Welsh and Airedale it took quite a few years for the next breed to gain recognized status. In fact, developments followed closely the pattern already studied with respect to Great Britain. The twelfth breed to gain status was the West Highland White Terrier when Talloch 116076, owned by Mrs. C. E. Bell of Springfield, Massachusetts, entered the records in 1908. Then came the Sealyham Terrier, Harfats Pride 141623 in 1911, owned by an old friend, August Belmont, Jr. Thereafter the several remaining breeds entered the stud book at various times.

Badger digging about 1560. From *La Venerie* by Jacques du Fouilloux. Tongs were used to keep the badger at a safe distance.

8

The Working Terrier

ALL Terriers were bred originally for work. Previous chapters have emphasized the extent of their work and the importance of their ability to do the kind of work they were bred for. Beauty as such was given little if any consideration but, as is often the case, nature took care of appearance in such a way that the dog was attractive as well as capable.

Terriers were used for fox, otter, weasel, hedgehog, stoat, badger, rats and other vermin and predatory animals, and naturally the Terriers required special abilities to carry out all such work. Thus various distinct breeds were developed, each with its specialized skills and the necessary physical attributes. Some had to go to earth in pursuit of the fox, others had to brave the holt of the otter, while some had to make their way down into rocky dens with narrow, rugged entrances. Many were expected to run with the Hounds, to swim rain-swollen streams, and work their way along the hedgerows.

A hedgerow must be seen to be appreciated. It is a tangled mass of hawthorn where bushy trees have been planted ten or fifteen feet apart, their branches trained laterally and intertwined among upright stakes placed between each pair of plants. The mass grows into a tangle, re-rooting itself along the way to form an almost impenetrable wall often ten feet high and as broad. Hewed to size and shape with an ax, these kept rows are neat appearing and fully as useful as any fence known to man.

The hunting of wildlife was a widely practiced sport in the Terrier's early days. Dog owners enjoyed the hunt and reveled in the companionship of others interested in the same pursuit. Lest the reader think that hunting was merely the wanton destruction of wild animals, as a sport it was necessary to control propagation required to preserve the natural resources of the countryside. In working the streams and the rivers the otter depleted the supply of fish; foxes pilfered poultry and killed domesticated animals as well as game, while other predators also, if left to increase without hindrance, would have had a disastrous effect upon the food sources of man.

Terriers also helped rid the farms and the cities of rats that consumed needed grain and added to the filth of city slums. Continuous war had to be waged against them. The Terrier's part in the struggle was of great importance and so recognized as the chief means of bringing the scourge under control. The destruction of domesticated animals by foxes was another problem which the Terriers helped to solve. In a letter written to *The Fanciers' Gazette* and quoted in *Dogs of Scotland* (1887), the correspondent tells of twenty lambs being killed in a single night by a marauding fox. In the Harding Cox' book, *Dogs by Well Known Authorities,* Colonel Malcolm, writing about West Highland White Terriers, lists an almost unbelievable inventory of his Highlanders' achievements in a five-year period. He says his Terriers killed a total of 603 foxes and four otters during that time, together with an unknown number of dens cleared of cubs.

The Terrier's work is well described in this excerpt from a poem by Dr. Gordon Stables:

> He'll face a foumert, draw a brock,
> Kill rats and whiterits by the score,
> He'll bang tod-lowrie frae his hole,
> Or slay him at his door.

Today, we can list few working Terriers. Most are pets, breeding stock or show animals. Their ability to work has never been tested nor are their owners often interested in determining these capabil-

66

Shelburne Border Terriers worry a woodchuck.

Three Borders finishing off a woodchuck.

Ch. Shelburne Slipper retrieving a duck.

ities. However, these same Terriers can work if given a chance and this phase of interest will be covered here. Also this chapter will include credit to the many distinct Terrier strains that never acquired breed status. There are quite a few of these in Britain and America that were carefully bred for a purpose which they well fulfilled, but due to circumstances they did not reach the dignity of breed distinction.

The Terrier instinct is bred into every Terrier worthy of the name. How many can recall the amazing aptitude their dog has for killing a stray rat that foolishly crosses its path? Others can remember the fight of one of their Terriers to finish a woodchuck. Still others have seen the rare conflict between a Terrier and an otter, a rugged battle but one in which Terrier spirit usually prevails. Thus, today's Terrier, no matter what the breed, still carries in its veins the blood of conflict and the instinct to do the job. Let's not change his conformation so that these traits and instincts cannot be used.

Amazing stories of the Terrier's abilities are found in Dr. E. S. Montgomery's book, *The Bull Terrier*. In this treatise, the good Doctor recounts the feats of his Bull Terriers. Clear instructions are given for training a dog to work on rat, muskrat, otter, badger, etc., and it is said that fox will be taken as easily as a rat. The Bull Terrier, whose heritage was not hunting but fighting, has been trained to hunt all of these predators. The Bull Terrier has a generous infusion of the blood of the White English Terrier, now extinct but a fine working Terrier in its day. Apparently, instinct lives long past the memory of men, and in the veins of every Terrier is the desire, and the ability to do the work for which his forebears were bred.

In spite of the scarcity of wildlife, there are still a hardy few who work their dogs. To this end information will be offered that may startle those naive persons who state unequivocally, "Terriers are never used any more to go to ground." At least two of the present-day breed specialty clubs are interested in maintaining working abilities in the Terrier. These are the American Sealyham Terrier Club and the Border Terrier Club of America.

The Sealyham Club has been at it longer and with more interest than any other organized group. It has offered working certificates since 1914 to dogs that have demonstrated the required courage

68

and ability. It is true that interest in this work is not general among club members, nevertheless there has always been a generous segment of the membership who believe in working their dogs. To date about fifty such certificates have been awarded, and to still the voices that say a working dog cannot have the quality required for the show ring, eight of the recipients have also been bench champions of record.

In order to gain the certificate the worker must: (a) Demonstrate willingness to go to ground in a woodchuck earth; and (b) face and hold its quarry and draw the same.

The last "digs" of which I am aware were held at the farms of Mrs. Frances Wells near New Carlisle, Ohio, where certificates were granted to several dogs. An interesting picture in this book shows a Sealyham facing a 'possum in a woodchuck earth. The outlook is sufficiently formidable to cause a less determined dog to leave, but the Sealyham drew the quarry and gained his coveted certificate.

Capt. Jocelyn Lucas, M.C. of England, has long been an advocate of working Terriers. This Sealyham enthusiast has used his dogs for work for many years. Also an authority on working Terriers he has written several interesting books and many articles on the subject, the titles of which appear in the bibliography.

According to my information, the Border Terrier Club of America is presently investigating the possibility of holding working trials for dogs of this breed. No doubt the format of the trials will follow, to a degree at least, the Sealyham design. In any case they will assure that the competing Terrier has the necessary courage and ability to do the work for which it was originally bred, before it is granted a working certificate. Fortunately, many members of the Border Terrier Club still work their dogs for their personal pleasure and most of these small, unspoiled Terriers are adept at gaining the best of their adversary whether it be woodchuck, 'possum, fox or what have you. Mrs. Webb pictures several of her Borders engaged in various phases of work ranging from fox to retrieving duck. All but one of the dogs pictured have gained the bench title of champion, again demonstrating that quality and work may go together.

Kerry Blue Terriers were once worked for sport and the All-Ireland Blue Terrier Club offered working certificates for gameness.

The working consisted of drawing a badger but not killing it. As soon as the brock was drawn, it would be grasped by the tail and pulled clear of the Terrier to live for sport another day. For this work the Kerry received a "Teastes Mor" certificate, meaning "great test." For lesser work a "Teastes Beag" certificate was awarded, meaning "little test." A full description of these tests may be found in *Hounds and Dogs* by Croxton Smith.

Airedales have been known for years as good working Terriers as used for a variety of pursuits including the hunting of mountain lion, wildcat and even deer. Largest of the Terrier breeds, the Airedale is capable of being used with good success on anything that lives. Actual photos of their feats in combating wild animals prove this statement.

The tractability of the Terrier and the Airedale in particular may be judged by an advertising catalogue published periodically by a large Airedale kennel during the 1920's. This catalogue offered Airedales trained to suit the purchaser. The list of pursuits for which they could be trained was as follows: police work, farm dogs, for sheep or cattle; hunting dogs for bear, wolf, fox, deer, wildcat, lynx, skunk, coon, opossum, etc.; water retrievers for duck, geese, rail, plover and snipe; and of course dogs for the largest market, pets. From this listing it is apparent that there is little an Airedale cannot do and the kennel, a widely known and reputable establishment, sold hundreds of dogs as advertised. It should also be said that the same kennels bred many champions from their own stock, again demonstrating that quality does not detract from working ability.

Some of the Terrier varieties which were carefully bred to bring out desired characteristics never gained the stature of recognition. Possibly this was because their breeding activities were limited either to a small area or to the efforts of single breeders. In either case the breed never became strong numerically and for this reason did not reach the show bench, a requisite today if the breed is to gain official recognition.

Probably the most famous of the unrecognized Terrier breeds was the "Jack Russell Terrier." This dog was a small deviation of the Wire Fox Terrier but was shorter on the leg and had a broader skull. In other respects it was akin to the Fox Terrier. The Jack

Francis Duckerfield Castley and his Harriers. By R. Woodman after Benjamin Marshall (1767–1835). Note the White English Terrier running with the Hounds.

Russell Terrier was a tremendous worker and today is becoming more important due to an apparent rebirth in interest that has occurred during the past two or three years. The breed was named after Rev. Jack Russell, its originator. More formally known as the Rev. John Russell, he lived a long and happy life in the 19th century His activities were so varied and colorful that they have been chronicled in several books, one of the best being *Memoir of Rev. John Russell* which sets forth in detail many of his experiences and escapades. So numerous were his forays into the field that one cannot but wonder when he had time for his flock though it was said he was an excellent preacher.

Russell was not unlike many others of the cloth during the same period. A great many of these sporting parsons who hunted with abandon were frequently engaged in a game of "hide and seek" with their Bishops who were trying to catch them "at play" but seldom were successful. Russell's book tells several delightful stories about these fruitless efforts.

71

A charming toast oft drunk in ale after a hard ride seems apropos—

> *Here's a health to the parson despising control*
> *Who to better his parish, his health, or his soul,*
> *— — — — On my honor I think he does each.*
> *Five days in the week follows the fox and the hound,*
> *On the sixth duly goes his parochial round,*
> *— — — — — And on Sunday devoutly can preach.*

Russell bought his first dog, a Terrier called "Trump," while a student at Oxford about 1813. From a detailed description of this dog she seemed to have been a rather nicely balanced white Fox Terrier, with a short but heavy wire coat. According to Miss Alys Serrell in her book *With Hound and Terrier in the Field* (1904) Russell had told her that his breed was established from the bitch Trump bred to a black and tan Terrier dog. Russell did not like his Terriers "hard." He never liked a dog that would kill but rather liked dogs that could run with the Hounds, could cover the retreats of the fox and, when required, could tease and worry the fox until the hunters arrived. His dogs went in packs and were tractable and intelligent. Since the parson was also addicted to badger digging, his dogs had to be equal to the occasion and again they did the job and would draw the badger with any of them.

The early Sealyham Terrier looked remarkably like a Jack Russell. As time went on the Sealyham's legs were shortened and the resemblance vanished. A good Jack Russell Terrier tipped the scales from 13 to 16 pounds. There are those writers who insist that the present-day wire-haired Fox Terrier goes back directly to the Jack Russell. Before this however, most Fox Terriers were of the smooth variety.

The Shelburne Terrier, though an excellent worker, was another breed that failed to gain official recognition. The Shelburne Terrier was developed in the United States by J. Watson Webb of Shelburne, Vermont. Mr. Webb found that fox holes in England were larger than those in America, in many cases having been made by badgers. He further noted that the Terriers of Britain were too large in most cases to be of use in this country. In America the fox often inhabited the earth of a woodchuck and therefore a relatively small Terrier was required. Webb went about breeding a Terrier

Mrs. Wells' Sealy draws a possum.   A Shelburne dog's first fox.

Badger baiting. From an etching by H. Alken, 1820. A Blue Paul Terrier is held by the scruff of the neck awaiting his turn at the unfortunate badger.

that would have the desirable attributes of the several breeds that go for fox and be of a size that could readily enter the earth, fasten to the fox and hold until drawn by the hunters. The Terriers did not have to run with the Hounds so they did require only enough running gear for digging and holding.

The Shelburne Terrier originally came from a Sealyham bitch imported into the United States about 1911 that was bred to a champion wire-haired Fox Terrier. The offspring from his mating was bred to a son of a Norfolk Terrier out of a West Highland White Terrier. This cross produced the desired dog; short in head and leg and much smaller than a Sealyham. This was the foundation stock for the Shelburne. During the following years the Terriers were bred to substantially eliminate white offspring even though a cross back to a Sealyham was carried out now and then to maintain size and improve head.

These little dogs weighed preferably about 12 pounds; were dead-game, faithful and hardy. A photo of "Peter," one of Mr. Webb's favorites is shown herein. I am informed that a few are even now kept at Shelburne where they still work with authority.

The Norfolk Terrier was another working breed originally produced by a man named Jones who lived near Leicester. The Norfolk was a working Terrier from the word go. It is said that the strain had a strong infusion of Irish Terrier blood though it was a smallish breed resembling the Norwich Terrier in most respects. Because of its chief breeder, the strain has also been called a "Jones Terrier," particularly in America where many of the small Terriers were imported. Today the Norwich Terrier takes the place of the Norfolk or Jones Terrier.

Many other breeds were used as working Terriers which, through refinement, eventually became lost in identity and were swallowed by one of the more generally recognized strains. One of these was the Ullswater, Reedwater or Elterwater Terrier. This small and very excellent worker is now known as the Border Terrier. The early dogs of these breeds differed in some small respects from the presently-known Border and preceded it or, in some cases, were bred and used concurrently with early dogs of the Border breed. The names have long since fallen into disuse and the breeds are now extinct.

74

Rat hunting. By T. S. Engelhart after Charles Hancock.

Working certificate issued by the American Sealyham Terrier Club to Cadwallader of Woodwell for gameness.

The Pittenweem Terrier is another lost breed that was much like the West Highland White Terrier. The name was used for a strain of the present breed and went back, as did all Highland breeds, to the old Scotch Terrier. The major point of interest was the white or rusty white color.

The Blue Paul or Blue Poll Terrier is here identified as a working Terrier for want of better classification. This strain was of the Bull Terrier family and, as the name suggested, came in a pleasing bluish slate color. The dog had all of the attributes of the Bull Terrier although it lacked the refinement of later animals. According to fragmentary descriptions now available, this Terrier was closer in conformation to the English Staffordshire Terrier than to the presently-known Bull Terrier.

The Blue Paul was classed as a Scotch fighter. The greatest breeding activity took place in the lowlands between Kirkintilloch and Edinburgh where the strain existed and flourished for about seventy or eighty years. There is no doubt that the Blue Paul variety of Bull Terrier had Scotch blood in its veins. Brown, when speaking of the third variety of the Scotch Terrier, mentioned that it was a larger dog up to 18 inches at the withers, and had longer legs than the rest of the tribe. "It is from this breed that the best bull-terriers have been produced," he wrote.

One of the first notices of the Blue Paul is seen in Alken's colored etching on badger baiting (1820). Here a white Bull Terrier and a Blue Paul Terrier are shown engaged in a badger-baiting contest. The white is at grips with the badger and the handler is attempting to loose the unfortunate animal by biting the Bull Terrier's tail. By 1880, or thereabouts, the strain began to lose size and the old sixty-pound heavyweights were no longer seen. The lightweights that came into vogue were not up to the work and with this deterioration the strain slowly slipped into oblivion.

Blue Pauls threw many colored offspring, mostly blues and brindles. Occasionally a red appeared which was called a "Red Smut" because of lack of clarity in the color. This type was never numerous and few references to it can be found though data are available that document its existence. The rare variety is mentioned to aid researchers who may come across the name in some obscure reference.

Several other breeds have been developed around the world that fall into the broad category of the working Terrier. One of the most intriguing of these is the Sealydale Terrier, a product of South African breeding acumen. As the name implies, this dog comes from a cross between the Sealyham and the Airedale Terrier. Oddly enough the color remains predominantly white with badger markings and the dog resembles the Jack Russell Terrier more than any other breed. In its native land the Sealydale is popular and, used as an all-purpose vermin dog, is doing a very creditable job.

A little known Irish breed is the Glen of Imaal Terrier. Named for its native habitat, the Glen of Imaal in County Wicklow, the dog has a long heritage as a fighting breed. In later years this Terrier was used as a badger dog. In Ireland it was first exhibited at Dublin in 1933. Resembling a short-legged Fox Terrier in conformation, the breed is soft-coated coming in wheaten, blue-brindle and blue-tan colors. Although measuring only about 14 inches at the withers the dog should weigh up to 35 pounds indicating a strongly muscled and cobby animal.

The Deutsche Jagdeterrier is a German hunting Terrier styled after the old Welsh Terrier in many respects. It has been speculated that the breed includes the blood of the Black and Tan Terrier. Black in color, the coat is marked with yellow or red to further the assumption as to derivation.

One of the oldest of all breeds is the Niam Niam, sometimes called the Nyam Nyam or Haute-Agoouc Terrier. Its antiquity may be traced to the Tesem, an Egyptian hunting dog dating back more than 4000 years. The present dog is a native of the Sudan, related to and resembling the Basenji. It has always been thought by this author that the Basenji more closely resembles a Terrier than a Hound. The upright ears, alert attitude and gaily carried curled tail are Terrier characteristics that have been indigenous to several African breeds for centuries. In fact, the old Egyptian Fox Dog illustrated in Rawlingson's *History of Ancient Egypt* (1881) dates back many centuries and is undoubtedly the progenitor of the Niam Niam, the Tesem and the Basenji. The Niam Niam is not well known in Europe or America although it was introduced into England in about 1925 and some specimens have been exhibited at continental European shows.

Working Terriers as distinct strains have, for the most part, become of small importance because of the steady march of civilization which has lessened the importance of the work of these fine little dogs. Of all the above, the Jack Russell is the only one that has not gained recognition and yet has maintained its identity. Possibly this is because Jack Russell Terriers have been in strong demand in England over the past few years.

Working Terriers were the forerunners of our present breeds since most were working Terriers before they gained breed recognition and made their appearance in the show ring. A tribute to the working Terrier, its ability and undeniable courage was written many years ago. No better way is known to close this chapter than with this salute:

> *Ay, see the hounds with frantic zeal*
> *The roots and earth uptear;*
> *But the earth is strong, and the roots are long,*
> *They cannot enter there.*
> *Outspeaks the Squire, 'Give room, I pray,*
> *And hie the Terriers in;*
> *The warriors of the fight are they,*
> *And every fight they win.*

> *Ring-Ouzel*

Col. E. D. Malcolm's West Highland working pack, 1905. Note chain couplings and variation in ear carriage.

9

Terrier Anatomy

WHETHER used for sport, for work or any other purpose whatsoever, the anatomy of the Terrier is the same as that of other types of dogs. Furthermore, the dog's skeletal structure is almost identical with that of man. The canine foreleg is made up of bones similar to those in the human arm; the length of the several bones differs but the basic structure does not. The pastern corresponds to man's wrist while the bones of the foot correspond to those in the fingers, the heel being similar to the union of the fingers with the palm of the hand. Actually the dog walks on his fingers in much the same manner as a man crawling on all fours.

The hind leg may be likened to a man's leg with different lengths of the bones. The dog walks on his toes, and his hock is like a combination of the heel and ankle joint of the man. In this connection, the hind leg with well-let-down hock improves leg action by increasing the drive as well as by lengthening the lower thigh which decreases the pull on the tendons.

This chapter will not delve deeply into basic anatomy since it is a subject of great complexity. It will, however, discuss certain structural deviations between the Terrier and most other breeds of dog. These differences, while minor in degree, are important to the dog's working ability and they sometimes cause concern to the fancier because of lack of understanding.

THE SKELETON

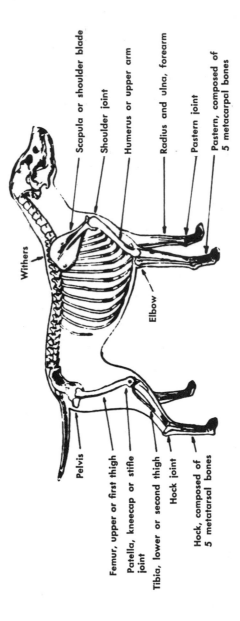

Withers

Scapula or shoulder blade

Shoulder joint

Humerus or upper arm

Radius and ulna, forearm

Pastern joint

Pastern, composed of 5 metacarpal bones

Elbow

Pelvis

Femur, upper or first thigh

Patella, kneecap or stifle joint

Tibia, lower or second thigh

Hock joint

Hock, composed of 5 metatarsal bones

Main bones and joints in the dog's running gear with their scientific and popular names.

The Terrier, unlike other dog breeds is basically a digger. For this reason most Terrier breeds have been modified to effect a compromise in bone structure which permits digging as an essential effort. To this end the Terrier's shoulder bones have slightly different proportions than those found in a runner, for example, a Greyhound. This does not mean that the fundamentals have been changed. So many persons think that a "Terrier" front requires an upright shoulder and that Terriers should walk with stilted and stiff movement. This is incorrect but the idea may have been spawned by the frequently used term "straight Terrier front." This does not mean an upright shoulder; it refers rather to a modification of the racing or running front where a shortening of the upper arm relative to the shoulder blade has been accomplished. This structural deviation offers better digging power through increased leverage. The lay-back remains unchanged.

This is a basic requirement, since lay-back permits reach and reach is responsible for a strong, steady stride that moves the dog over the ground with a minimum of effort. Obviously this was important in the days of fox-hunting when the Terriers occasionally had to run with the Hounds. Lay-back, or shoulder angulation is also important because it sets the dog's legs under the body and not at the front end. The old saw—"It's what's up front that counts" is indeed true for a dog without something in front of his legs is a sorry looking animal. (*See* chart.)

Lay-back of shoulder, or front angulation, must be balanced by proper hind angulation if the dog is to enjoy overall good movement. Unequal angulation between front and rear running gear causes poor movement. For example, if the front lacks lay-back or angulation, and the rear is well angulated, the dog will tend to "track" or "sidewheel" because the front is not covering as much ground as the rear and the rear is attempting to overtake it.

Similarly, if the front goes faster than the rear the dog drags behind and often appears to move quite badly although no apparent bone deformity can be detected. When both ends are poorly angulated the dog moves with short, quick strides and practically stands in one place—there is nothing more unpleasant to watch. In any case, because of his peculiarities every dog moves to best advantage at a specific pace and should be moved at the best

81

speed for the best movement and not at the standard "handler's gait" which is generally too fast for most Terriers.

Movement is the critical test of soundness in any breed of dog and this involves viewing the movement from front and rear as well as from the side. The desirable side movement has already been commented upon. When viewing movement from front and rear the legs of any breed of dog should move in generally parallel planes while moving slowly. The forelegs should swing freely fore and aft and the elbows should not be conspicuous. The hind legs should be separated and the hock joints should not point toward one another. Such indesirable structure is termed cow-hocks. The front feet should be spaced the same distance apart as the elbows and the hind feet are preferably the same distance apart as the hocks. As the speed of the dog increases there is a tendency in most breeds for the feet to draw together for changing the center of gravity to balance the dog. For this reason dogs of different sizes and weights should be moved at different paces to enjoy the best movement for judging purposes.

The several Terrier breeds have distinct and characteristic differences in their legs and feet. For example, the long-legged Terriers should all have straight legs with feet pointing straight ahead. No deviation from this structure is permitted and any dog with crooked legs or feet that turn in or out appears common. This is because a long-legged Terrier, when digging, throws the earth under his body and through his spread back legs.

The short-legged breeds are different. Because of their low station, these breeds cannot throw earth under their bodies. In fact if they did it would not take long before they had dug themselves in. Rather, they throw the earth sideways so that the low-slung body may pass through. In order to accomplish this it is necessary that the feet turn out slightly to guide the earth sideways of the body. Preferably the toeing-out is not great and it should always be equal with respect to both feet. A short-legged Terrier should never be penalized for this bone structure although you will sometimes hear persons faulting one of these dogs because of this characteristic requirement. Actually, feet pointing straight ahead on a short-legged breed are not correct and should be faulted although most judges do not look with disfavor on feet pointing straight ahead.

RIB STRUCTURE

Left—Round rib well sprung. Note how ribs take off from the backbone. *Center*—Well sprung rib with flattish side appearance. The take off is the same but the ribs cut in markedly and greater depth provides for heart and lung capacity. *Right*—A flat rib with poor spring. The ribs fall away from the backbone to produce a rib-cage that has insufficient capacity for proper functioning of the heart and lungs.

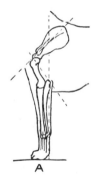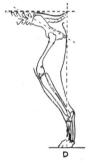

LEG STRUCTURE

A Terrier front with shortened or modified upper arm. It differs from the running or Hound front (*B*) where the upper arm is about equal in length with the shoulder blade. *C*—The same structure for a short-legged dog. Note all three fronts require the proper layback as indicated by dotted lines. *D*—Rear structure. The well-let-down hock is vertically placed when the dog stands.

The importance of the proper toeing-out is discussed by F. M. Ross in her treatise *The Cairn Terrier* (1925). She said, "No Cairn, however deep or in what kind of soil he goes to ground, ever closes himself in. This may be attributed to the turned-out feet which help move the earth sideways instead of directly behind the digging dog. Cairns, Westies, Scotties that work should all have this type of foot though accentuated turning out detracts from appearance and does not aid materially to the working character of the dog."

The short-legged breeds differ also from their long-legged cousins as concerned with straightness of leg. While a straight leg is highly desirable from the exhibition point of view it is seldom found on a dog that is properly constructed. Most short-legged Terriers have legs that are not perfectly straight and one will find that the elbows are not as close to the body as in the longer-legged breeds. Termed roominess behind the elbow this does not mean the dog is out at the elbow but merely that the elbow does not hug the body closely. This may be explained by the fact that the legs are spaced by the spacing of the upper arms. The body on most short-legged breeds is not round but slopes inward from the junction of the upper arm and the shoulder blade. It means that the body has fallen away from the leg structure at the elbow. This is correct, since if the elbow remains in close contact with the body, the legs will slope inward when viewed from the front and the feet will be quite close together.

These fundamental variations between long and short-legged breeds should be viewed with tolerance and understanding since they are necessary to working ability.

Bodies form another point of difference between the several breeds in the Terrier group. Many of the standards are not entirely clear on what is wanted. The term "well sprung rib" can be misleading unless modified by the statement "with body rounded" or some such qualification. Certain standards state that the ribs should be well sprung with depth and a flattish side appearance. Actually well sprung ribs are necessary in all cases. This means that the ribs should take off from the back bone in a more or less horizontal plane rather than taper downward immediately. Such a structure is required in order to insure adequate room for heart and lungs. If the ribs fall away rapidly by tapering downward without spring, heart and lung capacity maybe seriously limited and the dog incapable of performing duties requiring great exertion. This is why well sprung ribs are a necessity in every breed.

Flattish side appearance is noted when the ribs taper inward after their initial spring. This gives the rib cage a somewhat heart-shaped cross section. When the requirement is for well sprung ribs with narrow chest or similar wording, the structure is about the same. When a standard requires a rounded body or ribs well sprung and round it means that the ribs should not taper inward as rapidly and thus should offer a more or less rounded side appearance instead of a flattish side appearance. Bodies in this case are generally not as deep. (See chart)

Tail set is another point that warrants discussion. In those breeds where the tail is carried low, generally not over the level of the back, it appears to take off the back as a continuation of the spine. This occurs as a gentle curve from the end of the backbone. In the breeds that require an upright tail the tail should always be set on high. This means that the tail should "appear" to take off at the top of the backbone. Tail set is of great importance to the overall appearance of a Terrier. Those that require a high set-on do so because the structure effects an apparent shortening of the back. A low-set tail, carried upright, gives the appearance of a long back whereas a high set-on creates an illusion of a desirable short back. When showing any Terrier that requires a high set-on it is useful to press the dog's tail forward when the judge views the dog from the side. This enchances the illusion of shortness.

Those breeds that carry the tail down are for the most part longer-backed than the others. For this reason the tail carriage does not create any illusion but must be well carried to suggest proper breed character.

These are the major points in which Terrier anatomy differs from that of other dog breeds. Certain of these differences are also required in other breeds but for the most part they are indigenous to the Terrier and should be studied as a part of the dog.

10

Trimming and Conditioning

SINCE this book is of a general nature, no attempt will be made to offer detailed instructions for trimming and conditioning each of the twenty Terrier breeds. However, some general trimming instructions will be given together with advice universally applicable to all Terriers with respect to conditioning them for home or show.

All dogs require certain basic attentions if they are to be kept at the peak of condition and health. These several attentions are in some cases obvious and in others overlooked because of lack of knowledge or desire on the part of the owner. All dogs must be fed good, nourishing foods in sufficient quantities to keep them in good flesh without excessive fat. This is not always as easy as it sounds because some dogs are good doers and quickly take on fat which must be eliminated before they can be shown. Other animals are poor doers and these present the greatest problem.

Appetite is sometimes based upon exercise, and exercise is another of the basic attentions that should be given every dog. Too much exercise, while not usually harmful may keep the dog very thin; too little exercise, if he is a poor doer, will keep him from eating. In any case, exercise should be of two kinds, unsupervised and supervised. The first category permits the dog to run free in a yard or run for purposes of elimination and pleasure. The second, or supervised exercise, is for development purposes; it consists of walking the dog on a lead starting at about six months of age. He should be walked at the very least a half-mile per day.

Walking makes the dog easy to handle in the ring and it eliminates any later aversion to the lead. After one year of age, he should be walked at least two miles every day at a show gait and with his head held up. This teaches him proper show etiquette, tones up his muscles and improves his movement. Weakness in muscles of the pasterns, shoulders and hindquarters can all be improved by this effort. During this exercise period it is useful to stop now and then and pose the dog as you would in the ring. Also get strangers to go over him superficially to accustom him to being handled. If possible, the dog should be walked in congested areas periodically to familiarize him with strange sounds. A properly trained dog will always make more of himself in the ring than one that has not been trained.

A widely known handler, now a respected judge, told me that he always hired the youngsters in his town to take his dogs out, one by one, after school. In this manner the dogs got exercise and, even more important, they became accustomed to people, children and strange sounds—no wonder this man had good success in the ring for many years.

All dogs should have their nails trimmed very short. This may be done frequently with clippers and/or nail file. Twice a week is good since very little need be taken off each time to keep the nails back once they have been forced back sufficiently. This attention should start in puppyhood and continue through life. Long nails cause splayed feet and break down the pastern joints while often causing the dog to move poorly due to favoring his feet. Therefore, always do a little at a time and do it frequently.

While working on the nails surplus hair should be removed from between the foot pads. Some dogs grow more surplus hair than others but in all cases it should be kept short. Some can be pulled out while in other cases it must be cut out, preferably with curved blade, blunt-pointed scissors. Hair removed from between the pads eliminates wet pads and excessive licking which often causes weeping sores that are aggravated by constant licking. It also keeps the feet cleaner and more comfortable.

Ears and eyes require frequent care. Hair growing into the ear canals should be removed and the ears kept free from excessive wax. Frequent inspection will eliminate the possible danger of canker. Breeds with drop ears usually have more difficulty than prick-eared breeds but all need periodic attention. A swab of cotton on a toothpick or stick (sold commercially for baby care) dipped into rubbing alcohol may be used to clean away wax and may even be used to clean the ear canal if necessary. In the latter use, the swab should not be wet but merely damp. Thereafter, the ear should dried with a dry swab and then dusted lightly with boric acid powder. Never use an excess because the ear canal may become clogged with the powder. Use lightly and repeat once or twice. *Never* subject a dog to outside temperatures until the ears are completely dry. This should take an hour at least.

The eyes also require some attention but most Terriers do not have any great amount of eye difficulty. When a dog is healthy, the eyes should glisten and sparkle. Eyes are a good indicator of a dog's condition. In some instances and frequently because of external causes an otherwise healthy eye will collect matter in the corners. This should be removed daily with a bit of cotton. The eyes may weep excessively as caused by internal parasites, such as worms, or from a cold in the eyes. In the latter case, several eye ointments are available which will correct the condition. One per cent yellow mercuric oxide ophthalmic ointment has been used for years with good results. A quarter-inch of the ointment dispensed directly from the tube into a pocket made by pulling out the lower eyelid will generally help. If the weeping comes from worms or other internal difficulties a veterinarian should be consulted; however, if the dog is checked periodically worms are not ordinarily the cause.

Eye weeping in some long-coated breeds results from hair getting into the eyes, also there is a tendency in a few breeds to slight weeping that stains the eye corners. The eyes should be wiped clean each day to prevent staining of the hair.

The teeth require periodic cleaning. This varies with different dogs and different diets. Tartar may be removed when it begins to accumulate; it may be prevented by weekly rubbing the teeth with baking soda on a cloth. In most cases, however, it must be chipped or scraped off with a dental tool. Some dogs object to this attention; if so, it will be necessary to have a veterinarian do the job. In all cases removal of tartar keeps the breath sweet and prevents the possibility of loosening of teeth because of diseased gums.

The foregoing are some of the basic attentions that should be given to every dog, whether for show or for home. Followed carefully they will improve the dog's health, welfare and capability in the show ring and make him a pleasure to own.

Passing now to the more technical details of maintaining the Terrier's coat it will be found that all Terrier breeds require some trimming while some require a great deal. In this connection it is possible to classify all Terriers in two main categories: those that have heavy or rough coats and those that have smooth coats. The heavy-coated ones can be further divided into three main classes:

> Heavily trimmed wire-coated breeds.
> Heavily trimmed soft-coated breeds.
> Lightly trimmed or tidied-up breeds.

The smooth-coated dogs will be discussed first since the problems are fewer and the attention is generally not as difficult. In this class we find the two varieties of the Bull Terrier, the Smooth Fox Terrier, the Standard Manchester and the Staffordshire Terrier. All but the Fox Terrier may be treated the same and this entails frequent and preferably daily gloving and/or brushing. The glove should be a standard Terrier glove with fibre bristle facing, or a rough Turkish towel may be used as a substitute. This grooming brings out the coat oils, stimulates the hair follicles, produces healthy growth and maintains a good bloom. Nothing can take the place of daily grooming to keep the coat in shape and keep it coming. The stimulation improves hair growth and keeps the coat alive.

The stiff whiskers on the muzzle should be cut short and any long or straggling hairs around the ears or vent removed. The tail hair is sometimes tapered by various means, either a knife, scissors or sandpaper properly applied. Generally this is not necessary unless the dog grows a heavy coat. If he does it may also be necessary to thin out the hair on the neck which may be done with a stripping knife or thinning scissors carefully used to avoid "steps."

The Smooth Fox Terrier requires the same treatment as the other smooth-coated breeds. However, since the Smooth also may and probably does have some wire blood in his veins, the coat may grow considerably longer than that of other smooth-coated breeds. For this reason, it may be necessary to resort to an overall shaping up of the coat with a stripping knife used a little at a time and starting weeks before the first showing. Once the coat has been shaped it may be kept in condition by frequent light trimming.

All smooth-coated breeds except the colored Bull Terrier, Staffordshire and Manchester are predominantly white. They require cleaning for show. Overall washing (bath) with a few drops of bluing in the rinse water will do the trick although excessive bathing is not recommended. After the bath the dog should be thoroughly dried and chalk rubbed through the white parts of the coat in the

WEST HIGHLAND WHITE TERRIER TRIMMING CHART

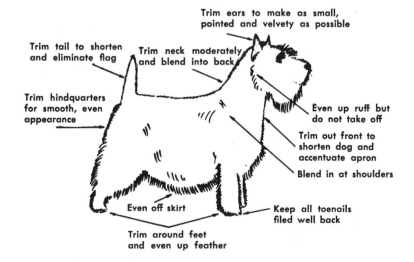

Trim ears to make as small, pointed and velvety as possible

Trim tail to shorten and eliminate flag

Trim neck moderately and blend into back

Trim hindquarters for smooth, even appearance

Even up ruff but do not take off

Trim out front to shorten dog and accentuate apron

Blend in at shoulders

Even off skirt

Keep all toenails filed well back

Trim around feet and even up feather

TRIMMING CHART FOR HEAVILY TRIMMED WIRE-COATED BREEDS

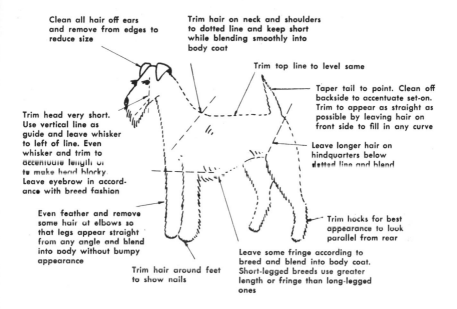

Clean all hair off ears and remove from edges to reduce size

Trim hair on neck and shoulders to dotted line and keep short while blending smoothly into body coat

Trim top line to level same

Taper tail to point. Clean off backside to accentuate set-on. Trim to appear as straight as possible by leaving hair on front side to fill in any curve

Trim head very short. Use vertical line as guide and leave whisker to left of line. Even whisker and trim to accentuate length or to make head blocky. Leave eyebrow in accordance with breed fashion

Leave longer hair on hindquarters below dotted line and blend

Even feather and remove some hair at elbows so that legs appear straight from any angle and blend into body without bumpy appearance

Trim hocks for best appearance to look parallel from rear

Trim hair around feet to show nails

Leave some fringe according to breed and blend into body coat. Short-legged breeds use greater length or fringe than long-legged ones

direction of the lie. This must be removed before showing; it is best done with a towel, brush or glove. If the dog is bathed it is best done the day before the show. A towel pinned around the dog's body will keep him clean in the home or on the bench until it is time to do him up for the ring. Heavier coated breeds may also require bathing but in most instances shampooing of the legs and whiskers with a thorough dry cleaning of the coat will suffice.

The lightly trimmed heavy-coated dogs include the Australian Terrier, the Border, Cairn, Dandie Dinmont, Norwich, Skye, and West Highland White Terrier. Of these, the Australian, Border, Norwich and Skye require very little trimming although the Skye needs a great deal of grooming to keep the coat at its best. All are double-coated dogs; they need brush work rather than combing which tends to remove too much undercoat. Of course a comb is the only means of eliminating tangles but if the dog is groomed enough these are kept at a minimum. In general, these four breeds need only to have the feet trimmed and surplus hair around the vent and on the tail shaped up. Thereafter brushing to remove tangles and a final combing before entering the ring is all that is required. The Skye of course must be combed to part the coat from the tip of the nose to the tip of the tail, so to speak, with a part right down the middle of the back. A little coat conditioner rubbed in will help to make it look its best.

These breeds, as all others, are frequently trimmed a bit here and there to improve their general outline and this is done only when you know the dog and the breed quite well. Judicious trimming should be carried out only after a bit of experimenting since hair removed cannot be quickly replaced. Removal of stray and straggling hair always "smartens up" any dog's appearance.

The Cairn and Westie are readied in about the same manner with the Westie using a bit more trimming than its cousin. Shoulders, hindquarters and neck are all improved with trimming to blend them into the remainder of the body. Of course the feather and tail, as with all dogs, need shaping and straightening to make them look their best. The trimming chart shows the general areas for trimming and it should be remembered that the main body coat should be kept about two inches in length. Under no circumstances should the ruff or frame around the head be removed; it spoils completely the character of the breeds.

The Dandie Dinmont requires a different treatment because of the ears and the topknot. Ears are cleaned off close, leaving hair at the top of the ears to be combed upward to join the topknot. The ear tips are not trimmed but left about an inch from the ends to form a tassle or tab. The inside of the ears should be clean. The sides of the skull are trimmed under the ears to make them lie close to the head. The rest is left untrimmed especially on the top of the head where the hair is used to form the topknot. Then the top of the nose or muzzle is cleaned off to accentuate the stop and the hair beneath the eyes is taken down to emphasize the large size of the eyes. Do not remove the "spectacles" around the eyes. The topknot should be groomed well and trimmed to present a rounded effect.

The remainder of the dog should be cleaned up to remove excess hair without destroying the double-coated effect or removing the pencilling in the body coat. Other trimming guides used with the other breeds are of course adhered to in order to present the best appearance. It should be remembered that the Dandie has a distinctive arch over his loin and nothing should be taken away that will destroy the effectiveness of this.

Airedales, Wire Fox Terriers, Irish, Lakeland, Miniature Schnauzers, Sealyhams, Scottish and Welsh Terriers all follow the same general pattern and all may be classed as heavily trimmed wire-coated breeds. All are plucked out about eight weeks before the first show and are permitted to grow a new coat. The feather, whiskers and belly coat is never removed since this requires many months to grow out. As the coat begins to come in, the head is kept close as is the neck and shoulders with the remainder of the coat being "teased" along with light trimming to make it tight. (*See* chart.)

Head trimming varies with the breed and the Lakeland and Welsh are trimmed to appear more blocky than the Wire, Irish or Airedale. The Lakeland and Miniature Schnauzer carry more eyebrow as a rule and the Schnauzer is left less hair on the hindquarters and more on the hocks than the others. In all of this group, the ears are trimmed close and clean inside and out.

The Sealyham follows about the same plan as the Wire Fox Terrier with a bit more coat carried under the body. The Scottish Terrier is shown today with a heavier coat than the rest and with profuse furnishings, otherwise it is trimmed about like the other breeds just discussed except for the ears. These are made to appear smaller by leaving tufts of hair at the inside near the skull which also makes them appear to be set higher.

In general all breeds in this group of heavily trimmed Terriers appear better the more they are worked on. Plucking improves color: tans appear deeper and blacks blacker as the trimming progresses. For this reason the process should be done frequently, especially on the head where trimming improves the texture and color of short hairs which otherwise may be soft and washed out in color. Repeated plucking also creates greater density, tightens the coat and makes it lie in place.

In all wire-coated breeds, except the Miniature Schnauzer, the coat may be kept in shape for a long time by getting it "rolling." This means that, by trimming, the coat is brought along so that it consists of three separate, distinct coat growths, one coming, one prime and one going. Working this type of coat requires gradual removal of the "going" coat so that it is all gone by the time the "prime" coat begins to go. By this time, of course, the coat that was coming has arrived and is "prime."

Terrier coats are for the most part double coats. They consist of a dense, soft undercoat and a hard, longer top coat. Usually brushing does not remove either coat although excessive combing will remove undercoat. When a double coat starts to blow, or lift, it is generally due to excessive undercoat. This calls for grubbing out some of the undercoat or the whole coat will go. This is best done with a carding comb or with a very fine-toothed comb. It should be done carefully and never should all undercoat be removed.

In all cases trimming or plucking is best done with thumb and forefinger. This is the way the old-time handlers did it and this is the way the coat can best be served. The old hair is removed so that new hair may come in. If you are not adept at this method, and few can do it today, the next best plan is to use a trimming knife. This can be a regular stripping comb (saw-toothed affair) or an old penknife with a dull blade can be used. The knife is held in the hand and the hair is grasped between it and the thumb and pulled. Dead hair will come out while most of the live hair will slip through.

Never use a razor on a double-coated dog. The razor cuts the hair off leaving the dead hair roots in place, retarding the growth of new hair and in general ruining coat texture. Razors are quick and easy but the results are disappointing. Their use is decried by most Terrier men and by judges.

The Miniature Schnauzer, because of the banded hair (dark ends with light roots) presents a problem different from any other breed in the group although Irish Terriers sometimes present a similar problem. Rolling the coat is difficult because it creates a multi-colored effect that makes the dog appear moth-eaten. For this reason most handlers bring a dog to its peak and show it during this period, usually about four to six weeks. They then take it down and wait for a new coat before starting out again. Others use the rolling technique but keep the coat quite short at all times so that the multi-colored effect is not so noticeable. Either method can be used and both are used successfully.

The remaining two breeds in the group fall in a different category, so far as trimming is concerned, than any others. The Bedlington and the Kerry Blue Terrier are heavy-coated breeds but neither is plucked—they are scissored dogs. This means that the art of barbering comes into the picture in much the same manner as with the Poodle. The virtue of a good coat in these breeds is a dense coat, rich and with a thick pile. This is generally accomplished by repeated scissoring which improves texture and density.

Both breeds have trimmed heads and ears. This may be done with the knife although many resort to clippers which does not enhance the texture or color of the hair. The ears of the Bedlington also require a tassle at the end, and the top of the head is adorned with a topknot fashioned in much the same manner as that of the Dandie.

The body of the Kerry should be scissored to resemble that of any other long-legged Terrier with greater length of hair. Thus many defects may be hidden by clever trimming. The Bedlington resembles the Dandie more closely than any other Terrier because of the top line, although the head differs widely as does the remainder of the body conformation. The Bedlington, like the Dandie must be trimmed to accentuate the arch while the tail has little hair left particularly from about half way to the tip and is cleaned down, often with clippers.

These are some of the problems encountered in trimming the various breeds of Terrier. The subject is one that never ends because each dog presents different problems and each requires a slightly different solution. The best approach is to follow a trimming chart and eye your work critically. Compare it with the dogs at the shows conditioned by experts, and make adjustments. Additional information may be obtained for specific breeds from the breed books noted in the bibliography. In all cases, mistakes will soon grow out to give the tyro trimmer a second or third chance.

Airedale Terrier, Ch. Westhay Fiona of Harham.

11

Terrier Breeds in America Today

TERRIERS have always enjoyed a young following of fanciers who have supported the several breeds in the group. This patronage, while still substantial, has lessened noticeably during the past two decades. The downtrend is mainly in evidence at dog shows where the interest is in animals with good conformation, but is not so apparent among pet-type breeders who find a large ready market for Terriers of all breeds.

This is proved by figures which show that the total number of Terriers registered during the five years from 1957 to 1961, inclusive, has risen from 20,075 to 28,200 while the total number exhibited at American Kennel Club licensed and member shows gained only from 23,712 to 28,700. Though more Terriers are being exhibited each year, the gain is slight and the ratio of show activity in Terrier breeds to that in other breeds is losing ground steadily. In spite of the decline the quality of Terrier exhibits is still high.

Possibly this trend is due to the substantial amount of expert trimming required by many breeds in the group. Today there are fewer professional handlers with Terrier background than in the early days of this century when large kennels had private handlers. The latter in turn employed apprentices who learned trimming the hard way. Today the private handler is virtually unknown and few handlers maintain kennels of a size to warrant the employment of an apprentice who may benefit from the experience.

The wire-haired Fox Terrier is one of the most difficult breeds to condition properly and to keep in top shape. The Irish Terrier, Welsh Terrier and Sealyham among others require a great deal of knowledge to bring the coat into full bloom. Many other breeds in the group need special coat care to a lesser but considerable degree.

Fanciers should become adept at trimming and conditioning their own dogs. The pleasure derived by so doing is rewarding and the fanciers certainly benefit from the knowledge gained. Increased technical knowledge of this nature gained by individual fanciers stabilizes the breeds and brings forward persons who are qualified to judge from actual contact rather than from mere reading. Too many of today's showgoers are interested only in winning and not in *knowing* what makes a winner. Firsthand knowledge derived from experience changes the outlook, brightens the show picture and makes the recipient of the knowledge respected by all.

In chapters to follow, concise histories and Standards of Perfection are offered for each breed in the Terrier group. In most cases, no extensive background is given since the basic heritage of all Terriers has already been explored in earlier chapters. The detailed background of the several breeds with respect to the names of dogs and their breeders is available in a number of excellent breed books. These books and articles are listed in the bibliography for the benefit of those who wish to add to their knowledge. Many of the articles come from the magazine, *Pure-Bred Dogs—The American Kennel Gazette* where Arthur Frederick Jones, managing editor, wrote each month about prominent kennels of various breeds. The Terrier articles will be found especially interesting to Terrier fanciers. Among other articles listed are those by A. Croxton Smith, an acknowledged authority and author on all breeds.

Complete rules and regulations governing dog shows will be found in the booklet, *Rules Applying to Registration and Dog Shows* obtainable from The American Kennel Club, 51 Madison Avenue, New York, New York. Information concerning parent breed specialty clubs is likewise available from the AKC.

Breed standards also are to be found herein. These standards are word patterns carefully written to guide fanciers in their breeding operations and judges in their show-ring appraisals. Approved by the AKC and by each specialty club involved, they are concise directives which detail the specifications of the ideal dog of each breed. They note also in certain cases, as disqualifications, traits and physical qualities considered detrimental.

In addition to disqualifications noted in breed standards, the AKC mentions a few applicable to all breeds, namely, the dog which is "blind, deaf, castrated, spayed, or which has been changed in appearance by artificial means except as specified by its breed standard, or a male which does not have two normal testicles normally located in the scrotum." Lameness does not disqualify if the show veterinarian pronounces it temporary, and things like the removal of dewclaws and the docking of the tail do not disqualify if such practices are not contrary to the standard.

Since Terrier breeds or kinds have been known by various names during the many years of their derivation, it is often difficult for readers of old books and periodicals to identify properly the different breeds discussed. Some names in use centuries ago are rarely encountered in modern works while others are used even today as nicknames or alternate names. In an effort to assist researcher and novice both I have compiled two alphabetical lists (*see* Appendix), arranged cross-reference fashion. This will enable readers to recognize with greater accuracy breeds as named in years gone by.

Peter, a Shelburne Terrier bred by J. Watson Webb.

12

Airedale Terrier

THE Airedale Terrier, largest of all the Terrier family, is often referred to as "the King of Terriers" because of his size and majestic outlook. Stonehenge first mentions the breed in his fourth edition of *The Dog In Health and Disease* (1886) where he says it is similar to the Irish Terrier differing "chiefly in color . . . and much fancied by pitmen" of the north country. This description was not very illuminating and certainly does not do the breed justice.

Actually, the Airedale Terrier was known for many years in the north country of England along the valley of the river Aire. Bred large, the dogs were used on water vermin, such as otter. Early writers credit the breed to offspring from a cross between large, wiry-coated English Terriers and Otter Hounds. This premise is well supported when one views an early Airedale Terrier with an Otter Hound of the same era. Illustrations of the two are offered for comparison.

The theory is further strengthened by other factors: for example, the coat of the Airedale has generally been of excellent texture. This was to be expected since the Otter Hound has always had a wiry coat and the Terrier cross was a wiry-coated dog. The progeny of the cross should excel in coat which makes it difficult today to appreciate an Airedale lacking proper coat texture. Size is another point marking the cross as a logical starting point for the present-day breed. No Terrier was known in the middle 1800's of a size approaching that of the Airedale. The Otter Hound, on the other hand, was a large dog standing 25 inches at the withers. This size, coupled with selection of large Terriers as breeding stock, undoubtedly can be credited for the present size of the breed.

Another point of interest is Airedale courage. Today the dog is used for anything and everything. He will hunt bear and lion and never back down. This indomitable spirit comes from his forebears. The Terrier has been established as including a bit of Bulldog blood for courage. The Otter Hound has always been known as a courageous dog or he would never have been of use for otter hunting. This courage was not indigenous to hounds that would back off when the going "got tough." Where the courage came from is not known, but Otter Hounds, unlike most docile hounds, have long been known as fighters when aroused. Naturally the cross of an Otter Hound and a Terrier would bring together courage plus tenacity, another of the Otter Hound's sterling attributes. For these reasons the Airedale Terrier must be fearless and majestic in appearance and action at all times and under any conditions.

According to Lee (1894) the dogs were found in various degrees of development for fifty years around Yorkshire, under the names of Bingley Terrier and Waterside Terrier. Since the greatest activity was adjacent to the Valley of the Aire it is not surprising that the name finally decided upon was Airedale Terrier, an alternate name used during the early days of the dog's exhibition. This occurred at the Birmingham show in 1883 where Airedales or Waterside Terriers had their first distinct classes. In 1886 the breed was given stud book rating under the single designation of Airedale Terrier.

The early dogs shown, reminiscent of the Hound cross, differed but little from their Otter Hound ancestors. As time went on the Terrier attributes were stressed to improve heads, ears and fine legs and feet. By 1891 the breed was of such quality that H. M. Bryan's entry of four tied for the honor of best Terrier team in show at Crystal Palace against competition that included eleven Terrier breeds. Dandie Dinmonts were the major competition and gained a similar high award.

Australian Terriers. *Left*—Ch. Cooees Stralean Aussie. *Right*—Ch. Tinee Town Traveler. Owners: Nell N. and Milton Fox.

Harold M. Florsheim's Airedale Terrier, Eng. and Am. Ch. Westhay Fiona of Harham, winner of 25 best in shows.

The present Airedale Terrier Club was not established in England until 1892 although there was an earlier group called the Airedale and Old English Terrier Club. The standard offered at that time was similar in most respects to the one used in this country although changes have since been made which specify height rather than weight limits, a sensible move since weight is not a proper criterion of a dog's size. Early standards suggested a 45-pound maximum while today's standard suggests a top height of 23 inches at the withers.

Ch. Master Briar (1897–1906) and his son Ch. Clonmel Monarch are two early dogs in the breed that helped bring about present-day refinement. Clonmel Monarch gave the breed tremendous impetus by claiming an unofficial best in show at Westminster in 1899. Holland Buckley, author of several Terrier books and later Hon. Secretary of the English Kennel Club, was a staunch supporter of this breed as evidenced by the repeated findings of his "Clonmel" prefix in the names of dogs known in the breed. In America Mr. C. H. Mason brought over the first Airedale by the name of Bruce, a dog shown in the "rough-haired Terrier" class at New York in 1881. It was not until 1898 that special classes were provided for the breed at New York. After this, Airedales began to move and such dogs as Clonmel Marvel and Clonmel Sensation gained prominence. Russell Johnson, Theodore Offerman and E. A. Woodward took the breed along during the early days of the century. By the 1920's the Airedale had become as popular as the wire-haired Fox Terrier and tremendous entries were found at most shows with a host of new fanciers entering the ring.

Several reasons may be advanced for this tremendous growth. First, two Airedales took top honors at Westminster within three years, Ch. Briergate Bright Beauty in 1919 and Ch. Boxwood Barkentine in 1922. These closely staged triumphs spotlighted the breed. When Warren G. Harding entered the White House as President of the United States in 1921, he was given an Airedale Terrier, Laddie Boy. This dog caught the public fancy and within a short time Airedales were in such demand that breeding efforts could not keep pace. Possibly this forward surge harmed the breed for, as in the case of other breeds, quality was neglected in an effort to raise puppies for the increasing market. Thereafter, breed popularity waned and fell to a low ebb in spite of an excellent Garden triumph by S. M. Stewart's Ch. Warland Protector of Shelterock in 1933.

Recently several excellent specimens have been shown and the Airedale is coming back. Breeders should remember, however, that this is a majestic dog and entries should exemplify the attribute. The Airedale should be fearless, not quarrelsome, but fully capable of and willing to take care of himself under any circumstance. One other admonition concerns ears, some of which still hark back to the Otter Hound ancestor. An Airedale's ears should hang on the sides of the head but should break or fold a bit above the top of the skull. Ears that are not characteristic destroy the typical expression.

In general the breed is doing well today and, in view of its sterling past record and acknowledged attributes, it is hoped that this renaissance will continue.

The Quorn Hunt, a typical hunt with its pack. Miss Serrell rode with this group many times.

13

Australian Terrier

BECAUSE of the relative newness of the Australian Terrier as a recognized breed in America, I have asked Mrs. Milton Fox to delineate the history of the breed with emphasis on its success in this country.

"The breed's beginnings go back many years. When the discoverers Tasmas and Cook first landed in the 'Down Under' continent they found much besides the natives that was unfamiliar. Among the strange features of this new world were foods, plants, birds, animals, wild and domestic, including the dog. The vague descriptions of the animal life leave much to our imagintion. It is known that men have sought to refine, domesticate and train some of these animals. How successful these refinements have been in regard to certain of the beasts is dubious. Here, confining ourselves to the dog, we may state unequivocably that improvements have been made! Temperamental and physical characteristics have now been adapted to associate closely with man's modern living requirements. Climatic, geographic and working variations are demonstrated in appropriate physical adaptations as a breed progresses.

"When Australians needed help to control rodents around waterfronts, gold mines and their 'stations' (i.e., ranches), they turned to their dogs and found the herding Kelpie type unsatisfactory for the work. The settlers therefore began propagating the small canine 'terrors' from the rough-coated, short-legged dogs from Britain which originally came with the first sailing ships. They were known then and now as having 'more courage per pound of live weight than any other animal on earth.'

"These little dogs, closely related to the early Scotch Terriers of Britain were first called Broken-coated Terriers in Australia. Rough and tough, they certainly were; associating closely with the hardy, independent pioneers, the dogs seemed to imbibe the characteristics of these masters. As fortune favored these early Australians, many soon lived in fancy houses and drove in splendid carriages behind prancing horses. Upon the carriage seat rode a good-looking Aussie (the endearing name that grew up with the breed). A fitting companion for drawing room or work outdoors, there is no breed quite like an Australian Terrier. To quote the late distinguished Frederick David, 'No one who has owned an Australian Terrier ever desires to own any other kind of dog!'"

"What most distinguishes them from other Terriers? Specifically, the attractive soft, light colored topknot, first emphasized to guard the eyes while 'going to ground' or tunneling; also, the dramatic frill around the neck which was originally grown for protective reasons. Both these features are at the same time attractive and useful. The Aussies' convenient 12–14 pound size places them among the smallest of the Terriers and distinguishes them from the majority. Each individual possesses its own special color tones, and physically and emotionally every Aussie has its own personality. For this reason it is difficult to exhibit a brace, because the variance in personality is reflected in expression. Even their voices vary; with a little attention it becomes easy to learn what each is telling us. To quote the Australian Terrier Club brochure, the Aussie is 'not snappy or yappy'; if he barks, it is for a good reason. Another means of contact between your Aussie and you is through the movement of the ears. If you watch these for reactions, you will discover they are incredibly sensitive.

"Even though the breed possesses rugged individualists and a 'none-look-alike' quality, it is essential that each representative combine with its own particular personality a certain definite uni-

American, Australian and New Zealand Ch. Merryvale Suzette. Owners: Nell N. and Milton Fox.

Cairn, Ch. Kilmet of Cairndania, owned by Mrs. Betty Hyslop.

Bedlington Terrier, Ch. Rock Ridge Night Rocket, a Westminster best-in-show winner. Bred and owned by Mr. and Mrs. William A. Rockefeller.

formity of basic standard requirements. This standard the world over has changed but little through the years. The American authorities, with vast experience, and upon studying the source and history of the breed, decided to accept a standard they considered best for America. Wisely enough, they are not influenced by the personal voices on the subject or the many opinions from other countries. To quote one of the breed's great enthusiasts, the late MacDonald Daly, 'First Australian dog shows were held in 1864, and in the 1880's classes were put on for *broken-coated terriers* of over seven pounds in weight or under seven pounds, further subdivided into *blue, sandy,* or any color other than *blue or sandy.*'

"From Daly and other reliable sources it is known that the ancestry of the Aussie includes blood from most of the early Scotch Terriers, such as Dandie Dinmonts, Skyes, etc., and later Yorkshire and possibly Irish and Black and Tan. At the present, no verified introduction of other breeds is known. In fact, from the time the breed achieved identity in Australia it has been kept quite pure and free from the infusion of foreign blood. In support of this statement is the fact that early Australian breeders had far less choice of the small, smart-working Terriers with which to interbreed their stock than did fanciers of the British Isles.

"In the late 1800's the first Australian Terrier Club was formed in the land 'Down Under' and from that time on Great Britain began importing. In 1933 the English Kennel Club granted the Australian Terrier a separate registry. In the United States, the breed has been known since about 1895 when the first Aussie came to America although breed recognition did not come until 1960.

"In more recent years Aussies were seen on Long Island estates and were imported by American service men after both World Wars. It was not until 1960 that the American Kennel Club officially accepted the breed, the first Terrier to be added to the group in twenty-four years. The first of the breed to be registered in the AKC Stud Book was Canberra Kookaburra R-258126 in 1960 and owned by I. M. Cecily Brush of Palo Alto, California. The first Aussie to gain an AKC title was Ch. Cooees Straleon Aussie owned by Mr. and Mrs. Fox of Point Pleasant, New Jersey. This recognition followed consistent, increased interest reflected by the Westminster Kennel Club shows in New York. This event had record-breaking entries of forty-four Australian Terriers in Miscellaneous

Classes in 1959 and fifty-eight entries in 1960. There was a noteworthy advancement for the breed as show and pet dogs in an increasing number of states. During these years, starting about 1956, a nucleus of a club began which is now a substantial group, incorporated and active. The Australian Terrier Club of America, founded in 1956, held its first Sanctioned 'A' Match, July 10, 1960, in Lakewood, New Jersey, only ten days after American Kennel Club official recognition. This successful event was followed by another match a year later, making possible the first specialty for the breed. There were over fifty dogs and seventy-seven entries on February 11, 1962, at the Associated Terriers' Clubs show in New York.

"The breed has benefited greatly by the excellent imports from Australia, New Zealand, England, and Ireland, although today American bloodlines have already grown strong enough to maintain quality and breed type. As in any breed, imports help maintain and improve quality when judiciously used in proper bloodlines.

"One can almost imagine that Australian Terriers themselves have pioneers' faith, sincerity, courage; indeed, the first people who struggle to promote a new breed in America today must also possess such fortitude, the sort of enthusiastic driving force which one has been conscious of ever since the A.T.C.A. was first founded. One might call it a spontaneous love affair between Americans and Aussies. This genuine emotion of the fanciers for their 'Down Under Darlings' (to borrow columnist Jack Baird's term) attracted outstanding writers who soon recognized the appeal the breed has for the U.S.A. and before long these hardy canine immigrants became as well-known in print as they have in American life. Frequently, particularly in the East, the breed is among the largest of the Terrier entries. Excellent specimens are seen in top places, even in brace classes and in the Terrier group rings.

For a true lover of dogs with prime devotion to Terriers, it is impossible not to have deep affection for the whole Terrier group. However, once acquainted with Aussies, one's admiration remains steadfast. As Jean McClure says: 'For the love of your life, choose an Aussie.' The unbounding devotion from puppyhood, the original manner of doing things, almost a sense of humor, the fact of their being so easy to care for, added to their protective, responsive natures, make them courageous companions beyond compare."

14

Bedlington Terrier

THE origin of the Bedlington Terrier is more obscure than that of most other varieties in the Terrier family. The low-set ears, the topknot, the roached back and the lithe, graceful, almost racy appearance are all attributes that defy explanation without bringing foreign blood into the background.

Undoubtedly, the English Terrier is the basis of this breed that came originally from the north counties of Northumberland, Cumberland and Westmorland. Since there is unquestioned consanguinity with the Dandie Dinmont, there must also be a very small amount of Scotch Terrier blood in its veins. Add to this mixture a trace of Otter Hound and a dash of Greyhound and you may have the basic ingredients which make the dog. To date, no authority has been able to offer a more reasonable explanation and most have bypassed the issue completely with literary agility.

In the early days, the Bedlington was known as a gypsy's dog. He traveled with tinkers and itinerants who journeyed from estate to estate plying their trades and wiles and the Terriers met great favor with the gentry by ridding the places of rats and other rodents.

Because of its place of origin, the Bedlington has been interchangeably referred to as a Rothbury, Rodberry, Northern Counties or Northumberland Fox Terrier. These names were abandoned, for the most part, by 1870 when the breed began to take shape and attract notice among fanciers. While the breed is of about the same antiquity as the Dandie Dinmont, it received its real beginnings around 1820 when a Joseph Ainsley purchased a dog named "Peachem" from William Cowen of Rothbury. This dog was bred to a bitch named "Phoebe," the offspring being a liver dog, "Piper," which belonged to James Anderson of Rothbury Forest. Piper was about 15 inches high and 15 pounds in weight; his coat was linty and his large ears hung close to the cheeks with feathering at the tips. Ainsley then obtained a bitch known as "Coates's Phoebe," a black-blue with a light-colored silky tuft of hair on her head. She was about 13 inches high and weighed 14 pounds. Ainsley bred her to Anderson's Piper. The offspring from this union, the first acknowledged Bedlington Terrier, was known as "Ainsley's Piper," a dog that sired many of the early dogs of the new breed.

The breed had its ups and downs for the next fifty years. Various bloods crept into the strain for one purpose or another, but in each case results were disappointing and fanciers reverted to the original type with a bit more leg to distinguish the breed from the somewhat doughty early specimens. Fast, courageous and intelligent the dogs had a tremendous hatred for vermin. They were dainty in appearance, easy to keep and made fine land or water dogs. Bedlingtons are reminiscent of sheep in appearance, and in manner are very docile and mild. They are, however, deadly fighters when pressed into action. This they accomplish without much noise and if three or more are so engaged, seldom more than one will emerge from the struggle. The puppies are born dark and the color clears in much the same manner as the Kerry Blue until they attain the attractive blue or liver color of the grown dog.

In 1870 the Bedlington, England, show had classes for the breed to mark its entry to the show ring, and in 1871 classes were provided at the great Crystal Palace show. The year 1877 marks the date that the National Bedlington Terrier Club was organized and this gave the breed real impetus with the backing of many influential persons who had become its devotees. By 1905 there were three specialty clubs in England helping the breed develop. In addition to the National Club they were the South of England

Bedlington Terrier Club and the Yorkshire Bedlington Terrier Club. To Mr. Harold Warnes' Ch. Cranley Blue Boy went the honor of best dog or bitch in show at Ipswich in 1906. This was the first high honor won by the breed but it was not the last.

In America by 1890 there were a few of the breed, mostly imports. Some were in Canada, others in the United States. The first Bedlington to become registered in the American Kennel Club stud book was Ananias 4475 owned by W. S. Jackson of Toronto. The Bedlington Terrier Club of America, founded in 1932, became a member of the American Kennel Club in 1936.

The breed has always enjoyed a modicum of popularity, not great enough to ruin its quality but sufficient to keep it before the eyes of the public. Probably one of the greatest boosts the breed has received was in 1948 when Ch. Rock Ridge Night Rocket captured the Westminster Kennel Club top award for best dog in show. He sandwiched this plum between best-in-show awards at the 1947 and 1948 Morris & Essex shows to claim the three top awards for the period. Of course, the dog's winning was not confined to these events but because of the stature of the shows the wins meant more to the breed than other triumphs.

Today we find the Bedlington in about the same condition as any other Terrier breed. Registrations are climbing but not in pace with other non-Terrier breeds. Many excellent specimens have been on the benches and seldom does a year go by when at least one Bedlington is not pushing for top Terrier.

Early Bedlington Terriers imported into the United States were larger than the forebears of the breed. For example, Sentinel 4479 by Pioneer ex Dusky, whelped August 31, 1883, a blue owned by W. S. Jackson, weighed 26 pounds and as the number indicates was registered simultaneously with Mr. Jackson's Ananias. Domino 6179, a bitch by Petrach ex Bagatelle, whelped September 1, 1881 and bred by A. Armstrong of Newcastle-on-Tyne and also owned by Jackson, weighed 22½ pounds while Tess Rock 9794, a light blue dog with a white spot on his chest, owned by E. D. Morgan, was a 25½-pounder. All of these Bedlingtons were being shown during the 1887 season at such events as New York, Hartford and Buffalo. They must have been large dogs since Coate's Phoebe and Anderson's Piper weighed 14 and 15 pounds respectively and were but an inch under top height limit of today's standard.

Prior to 1890 trimming was a serious offense in the eyes of the English Kennel Club; it became a point of controversy between the English Bedlington Terrier Club and the English Kennel Club. Some kennels at the time resorted to artful plucking but even this was frowned upon. Fanciers did not give up, however, and on January 7, 1890 the specialty group openly challenged the English Kennel Club on the issue when they voted to permit removal of "superfluous hair . . . as it is not done to deceive but to smarten the dog and show his shape and general contour. . . ." On February 4, 1890 the English Kennel Club capitulated with the proviso that superfluous hair "means old and dead coat." Removal of new coat or trimming of head and ears was still considered improper. Few worried about the admonition, and shaping of new hair as well as removal of dead hair went forward "to smarten the dog." Today we find the Bedlington a heavily trimmed dog with the coat shaped and trimmed to offer the very best appearance. The result of this trimming gives the dog an opportunity to do big winning since Terriers that grow heavy coats do not do well in the ring without trimming to accentuate their outline and "smarten" them up.

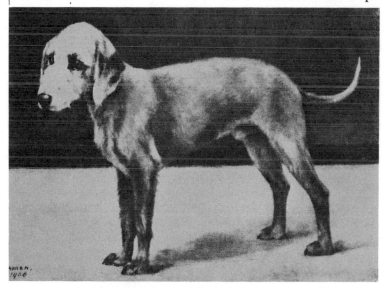

Once a top winner in England, the Bedlington Terrier, Ch. Cranley Blue Boy. From a painting by F. C. Fairman.

113

15

Border Terrier

THE Border Terrier is a relatively new breed in point of official recognition though the strain has been known for many years. It has been said that the Border, or "Ullswater Terrier," was known and bred pure since the 18th century by Lord Lonsdale and his descendants at Lowther where they were used regularly with the Hounds. This would indicate that dogs of the general stamp have been known for many years.

To this author's knowledge the present breed name first appears in Rawdon Lee's book *Modern Dogs* published in 1894 which gives an excellent and rather complete description of the dog, his background and work. Lee credits Jacob Robson of Byrness near Otterburn and his family with much of the breed's development. Robson was connected with the Border Foxhounds all his life and the name Border was also applied to Terriers used with the Hounds. Robson once stated that this type of Terrier had been bred and used in Northumberland and other border country for generations although the dogs did not carry the name.

In spite of this early knowledge, from about 1890, the breed was shown at small affairs under the category of "Any other breed or variety not classified." As late as 1913 when the breed was first registered with the English Kennel Club this broad, ambiguous

Sarah Swift's Dandie Dinmont, Ch. Flornell Beetham Skittle, dam of 8 champions.

Border Terrier winner, Ch. Portholme Mhor of Dalquest, owned by Dalquest Kennels.

classification was still used. In fact, it was not until 1920 when the English Kennel Club recognized the Border that the present name was used officially. This was the real beginning of its growth. Challenge certificates were then available, the first being offered at the 1920 Carlisle event. During the next ten years twenty-seven champions were made which indicated strong breed support.

In America, the first Border was registered and recognized in 1930. Eighteen had been exported from England before the registration appeared in the February 1930 stud book. The first dog, named Netherbyer's Ricky 719372, was registered by Don E. Hewat of North Adams, Massachusetts. Growth was not rapid after this beginning as relatively few were registered during the next ten years. After 1940 more and more appeared and today it is the rule to see good entries along the East coast indicating a steady breed growth.

The Border Terrier is a product of the Border country between England and Scotland. It is little wonder that he is related to the Dandie Dinmont and the Bedlington which explain the colors of blue and tan, grizzle and tan, and red that are permitted together with wheaten. These colors indicate Bedlington blood and although the present-day Border bears no resemblance to his forebear, the blood is there and with the Dandie background explains the determination with which a Border goes about his work. While the breed was first used on fox, it is a good hunter of any game. Major John Bell Irving, Master of the Dumfriesshire Otter Hounds writes eloquently of the abilities of the Border when used on otter. He says that "Sandy," one of his Borders, was a terror and was even known to attack a bullock and fasten onto his nose. After being introduced to otter, "he has never taken the slightest notice of the tame and harmless animals he was wont to assault." Sandy was a top-flight otter dog and he, with others of the pack, made the otter's life a precarious one, particularly when they were backed by the Otter Hounds.

It has been said that a Border is one of the few "unspoiled" Terriers. Fads and fancies have not caught up with the breed and its proponents today will not permit modification for the sake of mere beauty. Most of today's fanciers are interested in keeping the Border a working Terrier and some of them still work their dogs with good success. The Border Terrier Club of America is presently investigating working trials in an effort to maintain the abilities of the breed.

The Border Terrier is a fascinating little dog. Unlike that of any other Terrier, his head, broad in skull and short in foreface, resembles the otter, one of his most hated foes. His skin is also distinctive in that it is very loose-fitting and extremely thick. The hide of a Border may be grasped and pulled away from the body without making the dog uncomfortable. This tough, loose-fitting hide helps him in his work and protects him from the bites of his adversaries. The dog should be balanced and weigh from 12 to 15 pounds. He should have sufficient leg to be able to follow the fox hunt but should not be as leggy as the Lakeland or Fox Terrier. The coat is dense and harsh and naturally short so that it needs little trimming even for show. The dog requires all of the usual attributes of the Terrier in addition to the above special features. The Border is a delightful little dog, earnest in expression, friendly without being effusive and fully able to take care of himself under any circumstance.

The following excerpt offers the requirements of any worker in the Border Country and indicates why the Border Terrier is the rugged little dog that he is:

> *No product here the barren hills afford*
> *But man and steel, the soldier and his sword.*

Border Terrier, Ch. Dour Dare
owned by Dalquest Kennels.

16

Bull Terrier

THE Bull Terrier, often called the "White Cavalier," is one of the oldest breeds in the Terrier group to have been blest with identity. As early as 1822 the name *Bullterrier* can be found in the *Annals of Sporting* by Pierce Egan. Earlier artistic efforts show dogs strongly resembling the Bull Terrier, although these early animals are more like leggy Bulldogs with coarse, heavy jaws full of muscle and lacking today's desired quality of outline. Alken offered many efforts of fighting dogs of this general type as early as 1820 and these, with other art and writings, place the breed in an early position among identifiable Terriers.

The predecessor of the Bull Terrier was called a "Bull and Terrier" dog because of the crossing of Bulldogs with large White Terriers. The cross was used to obtain ferocity and tenacity with strength and courage. These two breeds had all of the necessary attributes, and those who wanted fierce fighters knew their breeding well. "Trusty" is one of the early Bull and Terrier crosses to be pictured in 1806 and the representation gave the dog the general appearance of a small white mixture of the breeds in question. Dogs of somewhat similar make are also shown in the aforementioned *Annals of Sporting* and in the *Sporting Magazine* (1832).

Since the Bulldog probably was derived from the Mastiff there

118

Ch. Heir Apparent of Monty-Ayr, first Am. bred Bull Terrier to win best in show in America. Bred by Dr. E. S. Montgomery.

Am. and Eng. Ch. Dulac Heathland's Commander, first male colored Bull Terrier to win best in show in America. Owned by Dr. E. S. Montgomery.

is little doubt that the Bull and Terrier cross had all the fierceness required for the fighting use to which the dog was to be put. The aforementioned Trusty was the first of the great fighting dogs.

The new breed began to take on some sort of identity around 1820–25 and "Brutus," known as a Bull Terrier and the property of Sir Edwin Landseer, was shown in 1824 in the *Annals of Sporting*.

From this day on the Bull Terrier became widely known through many authors who frequently identified the breed with fighting and equally distasteful pursuits. Charles Dickens depicted Bill Sykes' dog "Bull's-eye" as a fighting villain not unlike his master in the novel *Oliver Twist*. In fact, the breed gained a bad name as a fighting dog through the unsportsmanlike efforts of many of its supporters who used these brave dogs for work in the pits. The Westminster Pit was the most famous of these and many a dog fight was held in this arena of ill repute. Badger-baiting, dog fighting, and the matching of dogs with monkeys and bears were all "sports" of the early 1800's, and the Bull Terrier along with the Bulldog was an unhappy recipient of the "fame."

To Mr. James Hinks of Birmingham, England goes most of the credit for the development of the show type Bull Terrier. Hinks produced the white variety which has gained such high favor. The early development of this type or variety which began around the middle of the 19th century was founded on a cross of a White English Terrier with a Bull and Terrier dog. The breed prospered and its popularity increased steadily until abolition of ear cropping occurred in England in 1895 and in the U.S. shortly thereafter; this action lessened the demand for the breed on both sides of the Atlantic. However, good breeding of dogs with "fill" below the eyes and "downface" together with development of the prick ear, slowly restored the breed to favor. "Lord Gladiator," whelped in 1917 was probably the first Bull Terrier to have the much-prized profile.

The colored Bull Terrier was produced by crossing the Staffordshire Terrier (English variety) with the white Bull Terrier. The variety is old, possibly nearly as old as the "White 'un," but its popularity has never been as great. Possibly this is because the attributes of "downface" are not as visually apparent in the colored as in the white even though the bone structure is almost identical.

The colored Bull Terrier was accepted, but not without a vigorous struggle, and in 1936 the variety was recognized by the AKC.

The Bull Terrier, in spite of its rather unenviable beginning, has enjoyed an excellent press throughout the many years of its existence. This paradox is not without reason, for the breed has always been intelligent, lovable and extremely tractable. In fact, when not urged and trained to fight, the dog has all of the most desirable attributes of any breed. Sir Walter Scott was one of the first to recognize these and he wrote that his dog "Camp," a "bull-dog terrier," was "the wisest dog I ever had—He certainly had a singular knowledge of the spoken language." At Abbotsford one cannot but sense the attachment between the two when one sees the large painting (circa 1809) in the drawing room that shows Scott with Camp at his feet and the Greyhound "Percy" peering up at him. (See page 175 et seq. Complete Book of Dog Tales—Marvin, 1961.)

Richard Harding Davis also gave the breed a tremendous boost in writing the Bar Sinister, and no treatise on the breed would be complete without quotation of a layman's description. The layman, in this case, is that very fine author and dog lover, John Steinbeck, who describes the Bull Terrier quite accurately in well chosen words that offer insight into breed temperament:

"I have owned all kinds of dogs but there is one I have always wanted and never had. I wonder if he still exists. There used to be in the world a white, English Bull Terrier. He was stocky, but quick. His muzzle was pointed and his eyes triangular so that his expression was that of cynical laughter. He was friendly and not quarrelsome, but forced into a fight he was very good at it. He had a fine, decent sense of himself and was never craven. He was a thoughtful, inward dog, and yet he had enormous curiosity. He was heavy of bone and shoulder. Had a fine arch to his neck. His ears were sometimes cropped, but his tail never. He was a good dog for a walk. An excellent dog to sleep beside a man's bed. He showed a delicacy of sentiment. I have always wanted one of him. I wonder whether he still exists in the world." Bull Terriers today are quality animals. Their failings are relatively unimportant when viewed in light of their attributes. However, lovers of the breed should bear in mind that progress is rarely forthcoming without effort, and better fronts, shoulders, movement and more consistency in head structure are to be desired. This book will not attempt to go deeply into the breed's conformation or past history. The foregoing is sufficient general knowledge of breed derivation without delving deeply into its rich heritage. For those who wish to pursue more complete research, I have compiled a bibliography that offers a full range of excellent books and articles directed specifically to the Bull Terrier and all phases of the breed's development.

Before passing to this, a short history of the specialty club and the background of recognition of the breed together with notable changes in the standard of perfection will be of interest.

The Bull Terrier Club of America is one of the oldest of Terrier specialty clubs, having become a member of the American Kennel Club on September 23, 1897. The breed was recognized some six years before this date, and the white variety enjoyed a position at the shows from that time. The Standard of Perfection has been changed several times since its first writing; among the major modifications is the acceptance of the colored variety which occurred in 1936 much to the distress of some of the members of the parent club. Another major change concerns size. In the early standards the weight of the dog could vary from 12 to 60 pounds. This variation made it difficult to judge dogs of widely different weights on the same basis. The standard remained unchanged until 1936 when dogs under 25 pounds were classed as miniatures.

Cairn Terrier, Ch. Heathcairn Burleigh. Bred and owned by Mr. and Mrs. Carl E. Brewer.

17

Cairn Terrier

THE Cairn Terrier stems from the old Scotch Terrier and is therefore related to the Skye, Dandie Dinmont, Scottish and West Highland White. The Cairn, which was the last of these Scotch breeds to gain recognized breed status in either Great Britain or the United States, is probably the closest of all Scotch breeds to the conformation of their common progenitor.

Examination of the caricature signed by James Robertson (1835) will show a number of small Terriers scampering over the rocks in pursuit of an otter. These small dogs resemble today's Cairn Terrier more closely than any other Scotch breed unless it be the West Highlander which, except for color, is quite similar to its darker cousin. In fact, Cairns and Westies were interbred for many years to give greater substance to the Cairn progeny. This practice was a source of much controversy until about 1917 when the American Kennel Club refused to register the fruits of such unions.

The Cairn, as in the case of all the aforementioned breeds of Scotch descent, came originally from either the Isle of Skye, the other islands of the Western Hebrides, or the rocky slopes of the nearby Highlands of the Scottish mainland. These lands, rugged and bleak in character, presented a terrain that was a challenge to any dog. The wildlife had adequate cover in the rocky dens and cairns along the water and in the neighboring hills. Dogs used in this climate had to be rough and ready for any task, whether it involved an otter, a fox, or merely clearing the master's home of vermin. Fully up to any of these pursuits the Cairn has been a source of pleasure to owners from the first day the breed was identified until the present. One of the smallest of all Terriers, the Cairn has a big heart and an equally large share of independence and courage.

This last attribute has been documented many times in early books where the small Terriers have been trapped in rocky dens by rising tides and have had to fight for their lives with no chance of escape. In other instances the dogs have been known to squeeze their way between closely set rocks into a cairn where they have been trapped for days, unable to escape until starvation caused sufficient emaciation to permit them to extricate themselves. Upon their return home, starved and half dead, they would quickly regain their fervor for hunting within a few days. Such is the character of the dog—a delightful pet, buoyant and inquisitive in nature and hardy in health, a worthy member of the Terrier tribe.

The Cairn Terrier has been known by many names. In the beginning, the term Scotch Terrier or Highland Terrier was applied to the breed as these names were generic to all breeds of Scotch descent. Later, and after the Skye and Dandie Dinmont had gained identity, the names Short-haired Skye Terrier and Skye Otter Terrier were used in the Hebrides, while on the mainland the nickname of Tod-hunter was more common. Possibly these same names were sometimes applied to other dogs closer to the Westie or Scottie, but in the early days these three were often so similar in conformation that they were interbred with impunity. Beynon, in his book *The Popular Cairn Terrier* offers early pedigrees (1907) in which can be found known West Highlands, Scottish and Cairn Terriers, all in the lineage of a single dog. As an English judge once told me, "In the early 1900's, all three often came from the same litter . . . according to what the buyer wanted."

There can be no doubt that the West Highland White was an offshoot of the same basic blood that flows in the veins of the Cairn. I have a copy of a letter from one of the Malcolms stating that the West Highlander was derived because of a hunting accident which occurred after Col. E. D. Malcolm returned from the Crimean War. While shooting with his hunting pack of small Terriers, he killed one of the dark-colored ones, thinking it was a rabbit. This grieved him so much that he vowed he would only breed the light-colored dogs thereafter. Thus, by selection, he evolved the white strain and by the late 1800's he had eliminated the dark ones and had a breed of whites, or near whites. Other men, such as the Duke of Argyle, accomplished somewhat similar results, bringing about a separation of the two strains into distinct and reproducible breeds.

Cairns had an uphill fight to gain recognition in Britain. Short-haired Skyes were accorded a class at the 1909 Inverness show, and in 1910 the Cairn Terrier Club was organized. It was not until 1912 that independent registration was granted, and immediately thereafter breed popularity boomed until by the late 1920's Cairn registrations outstripped those of Scottish Terriers.

Early pioneers in the breed included Mrs. Alastair Campbell (Brocaire), whose dogs came from the short-haired Skyes known on the Isle of Skye as the "Waternish" strain, J. E. Kerr (Harviestoun), Errington Ross (Glenmhor), Baroness Burton (Dochfour), Martin McKinnon and Colonel Whitehead, among others. The bitch Tibbie of Harris was the first champion, while Mrs Campbell's Gesto was the first dog champion. These people, together with such Cairns as Harviestoun Raider, Skye Crofter, Roy Mhor, Inverness Doran, Firring Fling, Froach Gail, and Bagpipes, were responsible for the upswing of the breed in Britain. The last two dogs mentioned were instrumental in furthering the breed in America.

The destinies of Cairn Terriers in the United States are guided by the Cairn Terrier Club of America, formed in 1917 a year or so after the breed reached the American show bench. This was the ninth specialty club among Terrier breeds. Thereafter the Cairn prospered and the club grew strong. By 1922 entries at the shows were reasonably large, and from that time on the breed enjoyed a marked degree of popularity although it has never been hailed as a so-called popular breed.

Throughout the decades following organization of the Club, the membership has steadfastly opposed "popularizing" the breed by changing its characteristic conformation. Thus, today's Cairn still retains most of its early charm and has not been changed to suit the popular fancy for show purposes although a trend is developing towards shortening of the body, something that as yet does not have the support of the standard. In any event, today's Cairns are not the short-backed dogs seen in the Scottish Terrier ring but neither are they the relatively long-backed dogs of some thirty years ago. Furthermore, moderate trimming is being done by most successful exhibitors. The Cairn offers stiff competition in the group, where it looks as fit as the other members of this elite class.

In England Ch. Splinters of Twobees (whelped 1933) has had a tremendous influence on the breed. Ch. Bonfire of Twobees, a son and Ch. McJoe of Twobees, a grandson, were two big winners. Ch. Rufus of Rhu and Ch. Thistleclose Fling merit mention as does Ch. Unique Cottage Sir Frolic and Ch. Unique Cottage Black Gold. More recently Ch. Redletter McRufus, Ch. Redletter McBryan, Ch. Blencathra Rosanne and Ch. Oudenarde Light Melody have been making their presence felt in Britain among a host of other top dogs.

In this country a few of many that merit mention include Ch. Kilmet of Cairndania, Ch. Fiery Rob of Carysfort, Ch. Heathcairn Hector, Ch. Redletter Miss Splinters, Ch. Redletter McRuffie, Ch. Catescairn Camelot and Ch. Rossmar's Claruf O'Cairndania. Many more are worthy but space forbids. The names may be found in breed books listed in the bibliography section.

Present bench competitors include many fine American-breds together with a liberal offering of top imports. This provides a fine stud force from which the serious breeder may choose. As a result the breed is in a satisfactory condition, not overly popular, but supported by a host of loyal owners who breed intelligently with the best interests of the Cairn at heart.

The Cairn Terrier standard was up-dated in 1938 after several years of controversy to improve its clarity, reduce the top weight for dogs one pound and permit some tidying. It still included the many requirements that make a Cairn distinctive and give it character.

One major item frequently overlooked concerns the eyes. These should be dark hazel, not black, and they should be of medium size, not small and beady as suggested in some Terrier breeds. Eyes give character to the dog and proper eyes are an absolute necessity if a Cairn is to have its proper expression. The back should be of

126

medium length and the ribs deep with good spring but with a flattish side appearance so that the dog can pass through narrow openings.

Tail carriage is another point seldom understood. The tail should be carried up but not tight up as in the Wire Fox Terrier. Many top dogs carry the tail tight up; and while this is attractive it is not necessary and dogs that do not have the carriage should not be penalized.

Cairns, like Westies, must have relatively short heads with forefaces in balance and never longer than the skull. The long foreface ruins the expression. The Cairn's front feet may turn out slightly as in other Scotch breeds; this is not a fault but a characteristic. These are a few of the details characteristic of the Cairn that should be guarded by breeders as marks of distinction.

The first Cairn Terrier to gain registration in the *American Kennel Club Stud Book* was Sandy Peter Out of the West 173555 in 1913 to bring the fourteenth Terrier breed into the fold. He was owned by Mrs. H. F. Price of Noroton Heights, Connecticut.

Miss Sarah Swift's Ch. Waterbeck Watermark, the first Dandie Dinmont to win best in show in the United States. Sire of 25 titleholders.

18

Dandie Dinmont Terrier

THE Dandie Dinmont has the honor of being one of the first, if not the first, breed of Terrier to have an identifiable name. There is some dispute as to this fact but there can be no doubt that the name Dandie Dinmont appeared in Sir Walter Scott's novel *Guy Mannering* published about 1815 in the person of the owner of a tribe of small Terriers named "Auld Mustard," "Auld Pepper", "Young Mustard," "Young Pepper," etc. Accurately described, the dogs soon became known to all as "Dandie Dinmont's Terriers." The exact date the possessive was dropped is not known but undoubtedly the dogs in question were the same stamp we know today. Mr. James Davidson, said to have been the originator of the breed, was in real life a prototype of Dandie Dinmont. Mr. Davidson, lived in Hindlee in the Border country. The breed was also called a Hindlee and a Catcleugh Terrier; possibly this is why the name Dandie Dinmont was slow in being applied.

The Dandie Dinmont which came from the same basic stock as other Scotch breeds, goes back to the old Scotch Terrier for its early blood. Thus, the Dandie is related to the Scottish, Cairn, West Highland White and Skye Terrier albeit this relationship shows no crosses for well over one hundred years.

"First touching Dandies, let us consider with some scientific strictness what a Dandie specially is—." Carlyle.

128

Dr. M. J. Deubler's Ch. Salismore Playboy, Dandie of the
year 1960–61. From a pastel by Grace Wells.

The Dandie Dinmont is one of the most distinctive of Terrier
breeds. Because of the relatively large, low-carried ears and curved
top line the breed has been said to include some of the blood of the
Otter Hound and later to embrace a cross of the low-stationed
Hound (Dachshund-terrier). This last hypothesis was accepted by
Stonehenge and others who think the Hound blood came from
gypsy dogs brought across the channel on the numerous trips made
by travelers. The same premise is belittled by others although it
must be admitted that it appears well founded genetically. Regardless of the background, the Dandie has a distinctive top line
that sets it apart from the other Terrier breeds of Scotch descent.
This is often termed a "roach" but such nomenclature is improper.
A curved top line is more accurate and the structure a thing of
beauty when correct. Too few of today's dogs have this mark of
distinction. Many are level in top line and the curve is trimmed
onto the dog. Others are "high-sterned" and again trimming is
used to create an illusion. The curve over the loin is to be cher-
ished since it is distinctive and attractive.

Dandies, like all other short-legged Scotch breeds, tend to turn
out the front feet. This is correct as an aid in digging. Ears should
be low-set and generally long in leather. Too short leather permits
the ears to break too high when the dog comes to attention. The
eyes must be relatively large for correct expression. Small beady
eyes give an unnatural outlook not at all attractive, nor do they
fit with the massive skull, a hallmark of the breed.

129

Much controversy exists today concerning the top limit of 24 pounds for weight. In fact this has been argued for many years. This author contends that a dog properly sized as to height and in good working condition cannot weigh too much or too little. The weight of a properly sized dog takes care of itself provided the dog is in balance. Actually, if the dogs are considered too big, the maximum height limits should be reduced which will automatically take care of weight with balance. However, some of yesteryear's dogs were considerably larger than anything shown today. Rowland Johns in his book, *Our Friends the Dandie Dinmont and Skye Terrier* stated that dogs weighing 27 or 28 pounds were not uncommon in the 1870's and 1880's and that these dogs were good workers. This entire controversy should be based on *working* Terriers. Few are used for this purpose now, therefore few of the present protagonists in the weight controversy actually know whether today's "big" dog can work or not.

The Dandie is a dour, Scotch breed of dog, devoted to his master and generally tolerant of others. He likes to work and his ability to work was well put by Scott who said in *Guy Mannering* that the dog—"—regularly entered, first wi' rattans then we' stots or weasels and then wi' the tods, and brocks———fear naething tha ever cam' wi' a hairy skin un 't."

Since these dogs are individualists they frequently exhibit a canny awareness with strangers and strange sounds. This is particularly true with youngsters and may be mistaken for shyness. It is not! It is the true temperament of all Scotch breeds of dogs. I have owned, raised and observed many West Highland and Scottish Terriers with the same tendencies. Such youngsters mature into fine dogs, smart and true to their heritage.

This was acknowledged by many astute dog men years ago and even Stonehenge comments upon the tendency with a word of caution lest some discard such puppies. Speaking of Dr. William Brown's famous dog "John Pym" he offered the following advice— " 'Tis said . . . —Sometimes a Dandie pup of good strain may appear not to be game at an early age; but he should not be parted with on this account, because many of them do not show their courage till nearly two years old, and then nothing can beat them; this apparent softness arising, as I suspect, 'from kindness of heart'."

I liken a Dandie to the very fine description of a Terrier offered by an old Highland gamekeeper who, when asked about a certain Terrier of singular pluck and with more aloofness than the rest, said, "Oh, sir, life's full o' sairiousness to him—he just never can get enuff o' fechtin."

Proponents of the breed are fortunate in having available a classic work in the form of Charles Cook's book *The Dandie Dinmont Terrier*. Published in 1885, this is one of the very earliest books devoted entirely to one Terrier breed and gives the student an accurate background of the dog together with a sensible evaluation of the points. Seven etchings of Dandies help appraise the changes that have taken place through the ages.

The first showing in England in which the breed was named dates back to Manchester in 1861. Thereafter most shows had classes for the breed, while the Dandie Dinmont Terrier Club was founded fifteen years later in 1876. In the United States, the Dandie also had early beginnings; a dog named Bonnie Britton 4472 had the honor of gaining the first number in 1886. He was by Border Minstrel ex Wee Miss and was a pepper. Although shown several times he was not considered a top specimen. On the other hand, Robbie Burns was considered an excellent Dandie during the 1886–87 show season. He was a 20-pounder owned by James Rae of Buffalo and was by Habbie ex Nellie, whelped August 17, 1884 with George Graham of Scotland as his breeder. A mustard dog, King O' The Heather imported in 1887 and owned by Edward Brooks of Boston became the first American titleholder while Auld Pepper O' The Ark, a bitch and Auld Nick a dog were the first American-bred champions, gaining the honor in 1931 and indicating the emphasis that had been placed on imported stock.

Later dogs that bear mention as having a strong effect on the interests of the breed were Ch. Flornell Beetham Skittle and Ch. Waterbeck Watermark. The latter was the first Dandie to win best in show in this country while Ch. Salismore Playboy is a more recent consistent breed winner.

In Canada, Fan was registered as the first Dandie in that country's stud book. Fan carried the number 665 in Volume 1 dated 1889–91. The fortunes of the breed in this country are sponsored by the Dandie Dinmont Club of America. Organized in 1932 it has been a member of the American Kennel Club since 1936.

19

Fox Terrier

THE name Fox Terrier embraces two varieties of the breed, namely the Smooth and the Wire. From 1885 when the first Smooth was registered in this country there has been a shifting in popularity between them which has twice favored each variety.

In the beginning, the Smooth was the only registered Fox Terrier in the United States and not until 1887 did a Wire gain official recognition. After this date, the Wire gained slowly until about 1900 when the variety began to become quite popular. Thereafter, the Wire far outstripped the Smooth for several decades and, in fact, became the most popular of all Terriers, if not of all dogs. The condition was modified to a marked degree after the Smooth, Ch. Nornay Saddler, entered the show ring. The imported Saddler, a great winner in this country, dominated the ring for several years beginning in the late thirties. The effects of his popularity and his winning carried over until the middle forties when, the Wire regained the upper hand.

Smooths and Wires are true varieties and, according to the rules, may be interbred and the progeny registered according to coat. However, interbreeding has not been practiced for many years with the result that few fanciers breed both varieties. This has led to a separation of interest among Fox Terrier breeders and may have influenced the present general breed decline.

Ch. Nornay Saddler, whelped 1936, one of the greatest Smooths of all time. Owned by Wissaboo Kennels.

Ch. Hetherington Model Rhythm, Westminster 1946 best in show. Bred by T. H. Carruthers, 3rd.

Ch. Desert Deputy, a Saddler son. Owners: Mr. and Mrs. W. Holden White.

Until about 1943 the two varieties competed against one another for best of breed and the opportunity to compete in the Terrier group. This limited breed representation to one Fox Terrier in the Terrier group. In 1943, a rule change, which allowed the two varieties to compete in the group, often led to both Wire and Smooth placing among the four ribbon winners. This same situation, of course, applied to all breeds in which varieties were present. The change in the rules, while improving the winning record of the breed, did not do much to stimulate interest and the Fox Terrier is still struggling to regain its once dominant position.

Passing to the history of the breed in England we find that in 1863 the first Smooth Fox Terrier appeared in the ring at Birmingham and the Wire, then termed a "Rough" Fox Terrier had to wait until 1872 at Glasgow for classification which gave it identity. Thus, the British recognition of both varieties was quite a bit earlier than in this country but quite late in the general plan of dog shows which had admitted Terriers of various breeds since 1860. This was not because Fox Terriers were unknown but because the breed was used extensively by the hunting fraternity. No pack worthy of the name was without its Fox Terriers. In fact, the kennels of the better known hunts had strong Fox Terrier sections to go with their Hounds.

The Fox Terrier Club of England was founded in 1876 with such stalwarts as Francis Redmond and Harding Cox among the organizers. The following year the new club staged its first specialty show which had an amazing entry of 220 for Mr. Bassett to judge.

The Fox Terrier's background is as obscure as that of most Terriers. The term Fox Terrier is a confusing one for, as has been noted thoughout this book, the name was used to identify almost any dog that hunted fox and has frequently applied to a variety of the Scotch Terrier. However, the dog, as we know it today, undoubtedly came from English White Terrier and therefore the Smooth variety was probably the first evolved. The old English Terrier, a black and tan, brought out the color now found in both coats. The wiry texture of the Wire variety may have been derived from a cross with the Scotch Terrier which had a heavy, rough, wiry textured coat. No better explanation has been given than this one suggested by Stonehenge. Undoubtedly a trace of Bulldog may be found in the inheritance since it was used frequently in most Terrier breeds to bring out courage.

The Rev. Jack Russell offered a different but equally interesting background for the breed. He suggested that an English White Terrier be bred to an Italian Greyhound to improve the skin, that an offspring from this unión should be put to a Beagle to improve the ears which "are an eyesore," then, that a Bulldog should be introduced to improve courage. The composite animals from this polyglot became after due selection, the sires and dams of our modern Fox Terriers. Russell claimed ability to trace the blood of some of his Terriers well back into the 18th century. Whatever the background—and I do not wish to start a controversy that cannot be terminated—both coats of Fox Terrier were here to stay.

It is interesting to note that the standard for the Fox Terrier (both coats) has changed very little since the beginning. The original specification offered by Stonehenge was modified slightly by the Fox Terrier Club of England as noted in Lee's *Fox Terrier* (1889) and this standard was accepted by the American Club with no substantial alterations. Through the years the breed has changed in some respects but the standard remains the same except for the scale of points.

The most obvious changes (not found in the standard) are in head, where length is greater and width is less than in the past *and* in size where the large dog is now the rule rather than the exception. Of course the standard is sufficiently flexible to permit these modifications for no disqualification has ever been offered to limit size. This constancy of specification is mute testimony to the wisdom of the early breeders who knew what they wanted.

In 1885 the American Fox Terrier Club was founded with Lewis M. Rutherfurd, John E. Thayer and Edward Kelly as its first officers. It was the second specialty club in the United States (the Spaniel Club was the first) and the first of the specialty clubs to become a member of the American Kennel Club—this occurred in 1888. The present club seal, suggested by Messrs. Belmont, Hoey and Kelly in 1886, was first used on the title page of the specialty catalogue for 1887 and has been used ever since. In view of these auspicious beginnings it is small wonder that the Fox Terrier dominated the Terrier scene for many years.

Early honors in Fox Terriers were divided at the shows between a quartet of "greats"—Jock, Trap, Tartar and Rattler. The first two distinguished themselves at stud and their names will be found in many of today's extended pedigrees. These were followed by a host of illustrious dogs including Belgrave Joe and Ch. Spice. The latter with his more refined head started the trend apparent even today. Spice came to America in 1886 but was killed in a fight within the year. A dog named Gamester, imported by Newbold Morris about 1887 brought in the blood of Jock, Trap and Tartar. Actually, few good dogs in Britain remained there for wealthy fanciers headed by Belmont brought them over as soon as they made a name so that American bloodlines were heavy with imported blood.

Possibly two of the greatest Wires of the present century were Ch. Talavera Simon and Ch. Barrington Bridegroom. The latter was a strong influence in America where he was used for many years. Simon left his mark through a host of great show and stud dogs on both sides of the Atlantic. Later, American and English Ch. Gallant Fox of Wildoaks took over the title of top stud. An American-bred, he did his share here and was then exported to Britain where he carried on.

The illustrious history of the Fox Terrier may best be documented by listing the Westminster breed wins. Smooths and Wires both gained the honors and between them gave to the Fox Terrier more best-in-show wins at Westminster than is claimed by any other breed. Starting out with the first show to offer the award in 1907 we find Ch. Warren Remedy capturing the event and repeating for the next two years. Following this domination the fourth straight win was scored by another Smooth, Ch. Sabine Rarebit in 1910. Fox Terriers did not enter the picture again until 1916 and 1917 when George Quintard's great Wire, Ch. Matford Vic claimed the double triumph. Following these accomplishments the records show that the Wire Ch. Conejo Wycollar Boy won in 1920; Ch. Signal Circuit of Halleston (Wire) 1926; Ch. Talavera Margaret (Wire) 1928; Ch. Pendley Calling of Blarney (Wire), 1930 and 1931; Ch. Flornell Spicy Bit of Halleston (Wire) 1934; Ch. Flornell Spicy Piece of Halleston (Wire) 1937; and finally the last win claimed by the breed in 1946 when Ch. Hetherington Model Rhythm turned the trick. This means that Fox Terriers have won a total of fifteen top awards.

In spite of this amazing record, the fact that no top award has been gained for the past sixteen years indicates the decline of the breed which is further apparent from the reduced entries at Westminster and other shows throughout the country. Possibly one explanation is the difficulty in properly presenting the Wire. This cannot be offered as an excuse, however, in the case of the Smooth. Many believe that the deviations in conformation are responsible and that the temperament of the breed is less desirable than in the past. All of these excuses fail for one reason or another and the fact remains that the Fox Terrier, as is the case with most other Terrier breeds, needs strong support from its proponents. There is little wrong that cannot be overcome by fancier enthusiasm, something sadly lacking in many Terrier breeds.

Ch. Dusky Reine, an early Wire Fox Terrier winner, whelped 1899. From a painting.

20

Irish Terrier

THE Irish Terrier, "Daredevil" or "Mick" as he is sometimes called, is one of the two Terrier breeds indigenous to the Emerald Isle. However, the basic blood of the Irish, probably from Scotland, goes back to the old Scotch Terrier of the third variety, as described by Brown (*see* Chapter 4). This variety was larger and more on the leg than the usual Scotch Terrier and measured from 15 to 18 inches in height. It is said that this dog crossed with the Irish Wolfhound together with a trace of Black and Tan Terrier blood made the progenitors of the breed. Such an hypothesis is plausible and might well be accurate.

Many early fanciers and breed proponents decried this theory averring that the breed was known long before Scotch Terriers ever came to Ireland. However, since Belfast, where many of the prominent early fanciers lived, is quite close to Scotland and since there was a steady interchange of itinerant travelers between the two countries it is not difficult to envision the entry of the Scotch dog into Ireland or the interbreeding of this type of dog with dogs of Irish descent such as the Irish Wolfhound and its forerunners. Whatever the background, the Irish Terrier is a distinct breed today and has definite characteristics that stamp him as an Irishman through and through.

The nickname Daredevil was not applied because of lack of

courage as the Irish will tackle anything on four legs and more frequently than not will emerge the victor. In olden days the dog, like all his cousins, was used mainly for vermin. He was worked with rat, fox, badger, otter and would even take on a rabbit in the field, a chase that sometimes was not climaxed with the quarry. The dog was game, eager to work, determined and withal a lovable companion.

The show career of the breed began about 1873 when classes were accorded the Irish Terrier at the Dublin show. At the time, size must have varied widely since one class on the agenda was for dogs "under 9 pounds." Two years later the weight was changed and no dog under 12 pounds could be shown; the following year found 16 pounds the minimum.

The breed gained recognition rapidly because of its excellence and through the untiring efforts of several sturdy fanciers including a Mr. George Jamison, one of its enthusiastic supporters. In 1875 Jamison took "Sport" to Glasgow and won the breed. The following year he journeyed to Bristol, England (1876) with several dogs including "Spuds" (pictured) for the first exhibition of this new breed in that country. Three years later a group of fifty loyal fanciers met in Dublin to form a specialty club which was christened the Irish Terrier Club (1899) and later in the same year English enthusiasts organized in London to support this new group.

During the next decade a real Irish brawl developed within the club on two items. The first was size; there were many who wanted the Hiberian Daredevil to be a large animal. In fact, dogs weighing as much as 40 pounds were found on the benches and the wide variation in size (from the 16-pound minimum) caused a deterioration of the breed. Finally the weight question was settled with a maximum of 24 pounds the limit. Occurring sometime around 1891 this was a good move for it stabilized a point of real argument and eliminated the applicability of the then current poem which started:

> It's wonderful dogs they're breeding now
> Small as a flea or large as a cow. . . .

It will be recalled that the present American standard suggests a weight of 27 pounds as a maximum for dogs, with no disqualification set forth for dogs over this weight.

A concurrent "Donnybrook" was also in progress over the custom of cropping ears. Most of the early dogs in the breed had their ears cut. Many members of the club believed this to be improper and the argument raged for years. In 1888 the Irish Terrier Club finally passed a resolution condemning the custom and with this backing the English Kennel Club decreed that Irish Terriers whelped after December 31, 1889 could not be shown at English Kennel Club shows if they had cropped ears. This action ended the argument and the breed has been shown with natural, dropped ears ever since.

These interesting situations occurring during the early development of the breed should be carefully studied by today's breed proponents before changes are suggested in the breed standard. The size question plagues almost every breed. The Irish has been through it all since in the early days dogs under 9 pounds to over 40 pounds were known and accepted on the show bench. The specialty club stabilized the breed when it prescribed the upper and lower limits and it behooves today's fanciers to harken back to the old days and the reasons for these actions.

During the period of development from 1873 to 1900 the breed was gaining support in America. The first Irishman to be registered in this country was a bitch named Aileen 3306 owned by Dr. J. S. Niven of London, Ontario. The first Irish Terrier champion was crowned about 1888 when the English import Breda Tiny AKC 9140 claimed the title. The breed gained its biggest advantage in 1897 when the Irish Terrier Club of America came into being. This group gave the breed the strong backing required to effect steady and controlled growth.

A delightful description of the breed and its background was given by W. J. Cotton of Blessington, County Wicklow, who offered the following:

"To Sir Walter Raleigh, through potatoe skins and the Irish cottier (peasant farmers similar to crofters in Scotland) and hardships, we owe the Irish Terrier. When Ireland was more thickly inhabited, there were small parties of cottiers grouped together; each had his cabbage and potatoe garden badly fenced, and each family spent the greater portion of their time 'round the turf hearth, watching the murphies boil. The circle was incomplete, and liable to be disturbed in their beloved indolence, without a dog, which hissed

Martha G. Hall's Irish Terrier, Ch. Ahtram Golden Smasher.

Ch. One Particular

Irish Terrier, Ch. One Particular, owned by Mr. and Mrs. L. J. Long, Jr.

on when the neighboring pig or goat invaded the boundary of the estate. A large dog required too much support; one with some spice of pluck was, however, required in order to enforce its authority. The combination of Pat, pig, and potatoes, was conducive of rats—and rats, sport and rivalry. As such terriers were indiscriminately bred, and all ran wild, the dog with the most pluck exercised the largest influence on the breed. During the day, as described, these terriers lay at the fire, and at night, though the

141

pig might be given a corner of the cabin, the terrier was shown the outside of the door to guard the larder, which was the potato pit, look after the general safety of the estate, and to find a bed in a ditch or butt of a haycock. Generations of such treatment developed them into the 'pine knots' they are.

"Driving along the roads any hour of the night,—it is a matter of wonder how the inmates sleep and ignore the choruses of howls on moonlight nights. I believe mayself that the Irish garrisons distributed over the country the bulldog, which was used for crossing. As many native fanciers say to this day, there is nothing like a 'cras' of the bull and I think the Irish Terriers' disposition largely shows it. You will find them still in all types, long in leg, short on leg, and long in body, and crooked in legs, and of all colours, red, black, blue, brindle, and those with tan legs often have the best coats."—The quote goes on at length and will be extremely interesting to persons with genuine love of the Irishman. It can be read in full in Rawdon Lee's book, *Modern Terriers,* (Terrier Volume) 1st ed. (1894) pages 197 *et seq.*

Many fine Irish Terriers have graced the show benches in America through the many years the breed has been recognized. At the present time the Irish Terrier does not enjoy the popularity to which it is entitled and this lack of enthusiasm is probably due to the necessity of trimming which requires great skill if the coat color is to be brought to its peak. As in most whole-colored dogs, trimming changes color and it requires an expert to bring all parts of the body into uniform color simultaneously. Of course, companion dogs need not cause worry about these trivialities; they may be stripped occasionally and kept in satisfactory condition.

The breed has always enjoyed a host of prominent supporters and probably two of the most interesting who were exhibiting about the same time came from the ranks of politicians. Jimmie Walker, one-time mayor of New York City and a Tammany man was well known for his St. Timothy Kennels while Harrison Spangler of Cedar Rapids, Iowa was equally prominent in the Republican party and at one time was its national chairman. Perry Rice, long-time secretary of the American Kennel Club was another who will be remembered as will Ed (Pop) Sayres, a successful handler of Irish dogs who made history with Irish and Kerry Blue Terriers. So many others could be mentioned that it would be futile to start.

142

21

Kerry Blue Terrier

THE Kerry Blue Terrier is one of the two Terrier breeds recognized in the United States that claim the Emerald Isle as its home. Other Terrier breeds, such as the Soft-Coated Wheaten Terrier, stem from Ireland but have not as yet gained recognition in this country. The Kerry Blue Terrier is not an old breed when compared with the Manchester and the Dandie Dinmont but it is a distinctive breed that has improved tremendously during its short span of recognition.

While some supporters of the breed claim great antiquity for it, the fact still remains that the Kerry was not recognized in England until 1922 although the general type had been known for some time in County Kerry whence the name came. In fact, the first of the strain shown, called Irish Blue Terriers, were exhibited at Cork in 1913. There is also documentation of a substantial entry at Killarney in 1916. The breed gained official recognition in Ireland when the All-Ireland Kerry Blue Terrier Club was formed in July, 1920.

The blue-colored Terrier, known first as the Irish Blue and later as the Kerry Blue is beset by many claims as to origin. A cross of Irish and Bedlington Terrier is one of these while another mates the Bedlington to the Irish Wolfhound, still another claims a cross between the Bull Terrier and the Soft-Coated Wheaten Terrier while a fourth suggests an Irish Wolfhound crossed with a Soft-Coated Wheaten Terrier. All these breeds existed during the time the Kerry Blue was being developed so all the claims have some basis. Whatever theory is true there seemed to be a decided resemblance between the Soft-Coated Wheaten and the early dogs of the Kerry breed which lends credence to at least this one progenitor. Whether the remaining basic blood comes from the Bedlington, Irish Terrier, Bull Terrier or Irish Wolfhound remains a mystery—possibly all had their share in bringing about this very popular breed.

Whatever the background, there is no doubt that the Kerry has Irish traits and is fun loving and happy but will fight at the drop of a hat. This spirit is probably the reason the breed has met with such favor in the United States where a well trimmed Kerry is a "show-piece."

The breed was registered in the United States in 1922, the same year it was recognized in England. The first dog to gain the honor was Brian of Muchia 349159 owned by E. Swards of New York. This started a chain reaction that brought the breed into great prominence within the next twenty years. The Kerry Blue Terrier Club of America was formed and became a member of the American Kennel Club in 1926 which helped the breed by consolidating its supporters into an integrated group all working toward breed improvement.

While a number of persons contributed to the growth of the breed in this country there can be little argument that Ed (Pop) Sayres was the single figure responsible for the great strides the Kerry made during the 1930's and 1940's. Sayres was a handler of rare ability and his artistry in trimming the Kerry bought it from a lowly place among Terrier breeds into top contention. The writer can remember when Ben Edar Blaise and Ben Edar Bawcock were being shown. These were both great dogs in their day but a far cry from the clean, quality animals of today. Sayres showed them and by his own ability and perseverence won them acclaim. Blaise subsequently sired Ch. Rackety Packety Killmenskeg which in turn gave Sayres Ch. Bumble Bee of Delwin, by Bawcock. These two great bitches marked a turning point in the breed for in my opinion they were the first of today's Kerry type and they won

Kerry Blue, Ch. Rackety Packety Kilmenskeg, whelped 1933. Owned by Mr. and Mrs. William Fox.

many top awards with Sayres as handler. Many more followed with Ch. Fox Hill Thunderbolt one of the last greats to have been shown by "Pop."

During the period of from 1922 to date many other fanciers and handlers were developed who did their share in bringing the breed along. One of these bears mention because of the extensive kennel she maintained and because of the tremendous record made by her dogs. This was the late Mrs. F. Y. McEachren, a Canadian, owner of the Tailteann Kennels. One of her greatest Kerrys was a bitch Ch. Miss Show Off of Cognewaugh which made breed history followed by Ch. Tailteann's Marcie's Son. It would be unfair at this time not to list a few of the other Kerrys that did so well in the show ring and while the listing is by no means complete I doubt if anyone will take issue with the right of these dogs to be mentioned. They were: Ch. Blue Chip of Oakcrest, Ch. Blue Flame of Delwin, Ch. Michael of Somerset, Ch. Thorndale Blue Buddy, Ch. Conrad's Challenge, Ch. Deeds Show Off, Ch. Gered's Candy, Ch. Blue Bluster of Melbee, Ch. Michael of Som'set Jr., Ch. Truli Blu Roxiana, Ch. Bluemore's High Fidelity, Ch. Tregoad's Vicky's Cappy, etc.

During the thirties, a second specialty club known as the United

145

States Kerry Blue Terrier Club was formed. This apparent division in breed interest was resolved and on July 14, 1938 the Kerry Blue Terrier Club of America took in members of the United States Club and also appropriated the name of United States Kerry Blue Terrier Club. Thus, while the name has been changed, the club has enjoyed a continuous existence since its beginning in 1926.

Today, we find the Kerry Blue a real threat in any Terrier group. Refined and improved the breed presents an attractive exhibit at any show. Fanciers should heed the color called for in the breed name and eliminate the dark-hued ones as soon as possible. Too many Kerrys are seen of a "midnight blue" approaching a black. While this is all right for dogs under eighteen months of age there should certainly be a tinge of blue in the coat after that age. Kerrys today are also being shown with high breaking ears. While this may be attractive it is not in conformity with the standard which definitely requires the ear to break "slightly" above the level of the skull and to be carried forward close to the cheeks. The standard has been changed several times with deviations made to clarify various points. The size of the breed is down a bit from the original Irish standard which called for "not to exceed 21 inches at shoulder." Today's specification states a dog should never be over 20 inches and preferably about 18 to 19½ inches, one of the few specifications in the Terrier breeds to lower the top limit.

Other deviations concern coat texture, which while desired soft, did not penalize harsh jackets. The early standards also permitted blue and tan color, with the tan being on the head and legs. The present standard states the coat should be soft and that wiry, harsh or bristle coats should be severely penalized. Tan heads and legs are not now permitted. This last points to the early carry-over, probably from the Soft-Coated Wheaten ancester, and has now been bred out in almost every case.

The Kerry Blue Terrier has made tremendous strides in the short forty years of its recognized existence, quality is up and prestige is soaring. What will another forty years bring, surely improvement but nothing like what has been accomplished to date.

22

Lakeland Terrier

THE Lakeland Terrier, sometimes called the Fell or Patterdale Terrier is indigenous to the Lake District of England's Westmorland, Cumberland and Lancashire counties. This beautiful but rough land includes some of the highest mountains in England interspersed with sixteen lakes beautifully set in the rugged, rocky countryside. In this environment the Lakeland Terrier was developed to cope with the problems indigenous to the Lake District.

Patterdale, one of the many small villages in the area offered its name for the breed while others preferred calling the dog a Fell Terrier because of the rocky fells that formed the refuge from the rather large "Fell" foxes. The name Lakeland was finally accepted by the majority and fits the dog well.

The dog used with the Hound packs had to be dead game for its work. The Lakeland, unlike some Terriers that must mark the prey and await the hunters to dig it out, had to invade the very den of the Fell fox and the object was to kill. Thus, the Lakeland is not primarily a digging Terrier. Because the fox dens in the Lake country are rocky crevices that go deep into the mountainsides, the dog must be able to creep and squirm through narrow entrances between rock. For this reason the Lakeland must have a rather narrow chest and be of a rather flattish structure on the sides. No round barrel is seen or desired, rather a depth of chest is required to offer sufficient heart room and lung capacity. Since the dog must run with the Hounds and be sufficiently agile to clamber over the rocky ground he should be a trifle leggy as compared to a Welsh. These are distinctive points where the breed has attributes for a given purpose that should be jealously guarded by breeders.

It is said that a Lakeland can go through any opening that will pass its head. According to firsthand information this is true for a Lakeland will place its front legs forward and pass its head through an opening in the rock and then creep and crawl in. Obviously round-bodied dogs could not fulfill these requirements.

The breed probably came from the old-fashioned Black and Tan Terrier with a dash of Bedlington thrown in. This accounts for the color variations not found in other breeds of somewhat similar make.

The Lakeland did not attain identity until about 1921 when the Lakeland Terrier Association was formed in England, and it was not until about 1931 that the English Kennel Club offered challenge certificates in the breed. This does not mean that the dog was not shown because classes for "coloured working terriers" had been on the agenda for many years. In fact, John Peel and Tommy Dobson, early fanciers who bear mention, had authenticated pedigrees for these fine little dogs that dated back to around 1850. However, as in the case of most of our Terrier breeds specific recognition did not come soon nor was it easy.

Nevertheless, the breed is a good one and can be proud of its heritage which it is hoped will be maintained by present day enthusiasts so that its identity does not merge with that of the Welsh. Signs of this tendency crop up every so often and a strong specialty club appears to be the answer. A club of this character has been formed, called the United States Lakeland Terrier Club, but it is not as yet a member of the American Kennel Club.

Color was one of the original trademarks of the breed. Red-wheaten and blue-and-tan are the most characteristic colors which trace back to the Bedlington outcross. I was told many years ago by Tom Hosking, one of the founders of the Lakeland Terrier Association, that in the early days of the breed the blue-and-tans were the most prized with the red grizzle or wheaten the next most desired color. Of course according to present-day standards various color combinations are approved and accepted and should be judged without preference. It seems, however, that color is one factor that could be heeded to bring the breed greater autonomy over its Welsh cousin. Too often, while sitting at the ringside, one hears the Lakeland called a Welsh which could not be probable if the color were markedly different.

The breed is relatively new in the United States when compared to the Fox Terrier and the Bull Terrier. The first Lakeland to be registered was Egton What a Lad 938424 owned by R. A. A. Johnston in 1954.

Lakeland, Ch. Bowes Blue Lady of Opalea, imported from England for Mrs. Walter C. Foster.

23

Manchester Terrier

THE Manchester or Black and Tan Terrier is probably the oldest of all identifiable Terrier breeds. Sydenham Edwards depicted a Black and Tan in 1800 and even before this, Sartorius painted a Black and Tan running with a pack of Hounds. A portrait of this Terrier will be found in Alys Serrell's book, *With Hound and Terrier in the Field* (1904). Since this artist lived many years before Edwards it is reasonable to surmise that the breed was reproducible by 1800.

In spite of these comparatively early beginnings, the Black and Tan did not receive a distinctive name until some years later. Many references may be found to Terriers with smooth coats and colored black-and-tan but these, for the most part, were classified as Old English Terriers which included dogs of diminutive size indicating the Toy variety.

In Stonehenge's 3rd edition of *The Dog In Health and Disease* (1879) the term "Manchester Terrier" was mentioned for the first time although it was not popular and the more common term English Terrier continued to be used with Black and Tan as an alternative. Some oldtimers also called the dog a Rat-Terrier because of its excellent ratting ability. The name "Manchester" lacked early favor in England because it gave the locality around Manchester too much credit for the dog that was popular all over the country. In America the first dog of the breed to be recognized was Lever 7585 in 1887; he was classified as a Black and Tan Terrier. The name clung to the breed, as descriptive of its markings and color, until 1923 when the Manchester Terrier Club of America was formed and the name of the Standard officially changed. The Toy variety did not have a parent club until 1938 when the American Toy Manchester Terrier Club was organized and became a member of the American Kennel Club the same year.

The Standard Manchester did not fare too well, indeed the breed progressively lost popularity and support. About mid-year of 1952 the Manchester Terrier Club of America faded from the scene and the Standard was without organized breed representation. It is to the everlasting credit of the American Toy Manchester Terrier Club that the Standard and the Toy are now regarded as varieties of a single breed. This came about in 1958 when the organization proposed a new Standard of Perfection embracing two varieties to take the place of the two specifications for the then two separate breeds. The offer was approved by the American Kennel Club on December 9, 1958 and beginning with the year 1959 a single breed was recognized with two varieties. At the same time the American Toy Manchester Terrier Club changed its name to the American Manchester Terrier Club and became the parent breed club for both varieties.

This has undoubtedly strengthened the breed and healed some possible rifts that might have been present. It has also overcome a peculiar inconsistency which permitted interbreeding of Standards and Toys, even though they were separate and distinct breeds on the record. Such a practice had long been used to give substance and improved heads to Toys and to reduce size in Standards. Similar anomalies have been permitted in other breeds where the status has also changed from breeds to varieties of breeds.

The Manchester Terrier (including both varieties) is basically one of the two first known Terrier species. All Terriers were once classified as either Scotch or English Terriers and the English were in most cases quite similar to the Manchester of today, not as refined to be sure, but similar in general characteristics. For this reason, there is very little background that can be discussed about this breed other than that found in the earlier chapters of this book. Suffice it to say that the basic blood behind the Manchester is that of the early Hound with infusions of Bulldog, Greyhound and probably some Italian Greyhound in the smaller members of the tribe with a trace of Dachshund also being a possibility.

There have also been some improper breeding practices by a few unethical persons in the use of Chihuahuas and possibly Miniature Pinschers to gain diminutiveness. While the result was a smaller dog, the approach harmed the breed variety because it brought into the blood improper type evidenced by the appearance of apple heads with prominent eyes, points to be shunned in a Manchester of any size. The Toy variety particularly has been plagued for years by these early malpractices and knowledgeable breeders are making great progress towards eliminating evidences of the earlier offenses. Today, in the United States, we find the Standard and the Toy being judged by the same standard and requiring the same type in order to win although they remain in the Terrier and Toy groups respectively. The only difference is in size and ear requirements where cropping is not condoned in Toys but permitted in Standards. Also the button ear is satisfactory for the large dog but not permitted in the small one.

Size limits of the two have varied through the years, the minimum today being over 12 pounds for Standards and a maximum of 22. The Toys of course, must not exceed 12 pounds. The low limit for Standards has varied from 10 to 14 pounds and in 1922 the low limit for the Standard was 10 pounds while the Toy was not to exceed 7 pounds.

Probably one of the things that harmed the popularity of the Manchester (Standard) in England was the no-cropping edict which came about near the turn of the century and seriously hampered the growth in popularity of all breeds which normally required trimmed ears. The Bull Terrier suffered a similar set-back but breeders regained the dog's style by breeding for smaller ears which eventually became prick ears. Similar practices could be used with the Standard although to date only the Toy variety has been able to make the change. Possibly this is the reason that the popularity of the Toy has been greater than that of the Standard although anyone who has owned a "big" Manchester will vouch for its desirability.

Manchester Terrier, Canyon Crest's Magic Scot, owned by Mr. and Mrs. William O. Bagshaw.

The Bagshaws' winning Manchester brace, Ch. Canyon Crest Firecracker and Ch. Canyon Crest Fire Alarm.

The Manchester's markings are the hallmark of the breed where clarity and depth of color are very desirable. Head structure is also of great importance; clean and of good length, the head *should not be domed* but nearly flat between the ears. The domed head as noted before, is more prevalent in Toys than in Standards. Another definite breed characteristic is the arch over the loin so that the back joins the tail at the same height as the shoulder. This arch should present a graceful curve though not be accentuated into a defined roach. The Manchester should not resemble a Whippet nor should the back fall away behind the withers which is frequently the result of an exaggerated roach. Like the Dandie Dinmont, the Manchester has a characteristic gentle and graceful curve in the top line that, when proper, is very attractive but when not proper makes the dog appear ungainly.

Good coats are another attribute that should be stressed. Short-haired dogs frequently have thin, sparse hair indicating poor physical condition or a congenitally poor coat. The proper coat should be thick and glossy and never soft which generally accompanies long silky hair that is entirely improper.

In other respects, the Manchester follows the general requirements of most Terrier breeds: dark, small eyes, good feet and teeth, a relatively short body, well coupled and a Terrier character, fearless and proud, exhibiting quality in every move.

Since the consolidation of the breed, the Manchester Terrier faces an opportunity to become dominant with both varieties benefiting from the change. It is hoped that this condition will come to pass and since this book is directed to Terriers, it is especially hoped that the Standard quickly regains some of its lost popularity.

Ch. Sheepshead Lad, Kerry Blue Titleholder of the early 1930s. Owner: Mme. L. Soresi. Note the trim.

24

Miniature Schnauzer

HERE is the only breed presently recognized in the Terrier group that is not of basic British origin. Many have said that the Schnauzer is not a Terrier and should not be shown in the Terrier group. This view is held in Great Britain where the English Kennel Club classifies the Standard and the Miniature Schnauzer as non-sporting dogs. Even in Germany, its native land, the Schnauzer is not considered a Terrier. In this country a kind of anomaly arises out of the 1945 action of the Standard Schnauzer Club of America which requested the American Kennel Club to transfer the breed from the Terrier to the Working group, which was done on July 10, 1945. In spite of all of these conditions the Miniature Schnauzer remains classified as a Terrier in the United States and Canada.

The Schnauzer is of German derivation. Both the Standard and the Miniature have been known for many years in their native land. Records indicate that the Standard was observed in the middle 1800's while the Miniature came later, probably nearer the turn of the century. Originally known as a "Pinscher," the name Schnauzer came from the German "schnauze" (meaning snout), applied many years ago because of the short, heavy whiskers on the muzzle. The dog was derived from a cross of the black German Poodle and the wolfgrey Spitz blended with blood from the Ger-

155

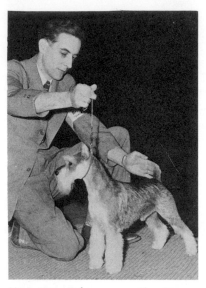 

Miniature Schnauzer, Ch. Dorem Display. Owner by Mr. and Mrs. Phil Meldon.

Miniature Schnauzer, Ch. Yankee Pride Colonel Stump. Owned by Mrs. Joseph Sailer.

man Pinscher. The Pinscher was a rough-coated dog which gave the breed its coat texture and also its Terrier characteristics since the Pinscher is said to have included some of the blood of the English Terrier, probably the Black and Tan. In fact, this was the only true Terrier blood infused into the strain. Nevertheless, the Schnauzer is a good ratter and will attack vermin of all kinds.

The presently known Standard Schnauzer is and was a medium-sized dog and the Miniature was derived from it by crossing with the Affenpinscher. The latter small dog brought down the size and endowed the Miniature with the undesirable, monkey-faced appearance so characteristic in early dogs of the variety. There may also have been a dash of Griffon in the basic blood of the Miniature; if this is true it would help to explain further the early head formation. The characteristic salt and pepper color came from the basic cross with the wolfgrey Spitz.

The development of the breed in America traces to the original specialty club known as the Wire-Haired Pinscher Club which was admitted to membership in the American Kennel Club on February 2, 1926. This was very near to the beginnings of American activity in the breed since the first Miniature was brought to this country by W. D. Goff of Concord, Massachusetts, in 1923. The Pinscher Club embraced both varieties of the breed, Standard and Miniature.

In 1927 the Club changed its name to the Schnauzer Club of America and held its first specialty show. Six years later, in 1933, the two varieties were acclaimed separate and distinct breeds when the Miniature fanciers split from the parent club and formed the American Miniature Schnauzer Club which has served the breed well since that time.

The first of the breed was registered in the 1926 *American Kennel Club Stud Book* as Schnapp v. Dornbusch of Hitofa 551063, an import owned by Frank Spiekerman of Greenwich, Connecticut, owner of the then powerful Hitofa Kennels. Hitofa also won the best-of-variety ribbon at the first specialty show with another import, Don v. Dornbusch, while Don's dam, Lenchen v. Dornbusch owned by the Brookmeade Kennels, was the first Miniature to gain the American title of champion in the same year. Moses Taylor, owned by Mrs. Slattery was the first American-bred to win the title, also in 1927. Thus, the year was a memorable one for the Miniature Schnauzer. It was marked with many "firsts."

Today, the Miniature Schnauzer is the most popular member of the Terrier group. It was not always so, for in the thirties and early forties the breed had a difficult time to become recognized as a contender in group competition. To the credit of some of the breed's early proponents the Miniature has advanced to its present position of prominence, for without their perseverance and loyalty, it would probably have fallen into obscurity. Curt Sohl (Kingswood), Mrs. Kerns (Wollaton), Dorothy Williams (Dorem), Leda Martin (Ledahof), Gene Simmonds (Handful), Mrs. Slattery (Marienhof), Mrs. Sailer, and Mrs. Woehling (Normack) are a few of the many whose interest was constant and whose faith in the breed did not waver.

To one dog goes a lion's share of the credit for the rapid advance in breed interest and the definite improvement in breed type. This was Ch. Dorem Display, whelped April 5, 1945. His appearance in the show ring marked a new era for the breed. Display might be termed a new type but I prefer to call him a "middle of

157

the road" type. He had a head and eye that was fully acceptable to Terrier judges. Better still, he passed his many fine points on to his progeny and thus created a new era for the breed. Some excellent dogs had been bred of the general type but there was none that dominated the shows like Display. This created interest because the dog was winning groups and best-in-show awards to prove his quality. His quality and showmanship put him in the spotlight and with him the breed enjoyed the public's acclaim.

Since the end of the war the breed has climbed steadily. More and more Miniatures are being bred and with the increase in numbers more are finding their way into the show ring where they are winning high honors to improve the breed's position in the dog world. Present-day fanciers should hark back to the thirties and take care to maintain the attributes that have made the breed great.

Today, there is a tendency toward over long forefaces, that are out of balance with the skull. The Schnauzer should not have a Fox Terrier's head; great length is not required or desired, in fact, it robs the breed of its true character. Another point that must be watched is soundness. Many Schnauzers do not move well. While this may not harm them in breed judging if the others are also moving poorly, it does have a bearing upon group placements. Schnauzers do not have to move poorly and many are as sound as any other Terrier. A little care in this respect will improve the overall picture and will keep the breed forging ahead.

Size also warrants mention because of a series of changes in the breed standard. The 1933 specification required dogs to measure under 13 inches at the withers and bitches under 12 inches with a disqualification for any over these heights. The Standard was changed in 1938 to suggest a size of from $11\frac{1}{2}$ to $13\frac{1}{2}$ inches with an ideal size approximating $12\frac{1}{2}$ inches. Disqualification was required for any dog over 14 inches. The Standard, changed again in 1958, now reads, "Size from 12 to 14 inches. Ideal size $13\frac{1}{2}$ inches." The disqualification now reads, "Dogs or bitches under 12 inches or over 14 inches." The obvious trend is up and these progressive changes have made larger dogs "legal." The trend will not aid the breed which should be a Miniature of the Standard size and should remain so. It is hoped that further increases will not be forthcoming.

25

Norwich Terrier

THE Norwich Terrier is a small dog exhibiting the same courage and determination as other and larger members of the Terrier tribe. Around 1870 these little red dogs were sold by a man named "Doggy" Lawrence to undergraduates at Cambridge who were wont to have their sport around a rat pit or hunting the rabbit, both of which pursuits were well suited to the dog.

The University of Cambridge includes among its many halls of learning Caius College, named for Johannes Caius who wrote the famous book *Of Englishe Dogges* in Latin in 1576. St. Peter's College is the oldest foundation in Cambridge having been established in 1257. Since St. Peter's College, Pembroke College, and St. Katherine's Hall were all situated on Trumpington Street, it was small wonder that this popular little dog was first known as the Trumpington Terrier.

At least one early author opined that the Norwich was nothing more than a small Irish Terrier but this premise was taken lightly because of variations that pointed to infusions of Black and Tan and the rough-coated stock of the Fox Terrier in the blend. In addition, the Irish Terrier was undoubtedly in the blood to account for the reddish color. Since the Norwich was a fine pack dog and ran well with the Hounds the dogs found their way into many kennels. Whatever the background the breed has all the Terrier characteristics that make these breeds so desirable.

Frank Jones, living near Leicester, bred these dogs in the early 1900's and some called them Norfolk Terriers but since he was quite successful in exporting them to American buyers they soon became better known as Jones Terriers. R. E. Strawbridge, of Philadelphia got a few and Mr. Webb (see Shelburne Terrier under Working Terriers) used one in the propagation of his famous Shelburne strain. Webb also suggests the Irish Terrier cross and further states that in 1911 the breed, also called Norfolk Terrier, was not a regular breed but quite popular as workers.

The original Norwich Terrier was known as far back as 1880 when Mr. Nichols of Norfolk bred small red dogs by that name. They were used with the Norwich staghounds under J. E. Cooke and thus gained their present name from the many that they were called. Mr. R. J. Read obtained a bitch from Cooke which was bred and was crossed with Bedlington and Staffordshire Bull Terriers and then outcrossed with small Irish Terriers. This produced Read's fine workers but as expected they were difficult to keep to a given type. After the first World War when the breed was nearly wiped out, Read renewed his breeding activities with greater success and improved and stabilized the strain. Mrs. Fagan of Kingsmead, Windsor was another early breeder. She started in 1914 with a bitch named Flossie bred by Jones. This bitch, though lost in an earth, produced some good stock.

Early dogs of the breed varied in coat length from rough to smooth while the ears varied from drop to prick with some cropped before the practice was banned.

The breed did not have easy sailing. Although of reasonably early beginnings it was not until 1932 that the English Kennel Club recognized it and the breed was first benched at the Richmond Championship show in July 1931. A prick-eared bitch named Airman's Storm owned by Mrs. Rodwell was the ultimate winner. She was one of the few at that time to have upright ears. Four years later in 1936 the American Kennel Club admitted the breed to the stud book. The first Norwich to gain registration was Witherslack Sport A-58858 owned by G. Gordon Massey of Trappe, Maryland, although to R. E. Strawbridge of Philadelphia goes the honor

Appealing head study of a drop-eared Norwich
Terrier as pictured by Dickson Green.

of bringing over the first of the breed in 1914, then known as a
Jones Terrier. His name was Willum Jones and he was one of
the original progenitors of the aforementioned Shelburne Terrier.

In the United States the destinies of the breed are guided by the
Norwich Terrier Club of America, a member of the American Kennel Club. The Norwich cannot be termed a popular breed since it
is one of the low registration breeds but it is well supported at
Eastern shows because of a few strong and enthusiastic kennels
which have kept the breed before the public.

Frankly, I cannot understand why these appealing little dogs
are not more popular. They exude personality and present a perky
and smart appearance. Further, they do not require much trimming, just a bit of light plucking to remove tufts and straggling
hairs and to improve the general outline. The head and tail require the most attention and a little work to smooth up the hair
is very beneficial. In general, however, the work is light and requires but a little time before each show. The attractive reddish
color makes them easy to keep clean and always neat, a grand
small dog.

26

Scottish Terrier

WILLIAM HAYNES once said, "All Dogs are good; any Terrier is better; a Scottish Terrier is the best." This is surely the belief of all owners of the breed. The dog is a distinctive animal, an individual with a temperament unlike that of any other Terrier and without doubt a delight to own.

The Scottish Terrier, Die-Hard or Aberdeen Terrier, is the most popular of any of the breeds derived from the old Scotch Terrier. This may be said because the breed is numerically superior to any other member of the Scotch clan whether in the show ring or in registration records. This is odd, since the Scottish Terrier was only the third breed to gain distinct identity of all the breeds derived from the "Old Scotch." Further, the Scottish deviates more drastically from its early progenitor in conformation than either the Dandie, Skye, Cairn or West Highland White, the remaining cousins of the Scotch family of dogs. Thus, the Scottie outstripped the Dandie and the Skye after a late start and still holds the advantage.

The Aberdeen Terrier, as the breed was first known, did not come into the show ring until about 1877 and the venture was not successful. As a result Aberdeens failed to gain continued classes in their name and were shown in the broad category of "Hard-coated Scotch Terriers" which covered many and varied dogs including Cairns and nondescript Scotch dogs of dubious lineage. From 1884 to 1886 a number of excellent Aberdeens came out and the breed began to gain a permanent foothold in the Scottish picture. Thereafter, classes were provided at most championship shows.

The Scottish Terrier was bred from the old Scotch Terrier—the first variety mentioned by Brown—but fails to resemble this early dog because of many man-made changes accomplished by breeding techniques well known to fanciers of the times. The head was lengthened and the legs were shortened so that the body was closer to the ground. This last change did not improve the dog for work since the breed needed body clearance to function properly among the rocky cairns of its native habitat. The body was also shortened appreciably as time progressed until today we find a very short-backed animal winning at the shows.

Early dogs in the breed were of almost any color except white. White markings were also objectionable. Ears were either erect or semi-erect to deviate from later standards. Early dogs shown in England included Dundee, K.C.S.B. 16818, a champion and a winner from 1884 through 1886, and said to be the best to that date; Ch. Skittles, K.C.S.B. 15974, a dark colored bitch that won well in 1884–85; Glen Greta, Ashley Charlie, Roger Rough and many more that were shown at the time.

According to Gray, the first demand for separate classes for a dog bearing the description of the later-named Scottish Terrier was found in the *Fancier's Gazette* in 1874. In 1875 classes were offered for "Scotch Terriers" with little or no entry responding. In 1876 Pig and Otter owned by Messrs. Carrick and Murray respectively were shown in the Skye Terrier classes. Both dogs resembled the breed and Otter, according to Gray, was a good representative of the breed. Exhibition of a prick or semi-prick-eared breed of hard-coated Terriers goes back to 1873 but no documentation can be found that these dogs resembled the Scottish more than the Cairn type.

Possibly we should give up conjecture and base the first claim for breed autonomy in the show ring on the 1884 date when we know of the dog Dundee, a big winner and an acknowledged Scottish Terrier as one of the contestants.

Incidentally, D. J. Thomson Gray's book, *The Dogs of Scotland* (1887), while covering all Scotch breeds of dog in varying degrees of thoroughness was slanted primarily toward the Aberdeen or Scottish Terrier and as such was probably the second book to have been written on a distinct Terrier breed, the first being Cook's fine book on the Dandie Dinmont.

In America, John H. Naylor is credited with importing the first of the breed. His Tam Glen, Heather and Bonnie Bell were exhibited at such shows as Chicago, Springfield, Illinois, Pittsburgh, and New York in 1883 and 1884 in classes for "Rough-haired Terriers," so we find that the breed was having the same difficulties gaining recognition in America as in England and Scotland. Shortly thereafter, and based upon the English recognition, the breed gained its goal and progress began. Naylor's Prince Charlie 3310 was the first to be registered in 1885.

In 1895 the Scottish Terrier Club of America was formed to further the fortunes of the breed. This group accepted the Scottish standard of 1888 and this was the specification by which the breed was judged until 1925. The Scottish Terrier Club of England, formed in 1882, preceded the Scottish Terrier Club of Scotland by six years. The latter group, odd as it may seem was not formed until 1888. It might be noted that before this, the standard given in Gray's book (probably the English standard) sets the weights for dogs at 14 to 18 pounds and for bitches from 13 to 17 pounds with heights from 9 to 12 inches. Under "Faults" we find, "Specimens over 18 pounds should not be encouraged."

In 1925 a committee of Henry Bixby, later executive head of the American Kennel Club, Robert Sedgwick, Henry T. Fleitmann, S. Edwin Megargee, Jr., noted animal artist, and Richard Cadwalader drew up a new standard which eliminated the "half-prick" ear; and modified the neck to permit greater length by the inclusion of the word "moderately" before short. Possibly the most important change was in body. Here the old wording "of moderate *length*" was changed to "moderately *short*." Thus, the moderately long-bodied dog of the past had been changed to a moderately short-bodied dog of the present. Many other minor changes and clarifications were made.

The 1925 standard was used until 1947 when a committee consisting of S. Edwin Megargee, Jr., Theodore Bennett, John Kemps

Mrs. Howe Low's homebred Norwich Terrier,
Ch. Upland Spring Jock.

Todhill Kennels' Scottie, Ch. Walsing Winning
Trick, imported by Mrs. John G. Winant.

Hillwood Kennels' Scottie, Am. and Eng. Ch. Merle-
wood Hopeful, an early winner of 1932.

and Maurice Pollak proposed a standard which was adopted in April of 1947 and which is still "gospel." The major changes at this time were two in number. First, the size was changed. Under the revision, the top weight was suggested to be from 19–22 pounds for dogs and from 18–21 pounds for bitches with a height of 10 inches for both sexes. Second, an addition dealing with character and showmanship was inserted under "Penalties." This section directs the judge to turn down any dog for winners that does not have head and tail up stating that these factors of showmanship should be penalized.

This was added to stop a trend then beginning to be noticeable in the ring. Scottish Terriers were being shown that had good conformation, but they were shy and timid. Certainly no Scottie worthy of the name should exhibit these tendencies. On the other hand, the breed is a dour one and a Scotsman that does not want to show will not show. This does not mean that the dog is shy or timid—any judge who knows the breed can see the character of the dog in the eyes. A smouldering, defiant look belies timidity and therefore the standard requirement places judges in a difficult position at times although it must be admitted that the change substantially eliminated the shy ones.

Study of the four standards, namely the one in force before 1888 through the present finds deviations that have practically made over the breed. First, the body has been shortened with a longer, more graceful neck. In fact, the dog is now termed a "short-bodied dog" while his ancestor was definitely a "long-bodied dog." Second, the weights for the breed have been increased while the height has been reduced. This means that the dog is definitely cobbier, more blocky in appearance than his racier forebear.

As previously noted, the weights set down in the first standard in Gray's book were: dogs 14 to 18 pounds and bitches 13 to 17 pounds with height from 9 to 12 inches at the withers. In the present standard weight is from 19 to 22 pounds for dogs and from 18 to 21 pounds for bitches with height not to exceed about 10 inches for either sex. Surely these figures indicate the trend and also offer evidence that the present breed is not being bred to follow the early working pattern which by now has been essentially lost.

The Scottish Terrier has enjoyed a host of big names among its

166

following. This has brought the breed a large amount of excellent publicity. S. S. Van Dine (the alias of Willard Huntington Wright), novelist and fancier, helped bring the breed before the public with his book *The Kennel Murder Case*. His Ch. Heather Reveller of Sporran was a big winner. Mrs. John G. Winant, wife of our wartime Ambassador to the Court of St. James was another who loved the breed and her Edgerstoune Kennels (now closed) are still considered one of the strongest ever. Her Ch. Walsing Winning Trick of Edgerstoune, made a record when he was shown with but a single breed defeat in his career and with more than a ninety-five percent record for going best in show; Westminster, Morris & Essex, Chicago International and the specialties were all among his conquests.

Dr. Fayette Ewing is one early breeder who should certainly be mentioned. He bought his first Scottie in 1897 and had an unfailing interest in the breed for over fifty years. Until his death, his Nosegay Kennels owned many of the best.

In the years that have passed many persons and kennels have had their share in making the breed what it is today. In the bibliography a number of available articles are listed; they discuss several of the more notable kennels of the past and also include a few that are still active.

Scottish Terrier literature also has the distinction of including two momentous works giving a complete pedigree background of all dogs and bitches in the breed that have completed championship requirements. The first, by the noted English authority, Dorothy S. Caspersz, was published in 1934 with supplements in 1950 and 1962. This of course deals in the main with British dogs of the breed. The second is a book issued in 1962 of American Scottish Terrier champions' pedigrees by T. Allen Kirk, Jr., M. D. which lists all United States champions.

> —*I ken the Terrier o' the North,*
> *I ken the towsy tyke—*
> *Ye'll search frae Tweed to Sussex' shore,*
> *But never find his like.*

167

27

Sealyham Terrier

THE Sealyham or Pembrokeshire Terrier is an old breed in England but relatively young in point of official recognition. It was not until 1908 that the Sealyham Terrier Club of Haverfordwest was formed, the first specialty group to support the breed. In 1910 the English Kennel Club permitted challenge certificates to be offered in the classes at the Great Joint Terrier show in London although there is evidence that the breed was shown first in Wales about 1903.

In the United States, the year 1911 was significant for the breed. It was recognized by the American Kennel Club with August Belmont's Harfat's Pride 151623, the first to gain registration. The first Sealyham was shown at San Mateo, California the same year. The American Sealyham Terrier Club was formed May 15, 1913 with Mr. Belmont as its president. Also in 1913 the first champion, an import by the name of The Varmint by Grip ex Tiny was crowned. Thus, the entire growth and recognition of the breed came about early in the present century.

Going back to Sealyham beginnings, we find many claims of the age of the breed. The poem found in Freeman Lloyd's *Dog Breeds of the World* in the October issue of the 1934 *American Kennel Gazette* is no exception. It reads as follows:

THE SEALYHAM TERRIER

Just as old as the hills is the Sealyham,
Mars was his sire and Diana his dam.
Near Treffgarne Ricks he was nutured and bred,
And there on the milk of the wolf he was fed,
And that made him sturdy, and strong for the chase,
Though the Glyn-y-mel Hounds might beat him a pace.
But 'tis not speed only that makes a good run,
That may last from morn' till set of the sun.
The Hounds were eager when they cried 'Gone Away!'
And you'd follow their music towards Fishguard Bay.
Yet sometimes they lost their endurance and breath,
But always the Terrier got in at the death!
When Sir Gwen Tucker, of Poictier's fame,
(He served the Black Prince) back to Sealyham came;
He laid his sword down—so the old books we read—
To found and to foster the Sealyham breed,
For ever and ever, his fine dog shall live,
And tho' he can't hear us! 'tis three cheers we give!
        —Rev. William Williams in *Our Dogs*

With regard to mention of the wolf in the above poem, it should be explained that nearby were Wolf's Castle and Wolf's Dale.

In spite of claims and legends, the first reasonably well documented information places the origin of the breed with the Edwardes family of Sealy Ham near Haverfordwest. Credited with the development of the strain in the middle 1800's Captain Edwardes was proud of their accomplishments in bolting the fox and destroying the otter. The dog at the time had a wiry jacket, was mostly white with badger markings and according to Rawdon Lee weighed around 18 pounds. The breed has always had unflinching courage and in spite of 20th century refinements can still take toll of vermin as will be noted later.

Captain Edwardes took his "Sealy Ham" Terriers with him wherever he went—it is said he even presided at a political meeting at Fishguard flanked by two of them as he sat on the platform. Edwardes was a careful breeder; one of his dogs, Tip, was named in the working Terrier entry in a catalogue at a Haverfordwest dog show about 1890. The entry stated, "pedigree known for one hun-

169

dred years, warranted to go to ground to fox, badger and otter;—."
Since there is no reason to doubt this statement it carries the origin
of the breed back many years before any public acknowledgment
was first made of the Sealyham or, for that matter, of any defined
breed of Terrier.

The Sealyham is probably derived from the Welsh Corgi as a
foundation. This was crossed with a Dandie Dinmont to offer true
Terrier blood which left its mark on the new breed and unques-
tionably added gameness. Some Bull Terrier was likewise added to
further improve gameness and to give strength to the jaw. Later
several crosses were used, the West Highland White to reduce
size and Wire-haired Fox Terriers to improve coats. In fact, many
early Sealyhams resembled a Fox Terrier more closely than any
other breed since they were well up on the leg. Sir Jocelyn Lucas
supports the aforementioned background which is certainly a mixture that combines many fine characteristics for any Terrier.

The American Sealyham Terrier Club is the only specialty club
in the Terrier group to offer working certificates at this time. (One
of these is shown in the chapter on Working Terriers.) This certificate, given for actual ground work on vermin, has been an interesting phase of Sealyham activities for many years with Carleton
Punch 195501 gaining the first award. To date some forty-seven
have gained the coveted certificate and seven of these were champions of record on the show bench.

Sealyham Terrier, Ch. Robin Hill
Sweet Sixteen, bred and owned by
Mrs. Robert B. Choate.

Sealyham Terrier, Ch. Robin Hill
Brigade, bred and owned by Mrs.
Robert B. Choate.

170

The Sealyham Terrier has enjoyed an excellent record at Westminster where the breed has been singularly successful. Ch. Barberryhill Bootlegger won best in show at "the Garden" in 1924 followed by Ch. Pinegrade Perfection in 1927 and Ch. St. Margaret Magnificent of Clairedale in 1936. In the past two decades the breed has declined in popularity, why, is not known since Sealyham Terriers have all the attributes that make a good show dog or pet. They are easy to keep, small enough for apartment living and they exhibit all the affection that can be desired. It is hoped the breed regains its past position soon.

The breed standard has been changed several times. The latest modification was the adoption of a scale of points in 1942, the present standard having been in vogue since 1935. This varies widely from the original standard which offered the following suggested type: "The ideal being the combination of the Dandie Dinmont with a Bull Terrier of twenty pounds, otherwise, any resemblance to a Fox Terrier in either make, shape, character, or expression should be heavily penalized."

The earlier standard included another revealing statement under color. It read, "Black is objectionable, even on the head and ears. A large black spot on the body should be almost a disqualification as showing Fox Terrier blood." This is interesting since it does not mention a tan or brown body spot as even being objectionable. The present standard merely states, "Heavy body markings and excessive ticking should be discouraged." Further, the size has been better designated by limiting the height at the withers to "about 10½ inches" rather than the previous wide limits of "9 to 12 inches at the shoulder, bitches somewhat smaller."

28

Skye Terrier

THE Skye Terrier has been known probably by more names than any other Terrier. It is difficult to document the beginnings of the breed since the various names cause confusion particularly because other Terriers have been called by the same generic names. The Skye, a breed of pure Scotch descent as the name implies, came originally from the Isle of Skye. For this reason it is not to be wondered that the early name, Isle of Skye Terrier, has been used nor is it difficult to reconcile the use of the generic terms, Highland and Scotch Terrier.

The breed is an old one and proponents who claim it to be as old as any Terrier have some basis for their claims. The original Scotch Terrier was described in some cases as a dog having long hair, and the drawing of an Isle of Skye Terrier in Smith's *Natural History of Dogs* (1839), is a very good representation of the breed leaving no doubt of its identity. Claims have been made also that all Scotch Terrier breeds originated from the Isle of Skye Terrier. Whatever the facts, there can be no doubt that it is an old breed and one that has held its identity without too great a change through the many years of its existence.

After reaching the mainland and becoming popular around Glasgow, the breed was known as: Glasgow Terrier, Clydesdale Ter-

Skye Terrier, Ch. Ivory Jock of Iradell, American-bred winner, bred and owned by Mrs. N. Clarkson Earl, Jr.

Glamoor Kennels' imported Ch. Evening Star de Luchar, top winning Skye, owned by Mrs. A. F. Goodman and Walter Goodman.

rier, Fancy Skye Terrier, Silky Skye Terrier and Paisley Terrier. All were directed in the main to an outgrowth of the breed which had a soft and sometimes silky coat. The most useful names were the Clydesdale or Paisley Terrier and these have remained with the offshoot of the breed and are still used, although the silky-coated ones have disappeared. The Clydesdale Terrier was an appealing dog with a bright steel blue coat, silky and long. Legs and feet were usually an attractive golden tan. Undoubtedly there was consanguinity with the Yorkshire or the Halifax Blue Tan. The close relationship between the Skye and the Clydesdale is shown by the name of an early specialty club called the Skye and Clydesdale Terrier Club. The blue dogs lost their popularity around the turn of the century and the breed lost its identity even though the name lived on.

Lee had little regard for the blue dogs while others praised them highly. In any event, shown in classes with the Skye until about 1887, they did their share of winning. The Skye lived on, however and today is as popular as ever.

Terriers by the name of Skye were exhibited at the first dog show to include Terriers. This was at Birmingham in 1860 under the broad classification of Scotch Terrier. One of the winners was listed as a White Skye, while another was designated as an imported Skye. The 1861 Birmingham fixture had the same classes as before but the Manchester event of the same year included a classification for Skyes together with classes for Scotch Terriers. Most shows after 1861 included the Skye as a separate breed among the several Terrier breeds and separate from the more general term of Scotch Terrier which often was broken into several goupings such as White Scotch, Fawn Scotch and Blue Scotch as noted at the 1863 London event. Subsequent shows expanded the classification and in the first edition of Stonehenge, the Skye is one of the four Terriers listed as distinct breeds.

In the United States the first Skye registered in 1887 was a dog named Romach 6184 owned by the Maizeland Kennels of Red Hook, New York. The breed was shown immediately and early records offer an interesting study of the type of dogs of that day. C. H. Mason's, *Prize Dogs* (1888) gives weights for some of these dogs and we find a wide variation indicating lack of uniformity.

For example, J. H. Naylor's Drollie, a dog by Prince Charlie ex

174

Nellie Grant, whelped in 1885 weighed 18 pounds, whereas F. P. Kirby's bitch Countess tipped the scales at 32 pounds. Another bitch, Highland Belle owned by Henry Stearns by Berkie ex Highland Mary, whelped in 1881 weighed only 12½ pounds while a dog Towsie 9152, by Jim ex Queen Mab, weighed 27 pounds. The weights of these dogs varied with later standards indicating that the early dogs were often quite large when compared to later specifications. In 1922 the United States standard suggested that dogs should be from 16 to 20 pounds with bitches 14 to 18 pounds. The height of dogs was given as 9 inches at the withers and bitches 8½ inches. This general specification remained in vogue until 1956 when a new standard was approved which raised the height to 10 inches and removed weight specifications. The 1955 English standard agrees in substance with the American but includes a weight of 25 pounds for the dog.

The Skye Terrier Club of America, organized in 1938, adopted in 1939 the standard of The Skye and Clydesdale Terrier Club of England (1923) which in turn adopted the description by permission of the Skye Terrier Club of Scotland. Presently we find the Skye Terrier in short demand and while relatively few are being shown, those that do reach the ring are high quality animals that make difficult competitors for all other breeds. Today's Skyes have long flowing coats of great elegance, and the silky hair of the Clydesdale branch is never found in the hard, straight top coat. The breed is one of the few that does not move with an elevated tail; it carries it in a graceful continuation of the top line and generally no higher than the back. The Skye is one of the few breeds that permit prick or drop ears although prick ears are more desirable because they appear more stylish. In fact, few drop-eared Skyes are being exhibited and none of the present top winners has them.

The Skye Terrier is one breed in the Terrier group that pays dividends for length of back. The standard offers measurements for an ideal dog 20 inches from chest bone to tail for a 10-inch height at the withers. Short-backed Skyes are generally penalized. The Skye is a Terrier through and through and this fact should not be forgotten. The breed is alert and intelligent and with its great heritage, it deserves greater popularity than it now enjoys.

29

Staffordshire Terrier

THE Staffordshire Terrier is a late-comer to the Terrier scene in America. The first of the breed was registered in 1936 after American Kennel Club recognition under the name Staffordshire Bull Terrier. In spite of this late acknowledgment, the breed is by no means a new one. In fact, the "Staff" comes from the old Bull and Terrier cross dating back to the early 1800's and has the same basic inheritance found in the Bull Terrier.

The breed had an unfortunate beginning when fighting stock was imported from England some time near the close of the Civil War. Propagation of the fighting strain was continued with the breed being known alternately in this country as American Bull Terrier, pit Bull Terrier or Yankee Terrier. None of these names could stamp out the breed's basic British heritage and finally, when AKC recognition came it did so with the breed carrying the name of its north-country birthplace in England.

Type on both sides of the Atlantic varied during the early years of its existence. In England heads deviated greatly but finally became stabilized with a short, heavy muzzle which was held in great esteem in the Cradley Heath district where many of these fighting dogs were raised and highly prized. In the United States the early representatives varied physically because type was not as important

English Ch. Luckystar of Bandits shows the type difference in American and English Staffs.

Staffordshire, Ch. Xpert Brindle Biff, sire of 13 champions and a big winner. Bred and owned by Clifford A. Ormsby.

as gameness which was the first requisite of a good pit dog.

The American version of the Staffordshire no longer resembles too closely the British breed of the same name. The American dogs are generally about ten to fifteen pounds heavier and approach more closely the Bull Terrier type than their English cousins which still offer strong visual proof of their heritage. The English dogs are smaller, lower to the ground and do not have the legs or heads of the American strain.

The Staffordshire Terrier was used to produce the Colored Bull Terrier. This occurred many years ago when the White Cavalier was bred with the colored Staff. The two breeds now vary widely although the American Staffordshire has overall lines more akin to the Bull Terrier than does its English cousin. Here the resemblance ceases for the Staff differs widely in head with a defined stop and pronounced cheek muscles together with ears that may be half-rose. Also, the Staffordshire may be any color except all white, but black and tan, liver and more than eighty percent white are not encouraged although such colors are sometimes seen at the shows.

The breed was originally fostered in the United States by the United Kennel Club under the name American or Pit Bull Terrier.

177

Much early progress was made prior to 1935 although the breed was considerably different than it is now. Such early dogs as Frisco Sport and The Blind Dog exemplified early variables of the breed. Sponsors of the Staffordshire worked for AKC recognition and were successful in 1936 when the breed was admitted to the stud book as the nineteenth Terrier to gain the honor. Wheeler's Black Dinah A-86066 was the first of the breed to be accorded a stud book number in 1936 and the following year Maher's Captain D became the first American Kennel Club Staffordshire champion.

The breed gained strong support from the national specialty club called the Staffordshire Terrier Club of America which was admitted to membership in the American Kennel Club in 1940. This quite active group sponsored specialty classes at the International Kennel Club of Chicago shows which won acclaim during the late 1940's when entries of fifty and over were the rule. Many fine dogs did much to bring the Staff into the limelight and contemporaries such as Ch. Doyle's Tacoma Flambeau, Ch. Topsy's Ghost and Ch. X-Pert Brindle Biff were a few of many that kept the breed before the public. In later years interest has seemed to slacken and entries are not as large as before. This does not help the breed and while the club still holds its specialty events they are not usually as well attended. Possibly one explanation for the decline is the loss of some of the early fanciers whose initial interest helped bring the breed to its pinnacle. It is hoped that others will take their places with the same degree of enthusiasm.

While the breed has enjoyed a degree of popularity all over the country, the Mid-West is the most active in breeding and exhibiting. This is probably due to the early beginnings during the days when pit dogs were used for fighting. Several of the periodicals associated with the "sport" were published in the Mid-West and the U.K.C. which first gave the breed recognition is located there.

The standard is the same now as when approved June 10, 1936. The dog has an excellent temperament and makes a fine and loyal companion.

30

Welsh Terrier

THE Welsh Terrier had its beginnings in early times and if legends are to be given credence, the breed is one of the oldest. In fact, an old Welsh poem written about 1450 describes these hardy little Terriers with some accuracy. A literal translation is:

> *You gave me a dignified (picked)*
> *stick—and a good bitch,*
> *A black red-bellied terrier bitch*
> *To Throttle the brown pole-cat*
> *And to tear up the red fox.*

Enlightening as regards working Terriers of the day, this describes unmistakably a red and black animal. Since the rough-coated Terrier was one of the first of this strain to be given notice it is reasonable to assume that this type of worker was known, used and held in high regard in Wales in the 13th century. Without doubt, this type was the progenitor of the present day Welsh Terrier.

In spite of these seemingly early beginnings it was not until about 1884 that any of the breed gained recognition or reached the show bench. Immediately thereafter the Welsh Terrier Club was formed in England in 1886. It did not take long for the breed to reach our shores for in 1888 Prescott Lawrence of Groton, Massachusetts registered the first under the name T'Other 9171. Simultaneously he registered another of a brace which carried the intriguing name of "Which" 9172, both registrations being entered in Volume 5 of the AKC Stud Book. The same year saw T'Other entered in the miscellaneous class at Westminster. Thereafter for a few years there was little activity in this country until the Welsh Terrier Club of America was organized in 1900, twelve years after the first Welshman gained registration. It has since grown into a strong group that supports the breed well.

Returning to the history of the breed, there is little documented background before the time it was recognized. Some say that pedigrees were kept by Welsh breeders as early as the middle of the 19th century but these would be of little real value in determining background since it was the acknowledged practice of the times to use dogs with hunting ability rather than with conformative excellence. For this reason, purity of blood was not as important as it is today. Further, common given names such as Bob, Sandy, Nellie and the like offered little chance to verify a pedigree, especially when the neighborhood had a dozen or more of each name, and each held in high regard by the owner.

In spite of this beclouded history there is little doubt that the old working, rough-coated Black and Tan Terrier had a great influence on present-day Welsh. Most of them came from North Wales where the early dogs were entered regularly in competitions held in conjunction with agricultural events. Here the dogs were often shown in classes for working Terriers and later, sometimes prefaced with Old English, an early Black and Tan Wire-Haired Terrier name used for the Welsh. Some even fell into the classification of "Any Variety Terriers." These rough dogs were a bit more on the leg than present-day animals; they had shorter, heavier heads and were not nearly as eye-catching as the smart Welshman of today.

In any event, the first show that included classes for the Welsh Terrier was the Lleyn and Eifionydd Agricultural Society event held at Pwllheli, North Wales in August of 1884 with a good entry present. In spite of this recognition the dogs were entered as Rough or Wire-haired Terriers at the Bangor Dog, Poultry, Pigeon,

Cage Bird and Horticultural show held in September of the same year. The following year the breed gained entry in the stud book in November of 1885. During this period, the alternate name of Old English Wire-Haired Black-and-Tan Terriers was still used and a group of fanciers endeavored to form a club under this name but failed. The probable reason was lack of purity. The Welsh Terrier Club emerged as the proper breed club and the breed gained the appropriate name of its homeland, a fitting tribute to the tenacity of the Welsh fanciers.

The first Welsh to gain a title in Britain was a bitch, Bangor Dau Lliw in 1885. She was followed to the title by Ch. Mawddwy Non-such, Ch. Dim Saesonaeg and later by a big winner Ch. Brynhir Ballad which won more than thirty championship certificates. The two champions pictured, Longmynd Chamberlain and Longmynd Enchantress, owned by Mrs. H. D. Greene, won their titles in 1905 and from the painting one can see the considerable difference in type from the modern Welsh.

The Welsh Terrier today is a stylish dog that wins nicely at most shows. It has done well at Westminster where an import, Ch. Flornell Rare-Bit of Twin Ponds won the supreme honor of best in show in 1944. On many other occasions Welsh have captured the always hot Terrier group. The dogs are gay and even in disposition and afraid of nothing to fulfill a traditional Welsh motto: Gwell Angau Na Cywilydd which translated means "Better death than shame."

Many other Welsh Terriers have distinguished themselves in the show ring to the ultimate benefit of the breed—Ch. Halcyon Playboy, Ch. Hotpot Harriboy of Halcyon, Ch. Twin Ponds Belle, Ch. Strathglass Admiral, Ch. Strathglass Venture's Lucifer, Ch. Toplight Template of Twin Ponds, Ch. Beelzebub of Alvin Farm, to name a few. In addition many loyal fanciers have kept the breed integrated. A great share of this credit should go to the Misses de Coppet who, for fifty years, supported the breed loyally. The death of these two was a great loss to the Welshman in this country as was also that of two others, Miss Jean Hinkle (Port Fortune) and Hugh Chisholm (Strathglass). The unfortunate passing of these fanciers within about four years deprived the breed of three strong kennels and had a noticeable effect on Welsh entries at the shows. While three or four large kennels are still active and doing well, the breed does suffer from lack of interest. In fact, except at a few shows in the East, Welsh entries are at their lowest ebb even though quality is still good.

The standard of the breed has had its changes and breed type has deviated from its early leggy conformation into a cobby, sturdy little dog. Today, we find two types being shown, one the true Welshman with proper wedge-shaped head, ears carried close to the cheeks and of the attractive "15 inches maximum" size. The other type is a bit more like a Fox Terrier, racier, with leaner, longer head, higher breaking ears and often a bit over the 15-inch maximum height. Both types win and win well since both are attractive but it is believed that the presence of two distinct types harms the breed since it confuses newcomers as to what is really wanted. Stabilization of type would surely help this fine breed regain its past popularity.

An ancient Welsh triad sets forth three things most distasteful to the true Cymro (Welshman). They are: "to look with one eye: to listen with one ear: to defend with one hand." Surely the Welsh Terrier does not fail to meet the test for he is an intense dog, one that looks with both eyes, listens with both ears and defends with the great vigor he has within him.

Ch. Twin Ponds Belle, winning American-bred Welsh Terrier. Owned by Mrs. Edward Alker.

Ch. Strathglass Bingo's Venture, sire of Belle. Owned by the Strathglass Kennels.

31

West Highland White Terrier

THE West Highland White Terrier is the all-white Terrier from Scotland. Affectionately known as the Westie or Highlander he stems from the same family of Scotch dogs as the Scottish, Dandie Dinmont and Cairn and Skye Terriers.

This family of dogs goes back to the old Scotch Terrier as basic progenitor. The latter differed widely from some of these present-day breeds but had basic characteristics still present in many dogs of Scotch heritage. This early breed was known in all colors from black to white, with pied and tans included. It was of a size approximating the present-day Westie and was known with prick and drop ears. The present separate strains were evolved by selection and inter-breeding sometimes with other Terriers of special abilities and the Westie thus emereged as an all-white huntsman and companion. The white color was purposely bred so that the dog could be distinguished easily from wildlife and small predatory animals during the hunt.

In the late 19th and early 20th centuries the West Highland was known as the Pittenweem, Roseneath or Poltalloch Terrier, the last two names having been borrowed from the estate names of the Duke of Argyll and Colonel E. D. Malcolm, two early breeders of the strain. In fact the latter generally is credited as originator of the breed having propagated Westies with diligence from the middle of the 19th century. The claim to breed antiquity is further strengthened by Sir Edwin Landseer's painting, *Dignity and Impudence* executed in 1839, which depicts an excellent head study of a West Highlander. As early as 1903 Colonel Malcolm fostered a change in name to West Highland White Terrier, indicative of the dog's habitat, in an effort to unify the fancy. This was officially accomplished and in 1907 the Crufts show had classes for the newly designated breed.

The Highlander was originally bred to be a hunter of small stature, great courage and unsurpassed determination. Being a Terrier he went to ground and fought within the earths of the fox and in the dens of the otter with equal skill and pluck. His fine double coat acted as a protection against the teeth of his foe and the ravages of the native climate. Colonel Malcolm, in his treatise on the breed, *The Dog* (Volume 1), *The Terriers*, edited by Harding Cox, records feats of unbelievable courage wherein the Westie was often out-weighed but never out-fought. The dog's indomitable spirit is best exemplified by the following statement made by Rowland Johns in *Our Friend the West Highland White:* "No water was ever too cold and no earth was ever too deep for them."

The Westie is a dog of undeniable charm. Scotch as a bagpipe, he is not so dour as other Scotch breeds. He likes people and is not aloof although his master and his master's family capture his great affection. Westies are fun-loving and gay, they enjoy a romp or play but are also content to remain indoors when necessity demands. They are not argumentative but will not back down to any adversary, regardless of size.

Like all Terriers, the Westie is hardy and needs little care other than good food, suitable exercise and the love and affection of a human being. They are easy to keep in shape with a daily brushing and need but little trimming to keep them looking fit. A grand breed, leaving nothing to be desired by a dog lover, young or old.

The show career of the Highlander has been relatively short when compared with many other breeds, and the first Westie was shown in the United States at Westminster in 1906 under the classification of "Roseneath" Terrier.

One point of the Highlander differs from some of the other short-legged Terriers, namely, the distinctive gait which resembles a

Mrs. John Marvin's West Highland, Ch. Cranbourne
Arial. From a painting by C. C. Fawcett, 1951.

West Highland, Ch. Elfinbrook Simon, best in show at Westminster, 1962.
Left to right—William Rockefeller, club president; George Ward, handler;
Heywood Hartley, judge. Imported and owned by Miss Barbara Worcester.

jaunty bounce. The Westies' hind legs are properly carried rather close together when moving instead of being spread wide as in some of the longer-legged breeds. The body is deep, the ribs are well sprung but with a rather flattish side appearance as opposed to a round barrel. The front feet turn out as is characteristic in all short-legged Terriers which require this stucture to permit digging. Generally speaking both feet should be symmetrical and turn out the same degree for show animals.

Pigmentation in the ears, around the eyes, on the pads and nails is always desirable and Westies develop their pigmentation as quickly as any breed after birth. The Highlander should not be too low stationed but should have sufficient length of leg to be able to scamper over rocky terrain. Very short-legged dogs are not in proportion.

Heads require some consideration today with overly long forefaces being seen too frequently. The foreface of a Westie should be about the same length as the skull and a proper length of foreface goes a long way towards giving the desired expression. This is also enhanced by eyes which should be wide-set and small but not beady, and should be of dark hazel color rather than jet black.

The breed in the United States is guided by the West Highland White Terrier Club of America which was admitted to American Kennel Club membership on September 21, 1909. The Standard of Perfection was approved by the AKC, December 21, 1909, although the breed was admitted to the stud book in 1908.

First Westie to gain registration in the American Kennel Club Stud Book was Talloch 116076 in 1908, owned by Mrs. Clinton E. Bell of Springfield, Massachusetts, while the English import, Cream of the Skies, AKC 124682 was the first of the breed to gain a United States championship in 1909.

The standard has been changed but little since its initial approval. Size has been modified to lessen the earlier wide latitude of from 8 to 12 inches at the withers and notice has been included that the dog should "be tidied up." Otherwise no significant changes have been made.

186

32

Terrier Breed Standards

Courtesy, The American Kennel Club

Airedale Terrier

Head—Should be well balanced with little apparent difference between the length of skull and foreface. *Skull* should be long and flat, not too broad between the ears and narrowing very slightly to the eyes. Scalp should be free from wrinkles, stop hardly visible and cheeks level and free from fullness. *Ears* should be V-shaped with carriage rather to the side of the head, not pointing to the eyes, small but not out of proportion to the size of the dog. The topline of the folded ear should be above the level of the skull. *Foreface* should be deep, powerful, strong and muscular. Should be well filled up before the eyes. *Eyes* should be dark, small, not prominent, full of terrier expression, keenness and intelligence. *Lips* should be tight. *Nose* should be black and not too small. *Teeth* should be strong and white, free from discoloration or defect. Bite either level or vise-like. A slightly overlapping or scissors bite is permissible without preference.

Neck—Should be of moderate length and thickness gradually widening towards the shoulders. Skin tight, not loose. *Shoulders and Chest*—Shoulders long and sloping well into the back. Shoulder blades flat. From the front, chest deep but not broad. The depth of the chest should be approximately on a level with the elbows.

Body—Back should be short, strong and level. Ribs well sprung. Loins muscular and of good width. There should be but little space between the last rib and the hip joint. *Hindquarters*—Should be strong and muscular with no droop. *Tail*—The root of the tail should be set well up on the back. It should be carried gaily but not curled over the back. It should be of good strength and substance and of fair length. *Legs*—*Forelegs* should be perfectly

187

straight, with plenty of muscle and bone. *Elbows* should be perpendicular to the body, working free of sides. *Thighs* should be long and powerful with muscular second thigh, stifles well bent, not turned either in or out, hocks well let down parallel with each other when viewed from behind. *Feet* should be small, round and compact with a good depth of pad, well cushioned; the toes moderately arched, not turned either in or out.

Coat—Should be hard, dense and wiry, lying straight and close, covering the dog well over the body and legs. Some of the hardest are crinkling or just slightly waved. At the base of the hard very stiff hair should be a shorter growth of softer hair termed the undercoat. *Color*—The head and ears should be tan, the ears being of a darker shade than the rest. Dark markings on either side of the skull are permissible. The legs up to the thighs and elbows and the under-part of the body and chest are also tan and the tan frequently runs into the shoulder. The sides and upper parts of the body should be black or dark grizzle. A red mixture is often found in the black and is not to be considered objectionable. A small white blaze on the chest is a characteristic of certain strains of the breed.

Size—Dogs should measure approximately 23 inches in height at the shoulder; bitches, slightly less. Both sexes should be sturdy, well muscled and boned.

Movement—Movement or action is the crucial test of conformation. Movement should be free. As seen from the front the forelegs should swing perpendicular from the body free from the sides, the feet the same distance apart as the elbows. As seen from the rear the hind legs should be parallel with each other, neither too close nor too far apart, but so placed as to give a strong well-balanced stance and movement. The toes should not be turned either in or out. Yellow eyes, hound ears, white feet, soft coat, being much over or under the size limit, being undershot or overshot, having poor movement, are faults which should be severely penalized.

SCALE OF POINTS

Head	10	Color	5
Neck, shoulders and chest	10	Size	10
Body	10	Movement	10
Hindquarters and tail	10	General characteristics and	
Legs and feet	10	expression	15
Coat	10	Total	100

Approved July 14, 1959

Australian Terrier

General Appearance—A small, sturdy, rough-coated terrier of spirited action and self-assured manner.

Head—Long, flat-skulled, and full between the eyes, with the stop moderate. The muzzle is no longer than the distance from the eyes to the occiput. Jaws long and powerful, teeth of good size meeting in a scissors bite, although a level bite is acceptable. Nose black. *Ears* set high on the skull and well apart. They are small and pricked, the leather either pointed or slightly rounded and free from long hairs. *Eyes* small, dark, and keen in expression; not prominent. Light-colored and protruding eyes are faulty.

Neck—Inclined to be long, and tapering into sloping shoulders; well furnished with hair which forms a protective ruff.

Body—Low-set and slightly longer from the withers to the root of the tail than from the withers to the ground. *Chest* medium wide, and deep, with ribs well sprung but not round. Topline level. *Tail* set on high and carried erect but not too gay; docked leaving two fifths. *Legs and Feet*—Forelegs straight and slightly feathered to the carpus or so-called knee; they are set well under the body with elbows close and pasterns strong. Hindquarters strong and well muscled but not heavy; legs moderately angulated at stifles and hocks, with hocks well let down. Bone medium in size. Feet are small, clean, and catlike, the toes arched and compact, nicely padded and free from long hair. Nails strong and black.

Coat—Outer coat harsh and straight, and about two and one half inches all over the body. Under coat short and soft. The topknot, which covers only the top of the skull, is of finer texture and lighter color than the body coat.

Color—May be blue-black or silver-black, with rich tan markings on head and legs. The blue-black is bluish at the roots and dark at the tips. In the silver-blacks each hair carries black and silver alternating with black at the tips. The tan is rich and deep, the richer the better. Also, sandy color and clear red are permissible but not as desirable, other things being equal, as the blue and tan. In the sandies, any suggestion of shading or smuttiness is undesirable.

Gait—Straight and true; sprightly, indicating spirit and assurance.

Temperament—That of a hard-bitten terrier, with the aggressiveness of the natural ratter and hedge hunter, but as a companion friendly, affectionate, and biddable.

Size—Shoulder height, about 10 inches. Average weight 12 to 14 pounds.

Approved September 13, 1960

Bedlington Terrier

Skull—Narrow, but deep and rounded, high at the occiput, wedge-shaped, covered with profuse topknot, which should be nearly white, and, when trimmed, should give a Roman nose appearance. *Jaws*—Long and tapering. There must be no "stop" and the line from occiput to nose end straight and unbroken. Well filled up beneath the eye. Close fitting lips, no flews. *Teeth* —Level or pincer-jawed. The teeth should be large and strong. *Nose*—The nostrils must be large and well defined. Blues and blue and tans have black noses; livers, sandies, etc., have brown noses. *Eyes*—Small, bright and well sunk. The ideal eyes have the appearance of being triangular. Blue should have a dark eye; blue and tans have light eyes with amber lights; liver and sandies have a light hazel eye. *Ears*—Moderate sized, filbert shaped; set on low and hanging flat to the cheek. They should be covered with short, fine hair, with a fringe of silky hair at the tip.

Legs and Feet—Muscular and moderate length. The hind legs, by reason of the roach back and arched loin, have the appearance of being longer than the forelegs. The forelegs should be straight, with a moderately wide chest and hare-feet.

Body—Muscular, yet markedly flexible. Flat-ribbed and deep through the brisket, well ribbed up. The chest should be deep and fairly broad. The back should be roached and the loin markedly arched. Light, muscular, galloping quarters, which are also fine and graceful. *Neck*—Long, tapering arched neck, deep at the base. The neck should spring well from the shoulders, which should be flat, and head should be carried high.

Coat—The coat is very distinctive and unlike that of any other terrier in that it should be thick and linty (not wiry), and when in show condition should not exceed one inch in length. It should be brushed on the body and back from the root of the tail toward the head, and should not lie flat against the body. There should be an absence of hair on the ears except at the tip, where the *fringe* should be from one-half to one inch long. The hair on

190

the legs should be slightly longer and straighter than that of the body. The topknot should be highest at the occiput and taper gradually to just in back of the nose. It (the topknot) should be rounded from side to side from an imaginary line drawn from the outer corner of the eye to the top of the ear on one side to a like line on the opposite side.

Tail—Of moderate length, thick at the root, tapering to a point and gracefully curved, slightly feathered, 9 to 11 inches long, scimitar shaped, carried elevated but not over the back.

Color—Blue, blue and tan, liver, liver and tan, sandy, sandy and tan.

Height—About 15 or 16 inches. *Weight*—Dogs, about 24 pounds; bitches, about 22 pounds.

Action—Very distinctive. Rather mincing, light and springy, must gallop like a Greyhound, with the whole body.

General—A graceful, lithe but not shelly, muscular dog, with no sign of coarseness or weakness. The whole head should be pear-shaped or wedge-shaped. The expression in repose is mild and gentle. When roused, the eyes should sparkle and the dog look full of temper and courage.

VALUE OF POINTS

Head	20	Eyes		5
Size	10	Nose		5
Teeth	10	Body		15
Color	5	Coat		10
Legs and feet	10	Tail		5
Ears	5	Total		100

Approved February 17, 1937

Border Terrier

Since the Border Terrier is a working terrier of a size to go to ground and able, within reason, to follow a horse, his conformation should be such that he be ideally built to do his job. No deviations from this ideal conformation should be permitted, which would impair his usefulness in running his quarry to earth and in bolting it therefrom. For this work he must be alert, active and agile, and capable of squeezing through narrow apertures and rapidly traversing any kind of terrain. His head, "like that of an otter," is distinctive, and his temperament ideally exemplifies that of a Terrier. By nature he is good-tempered, affectionate, obedient, and easily trained. In the field he is hard as nails, "game as they come" and driving in attack. It should be the aim of Border Terrier breeders to avoid such over-emphasis of any point in the Standard as might lead to unbalanced exaggeration.

General Appearance—He is an active terrier of medium bone, strongly put together, suggesting endurance and agility, but rather narrow in shoulder, body and quarter. The body is covered with a somewhat broken though close-fitting and intensely wiry jacket. The characteristic "otter" head with its keen eye, combined with a body poise which is "at the alert," gives a look of fearless and implacable determination characteristic of the breed. The proportions should be that the height at the withers is slightly greater than the distance from the withers to the tail, *i.e.* by possibly 1–1½ inches in a 14-pound dog.

Weight—Dogs, 13–15½ pounds, bitches, 11½–14 pounds, are appropriate weights for Border Terriers in hard-working condition.

Head—Similar to that of an otter. Moderately broad and flat in skull with plenty of width between the eyes and between the ears. A slight, moderately broad curve at the stop rather than a pronounced indentation. Cheeks slightly full. *Ears*—Small, V-shaped and of moderate thickness, dark preferred. Not set high on the head but somewhat on the side, and dropping forward close to the cheeks. They should not break above the level of the skull. *Eyes*—Dark hazel and full of fire and intelligence. Moderate in size, neither prominent nor small and beady. *Muzzle*—Short and "well filled." A dark muzzle is characteristic and desirable. A few short whiskers are natural to the breed. *Teeth*—Strong, with a scissors bite, large in proportion to size of dog. *Nose*—Black, and of a good size.

Neck—Clean, muscular and only long enough to give a well-balanced appearance. It should gradually widen into the shoulder. *Shoulders*—Well laid back and of good length, the blades converging to the withers gradually from a brisket not excessively deep or narrow. *Forelegs*—Straight and not too heavy in bone and placed slightly wider than in a Fox Terrier. *Feet*—Small and compact. Toes should point forward and be moderately arched with thick pads.

Body—Deep, fairly narrow and of sufficient length to avoid any suggestion of lack of range and agility. Deep ribs carried well back and not oversprung in view of the desired depth and narrowness of the body. The body should be capable of being spanned by a man's hands behind the shoulders. Back strong but laterally supple, with no suspicion of a dip behind the shoulder. Loin strong and the under line fairly straight. *Tail*—Moderately short, thick at the base, then tapering. Not set on too high. Carried gaily when at the alert, but not over the back. When at ease, a Border may drop his stern.

Hindquarters—Muscular and racy, with thighs long and nicely molded, Stifles well bent and hocks well let down.

Coat—A short and dense undercoat covered with a very wiry and somewhat broken top coat which should lie closely, but it must not show any tendency to curl or wave. With such a coat a Border should be able to be exhibited almost in his natural state, nothing more in the way of trimming being needed than a tidying-up of the head, neck and feet. *Hide*—Very thick and loose fitting.

Movement—Straight and rhythmical before and behind, with good length of stride and flexing of stifle and hock. The dog should respond to his handler with a gait which is free, agile and quick.

Color—Red, grizzle and tan, blue and tan, or wheaten. A small amount of white may be allowed on the chest but white on the feet should be penalized.

SCALE OF POINTS

Head, ears, neck and teeth ..	20	Back and loin	10
Legs and feet	15	Hindquarters	10
Coat and skin	10	Tail	5
Shoulders and chest	10	General appearance	10
Eyes and expression	10	Total	100

Approved March 14, 1950

Bull Terrier

WHITE

The Bull Terrier must be strongly built, muscular, symmetrical and active, with a keen determined and intelligent expression, full of fire but of sweet disposition and amenable to discipline.

The Head should be long, strong and deep right to the end of the muzzle, but not coarse. Full face it should be oval in outline and be filled completely up giving the impression of fullness with a surface devoid of hollows or indentations, *i.e.*, egg shaped. In profile it should curve gently downwards from the top of the skull to the tip of the nose. The forehead should be flat across from ear to ear. The distance from the tip of the nose to the eyes should be perceptibly greater than that from the eyes to the top of the skull. The underjaw should be deep and well defined. *The Lips* should be clean and tight. *The Teeth* should meet in either a level or in a scissors bite. In the scissors bite the upper teeth should fit in front of and closely against the lower teeth, and they should be sound, strong and perfectly regular.

The Ears should be small, thin and placed close together. They should be capable of being held stiffly erect, when they should point upwards. *The Eyes* should be well sunken and as dark as possible, with a piercing glint and they should be small, triangular and obliquely placed; set near together and high up on the dog's head. *The Nose* should be black, with well developed nostrils bent downwards at the tip.

The Neck should be very muscular, long, arched and clean, tapering from the shoulders to the head and it should be free from loose skin. *The Chest* should be broad when viewed from in front, and there should be great depth from withers to brisket, so that the latter is nearer the ground than the belly.

The Body should be well rounded with marked spring of rib, the back should be short and strong. The back ribs deep. Slightly arched over the loin. The shoulders should be strong and muscular but without heaviness. The shoulder blades should be wide and flat and there should be a very pronounced backward slope from the bottom edge of the blade to the top edge. Behind the shoulders there should be no slackness or dip at the withers. The underline from the brisket to the belly should form a graceful upward curve.

The Legs should be big boned but not to the point of coarseness; the forelegs should be of moderate length, perfectly straight, and the dog must stand firmly upon them. The elbows must turn neither in nor out, and the pasterns should be strong and upright. The hind legs should be parallel viewed from behind. The thighs very muscular with hocks well let down. Hind pasterns short and upright. The stifle joint should be well bent with a well developed second thigh. *The Feet* round and compact with well arched toes like a cat.

The Tail should be short, set on low, fine, and ideally should be carried horizontally. It should be thick where it joins the body, and should taper to a fine point.

The Coat should be short, flat, harsh to the touch and with a fine gloss. The dog's skin should fit tightly. *The Color* should be pure white, though markings on the head are permissible. Any markings elsewhere on the coat shall disqualify.

Movement. The dog shall move smoothly, covering the ground with free, easy strides, fore and hind legs should move parallel each to each when viewed from in front or behind. The forelegs reaching out well and the hind legs moving smoothly at the hip and flexing well at the stifle and hock. The dog should move compactly and in one piece but with a typical jaunty air that suggests agility and power.

Faults. Any departure from the foregoing points shall be considered a

194

fault, and the seriousness of the fault shall be in exact proportion to its degree, *i.e.* a very crooked front is a very bad fault; a rather crooked front is a rather bad fault; and a slightly crooked front is a slight fault.

DISQUALIFICATION

Color—Any markings other than on the head shall disqualify.

COLORED

The Standard for the Colored Variety is the same as for the White except for the sub-head "Color" which reads: *Color.* Any color other than white, or any color with white markings. Preferred color, brindle. A dog which is predominately white shall be disqualified.

DISQUALIFICATION

Color—Any dog which is predominantly white shall be disqualified.
Approved December 11, 1956

Cairn Terrier

General Appearance—That of an active, game, hardy, small working terrier of the short-legged class; very free in its movements, strongly but not heavily built, standing well forward on its forelegs, deep in the ribs, well coupled with strong hindquarters and presenting a well proportioned build with a medium length of back, having a hard, weather-resisting coat; head shorter and wider than any other terrier and well furnished with hair giving a general foxy expression.

Skull—Broad in proportion to length with a decided stop and well furnished with hair on the top of the head, which may be somewhat softer than the body coat. *Muzzle*—Strong but not too long or heavy. Teeth large —mouth neither overshot or undershot. Nose black. *Eyes*—Set wide apart, rather sunken, with shaggy eyebrows, medium in size, hazel or dark hazel in color, depending on body color, with a keen terrier expression. *Ears*—Small, pointed, well carried erectly, set wide apart on the side of the head. Free from long hairs.

Tail—In proportion to head, well furnished with hair but not feathery.

Carried gaily but must not curl over back. Set on at back level.

Body—Well muscled, strong, active body with well-sprung, deep ribs, coupled to strong hindquarters, with a level back of medium length, giving an impression of strength and activity without heaviness. *Shoulders, Legs and Feet*—A sloping shoulder, medium length of leg, good but not too heavy bone; forelegs should not be out at elbows, and be perfectly straight, but forefeet may be slightly turned out. Forefeet larger than hind feet. Legs must be covered with hard hair. Pads should be thick and strong and dog should stand well up on its feet.

Coat—Hard and weather resistant. Must be double-coated with profuse harsh outer coat and short, soft, close furry undercoat. *Color*—May be of any color except white. Dark ears, muzzle and tail tip are desirable.

Ideal Size—Involves the weight, the height at the withers and the length of body. Weight for bitches, 13 pounds, for dogs, 14 pounds. Height at the withers—bitches, 9½ inches, dogs, 10 inches. Length of body from 14¼ to 15 inches from the front of the chest to back of hindquarters. The dog must be of balanced proportions and appear neither leggy or too low to ground; and neither too short or too long in body. Weight and measurements are for matured dogs at two years of age. Older dogs may weigh slightly in excess and growing dogs may be under these weights and measurements.

Condition—Dogs should be shown in good hard flesh, well muscled and neither too fat or thin. Should be in full good coat with plenty of head furnishings, be clean, combed, brushed and tidied up on ears, tail, feet and general outline. Should move freely and easily on a loose lead, should not cringe on being handled, should stand up on their toes and show with marked terrier characteristics.

FAULTS

1. *Skull*—Too narrow in skull. 2. *Muzzle*—Too long and heavy a foreface; mouth overshot or undershot. 3. *Eyes*—Too large, prominent, yellow, and ringed are all objectionable. 4. *Ears*—Too large, round at points, set too close together, set too high on the head; heavily covered with hair. 5. *Legs and Feet*—Too light or too heavy bone. Crooked forelegs or out at elbow. Thin, ferrety feet; feet let down on the heel or too open and spread. Too high or too low on the leg. 6. *Body*—Too short back and compact a body, hampering quickness of movement and turning ability. Too long, weedy and snaky a body, giving an impression of weakness. Tail set on too low. Back not level. 7. *Coat*—Open coats, blousy coats, too short or dead coats, lack of sufficient undercoat, lack of head furnishings, lack of hard hair on the legs. Silkiness or curliness. A slight wave permissible. 8. *Nose*—Flesh or light-colored nose. 9. *Color*—White on chest, feet or other parts of body.

Approved May 10, 1938

Dandie Dinmont Terrier

Head—Strongly made and large, not out of proportion to the dog's size, the muscles showing extraordinary development, more especially the maxillary. *Skull* broad between the ears, getting gradually less towards the eyes, and measuring about the same from the inner corner of the eye to back of skull as it does from ear to ear. The forehead well domed. The head is *covered* with very soft silky hair, which should not be confined to a mere topknot, and the lighter in color and silkier it is the better. The *Cheeks,* starting from the ears proportionately with the skull have a gradual taper towards the muzzle, which is deep and strongly made, and measures about three inches in length, or in proportion to skull as 3 is to 5. The *Muzzle* is covered with hair of a little darker shade than the topknot, and of the same texture as the feather of the forelegs. The top of the muzzle is generally bare for about an inch from the back part of the nose, the bareness coming to a point towards the eye, and being about 1 inch broad at the nose. The nose and inside of *Mouth* black or dark-colored. The *Teeth* very strong, especially the canines, which are of extraordinary size for such a small dog. The canines fit well into each other, so as to give the greatest available holding and punishing power, and the teeth are level in front, the upper ones very slightly overlapping the under ones. (Many of the finest specimens have a "swine mouth," which is very objectionable, but it is not so great an objection as the protrusion of the underjaw.)

Eyes—Set wide apart, large, full, round, bright, expressive of great determination, intelligence and dignity; set low and prominent in front of the head; color, a rich dark hazel. *Ears*—Pendulous, set well back, wide apart, and low on the skull, hanging close to the cheek, with a very slight projection at the base, broad at the junction of the head and tapering almost to a point, the forepart of the ear tapering very little—the tapering being mostly on the back part, the forepart of the ear coming almost straight down from its junction with the head to the tip. They should harmonize in color with the body color. In the case of a Pepper dog they are covered with a soft straight brownish hair (in some cases almost black). In the case of a Mustard dog the hair should be mustard in color, a shade darker than the body, but not black. All should have a thin feather of light hair starting about 2 inches from the tip, and of nearly the same color and texture as the topknot, which gives the ear the appearance of a *distinct point*. The animal is often 1 or 2 years old before the feather is shown. The cartilage and skin of the ear should not be thick, but rather thin. Length of ear from 3 to 4 inches.

Neck—Very muscular, well-developed and strong, showing great power of resistance, being well set into the shoulders.

Body—Long, strong and flexible; ribs well sprung and round, chest well developed and let well down between the forelegs; the back rather low at the shoulder, having a slight downward curve and a corresponding arch over the loins, with a very slight gradual drop from top of loins to root of tail; both sides of backbone well supplied with muscle. *Tail*—Rather short, say from 8 inches to 10 inches, and covered on the upper side with wiry hair of darker color than that of the body, the hair on the under side being lighter in color and not so wiry, with nice feather about 2 inches long, getting shorter as it nears the tip; rather thick at the root, getting thicker for about four inches, then tapering off to a point. It should not be twisted or curled in any way, but should come up with a curve like a scimitar, the tip, when excited, being in a perpendicular line with the root of the tail. It should neither be set on too high nor too low. When not excited it is carried gaily, and a little above the level of the body.

Legs—The forelegs short, with immense muscular development and bone, set wide apart, the chest coming well down between them. The feet well formed *and not flat*, with very strong brown or dark-colored claws. Bandy legs and flat feet are objectionable. The hair on the forelegs and feet of a Pepper dog should be tan, varying according to the body color from a rich tan to a pale fawn; of a Mustard dog they are of a darker shade than its head, which is a creamy white. In both colors there is a nice feather, about two inches long, rather lighter in color than the hair on the forepart of the leg. The hind legs are a little longer than the forelegs, and are set rather wide apart but not spread out in an unnatural manner, while the feet are much smaller; the thighs are well developed, and the hair of the same color and texture as the forelegs, but having no feather or dewclaws; the whole claws should be dark; but the claws of all vary in shade according to the color of the dog's body.

Coat—This is a very important point; the hair should be about 2 inches long; that from skull to root of tail, a mixture of hardish and soft hair, which gives a sort of crisp feel to the hand. The hard should not be wiry; the coat is what is termed piley or penciled. The hair on the under part of the body is lighter in color and softer than on the top. The skin on the belly accords with the color of dog. *Color*—The color is pepper or mustard. The pepper ranges from a dark bluish black to a light silvery gray, the intermediate shades being preferred, the body color coming well down the shoulder and hips, gradually merging into the leg color. The mustards vary from a reddish brown to a pale fawn, the head being a creamy white, the legs and feet of a shade darker than the head. The claws are dark as in other colors. (Nearly all Dandie Dinmont Terriers have some white on the chest, and some have also white claws.)

Size—The height should be from 8 to 11 inches at the top of shoulder.

Length from top of shoulder to root of tail should not be more than twice the dog's height, but preferably 1 or 2 inches less. *Weight*—The preferred weight from 18 to 24 pounds. These weights are for dogs in good working condition.

The relative value of the several points in the standard are apportioned as follows:

Head	10	Legs and feet	10
Eyes	10	Coat	15
Ears	10	Color	5
Neck	5	Size and weight	5
Body	20	General appearance	5
Tail	5	Total	100

Approved May 10, 1960

Fox Terrier

SMOOTH

The following shall be the standard of the Fox Terrier amplified in part in order that a more complete description of the Fox Terrier may be presented. The standard itself is set forth in ordinary type, the amplification in italics.

Head—The skull should be flat and moderately narrow, gradually decreasing in width to the eyes. Not much stop should be apparent, but there should be more dip in the profile between the forehead and the top jaw than is seen in the case of a Greyhound. The cheeks must not be full. The ears should be V-shaped and small, of moderate thickness, and drooping forward close to the cheek, not hanging by the side of the head like a Foxhound. *The topline of the folded ear should be well above the level of the skull.* The jaws, upper and lower, should be strong and muscular and of fair punishing strength, but not so as in any way to resemble the Greyhound or modern English Terrier. There should not be much falling away below the eyes. This part of the head should, however, be moderately chiseled out, so as not to go down in a straight slope like a wedge. The nose, toward which the muzzle must gradually taper, should be black. *It should be noticed that although the foreface should gradually taper from eye to muzzle and should tip slightly at its juncture with the forehead, it should not "dish" or fall*

199

away quickly below the eyes, where it should be full and well made up, but relieved from "wedginess" by a little delicate chiseling. The eyes and the rims should be dark in color, *moderately* small and rather deep-set, full of fire, life and intelligence and as nearly as possible circular in shape. *Anything approaching a yellow eye is most objectionable.* The teeth should be as nearly as possible together, *i.e. the points* of the upper (*incisors*) teeth on the outside of or *slightly overlapping* the lower teeth. *There should be apparent little difference in length between the skull and foreface of a well-balanced head.*

Neck—Should be clean and muscular, without throatiness, of fair length, and gradually widening to the shoulders. *Shoulders*—Should be long and sloping, well laid back, fine at the points, and clearly cut at the withers. *Chest* —Deep and not broad. *Back*—Should be short, straight (*i.e. level*), and strong, with no appearance of slackness. *Brisket should be deep, yet not exaggerated. Loin*—Should be very powerful, *muscular* and very slightly arched. The foreribs should be moderately arched, the back ribs deep *and well sprung,* and the dog should be well ribbed up.

Hindquarters—Should be strong and muscular, quite free from droop or crouch; the thighs long and powerful; *stifles well curved and turned neither in nor out;* hocks *well bent* and near the ground *should be perfectly upright and parallel each with the other when viewed from behind,* the dog standing well up on them like a Foxhound, and not straight in the stifle. *The worst possible form of hindquarters consists of a short second thigh and a straight stifle. Stern*—Should be set on rather high and carried gaily, but not over the back or curled. It should be of good strength, anything approaching a "pipe-stopper" tail being especially objectionable. *Legs*—The forelegs viewed from any direction must be straight with bone strong right down to the feet, showing little or no appearance of ankle in front, and being short and straight in pasterns. Both forelegs and hind legs should be carried straight forward in traveling, the stifles not turning outward. The elbows should hang perpendicularly to the body, working free of the sides. *Feet*—Should be round, compact and not large; the soles hard and tough; the toes moderately arched and turned neither in nor out.

Coat—Should be smooth, flat, but hard, dense and abundant. The belly and under side of the thighs should not be bare. *Color*—White should predominate; brindle, red, or liver markings are objectionable. Otherwise this point is of little or no importance.

Symmetry, Size and Character—The dog must present a generally gay, lively and active appearance; bone and strength in a small compass are essentials, but this must not be taken to mean that a Fox Terrier should be cloddy, or in any way coarse—speed and endurance must be looked to as well as power, and the symmetry of the Foxhound taken as a model. The terrier, like the hound, must on no account be leggy, nor must he be too short in the leg. He should stand like a cleverly made hunter, covering a lot of ground,

200

yet with a short back, as before stated. He will then attain the highest degree of propelling power, together with the greatest length of stride that is compatible with the length of his body. Weight is not a certain criterion of a terrier's fitness for his work—general shape, size and contour are the main points; and if a dog can gallop and stay, and follow his fox up a drain, it matters little what his weight is to a pound or so. *According to present-day requirements, a full-sized, well-balanced dog should not exceed 15½ inches at the withers, the bitch being proportionately lower—nor should the length of back from withers to root of tail exceed 12 inches, while, to maintain the relative proportions, the head should not exceed 7¼ inches or be less than 7 inches. A dog with these measurements should scale 18 pounds in show condition—a bitch weighing some 2 pounds less—with a margin of 1 pound either way*

Balance—*This may be defined as the correct proportions of a certain point, or points, when considered in relation to a certain other point or points. It is the keystone of the terrier's anatomy. The chief points for consideration are the relative proportions of skull and foreface; head and back; height at withers and length of body from shoulder-point to buttock —the ideal of proportion being reached when the last two measurements are the same. It should be added that, although the head measurements can be taken with absolute accuracy, the height at withers and length of back and coat are approximate, and are inserted for the information of breeders and exhibitors rather than as a hard and fast rule.*

Movement—*Movement, or action, is the crucial test of conformation. The terrier's legs should be carried straight forward while traveling, the forelegs hanging perpendicular and swinging parallel with the sides, like the pendulum of a clock. The principal propulsive power is furnished by the hind legs, perfection of action being found in the terrier possessing long thighs and muscular second thighs well bent at the stifles, which admit of a strong forward thrust or "snatch" of the hocks. When approaching, the forelegs should form a continuation of the straight line of the front, the feet being the same distance apart at the elbows. When stationary, it is often difficult to determine whether a dog is slightly out at shoulder, but, directly he moves, the defect—if it exists—becomes more apparent, the forefeet having a tendency to cross, "weave," or "dish." When, on the contrary, the dog is tied at the shoulder, the tendency of the feet is to move wider apart, with a sort of paddling action. When the hocks are turned in—cowhock— the stifles and feet are turned outwards, resulting in a serious loss of propulsive power. When the hocks are turned outwards the tendency of the hind feet is to cross, resulting in an ungainly waddle.*

N.B.—*Old scars or injuries, the result of work or accident, should not be allowed to prejudice a terrier's chance in the show ring, unless they interfere with its movement or with its utility for work or stud.* •

This variety of the breed should resemble the smooth sort in every respect except the coat, which should be broken. The harder and more wiry the texture of the coat is, the better. On no account should the dog look or feel woolly; and there should be no silky hair about the poll or elsewhere. The coat should not be too long, so as to give the dog a shaggy appearance, but, at the same time, it should show a marked and distinct difference all over from the smooth species.

SCALE OF POINTS

Head and ears	15	Legs and feet	15
Neck	5	Coat	15
Shoulders and chest	10	Symmetry, size and	
Back and loin	10	character	10
Hindquarters	15	Total	100
Stern	5		

DISQUALIFICATIONS

Nose—White, cherry or spotted to a considerable extent with either of these colors. Ears—Prick, tulip or rose. Mouth—Much undershot, or much overshot.

Irish Terrier

Head—Long, but in nice proportion to the rest of the body; the skull flat, rather narrow between the ears, and narrowing slightly towards the eyes; free from wrinkle, with the stop hardly noticeable except in profile. The jaws must be strong and muscular, but not too full in the cheek, and of good punishing length. The foreface must not fall away appreciably between or below the eyes; instead, the modeling should be delicate and in contradistinction, for example, to the fullness of foreface of the Greyhound. An exaggerated foreface, which is out of proportion to the length of the skull from the occiput to the stop, disturbs the proper balance of the head, and is not desirable. Also, the head of exaggerated length usually accompanies oversize or disproportionate length of body, or both, and such conformation is not typical. On the other hand, the foreface should not be noticeably shorter than is the skull from occiput to stop. Excessive muscular development of the cheeks, or bony development of the temples, conditions which are described by the fancier as "cheeky," or "strong in head," or "thick in skull," are objectionable. The "bumpy" or "alligator" head, sometimes described as the "taneous" head, in which the skull presents two lumps of bony structure with or without indentations above the eyes, is unsightly and to be faulted. The hair on the upper and lower jaw should be similar in quality and texture to that on the body, and only of sufficient length to present an appearance of additional strength and finish to the foreface. The profuse, goatlike beard is unsightly and undesirable, and almost invariably it betokens the objectionable linty and silken hair in the coat.

Teeth—Should be strong and even, white and sound; and neither overshot nor undershot. *Lips*—Should be close and well-fitting, almost black in color. *Nose*—Must be black. *Eyes*—Dark hazel in color; small, not prominent; full of life, fire and intelligence. The light or yellow eye is most objectionable.

Ears—Small and V-shaped; of moderate thickness; set well on the head, and dropping forward closely to the cheek. The ear must be free of fringe, and the hair much shorter and somewhat darker in color than on the body. A "dead" ear, houndlike in appearance, must be severely penalized. It is not characteristic of the Irish Terrier. An ear which is too slightly erect is undesirable.

Neck—Should be of fair length and gradually widening towards the shoulders; well and proudly carried, and free from throatiness. Generally there is a slight frill in the hair at each side of the neck, extending almost to the corner of the ear. *Shoulders and Chest*—Shoulders must be fine, long, and sloping well into the back. The chest should be deep and muscular, but neither full nor wide.

Back and Loin—The body should be moderately long—neither too long nor too short. The short back, so coveted and so appealing in the Fox Terrier, is *not* characteristic of the Irish Terrier. It is objectionable. The back must be symmetrical, strong and straight, and free from an appearance of slackness or "dip" behind the shoulders. The loin strong and muscular, and slightly arched. The ribs fairly sprung, deep rather than round, with a well-ribbed back. The bitch may be slightly longer in appearance than the dog. *Hindquarters*—Should be strong and muscular; powerful thighs; hocks near the ground; stifles moderately bent. *Stern*—Should be docked, and set on rather high, but not curled. It should be of good strength and substance; of fair length and well covered with harsh, rough hair, and free from fringe or feather. The three-quarters dock is about right.

Feet and Legs—The feet should be strong, tolerably round, and moderately small; toes arched and turned neither out nor in, with black toenails. The pads should be deep, not hard, but with a pleasing velvety quality, and perfectly sound; they must be entirely free from cracks or horny excrescences. Corny feet, so-called, are to be regarded as an abominable blemish; as a taint which must be shunned. Cracked pads frequently accompany corny growths, and these conditions are more pronounced in hot and dry weather. In damp weather and in winter such pads may improve temporarily, but these imperfections inevitably reappear and the result is unsound feet, a deplorable fault which must be heavily penalized. There seems to be no permanent cure for this condition, and even if a temporary cure were possible, the disease is seldom, if ever, eradicated, and undoubtedly it is transmitted in breeding. The one sure way to avoid corny and otherwise unsound feet is to avoid breeding from dogs or bitches which are not entirely free from this taint. Legs, moderately long, well set from the shoulders, perfectly straight, with plenty of bone and muscle; the elbows working clear of the sides; pastern short, straight, and hardly noticeable. Both forelegs and hind legs should move straight forward when traveling; the stifles should not turn outward. Cowhocks—that is, where the hocks are turned in, and the stifles and feet turned out, are intolerable. The legs should be free from feather, and covered, like the head, with hair of similar texture to that on the body, but not so long.

Coat—Should be dense and wiry in texture, rich in quality, having a broken appearance, but still lying fairly close to the body, the hairs growing so closely and strongly together that when parted with the fingers the skin is hardly visible; free of softness or silkiness, and not so long as to alter the outline of the body, particularly in the hindquarters. At the base of the stiff outer coat there should be a growth of finer and softer hair, differing in color, termed the undercoat. Single coats, which are without any undercoat, and wavy coats, are undesirable; the curly coat is most objectionable. On the sides of the body the coat is never as harsh as on the back and the quarters, but it should be plentiful and of good texture. *Color*—Should be whole-colored; the bright red, red wheaten, or golden red colors are preferable. A small patch of white on the chest, frequently encountered in all whole-colored breeds, is permissible but not desirable. White on any other part of the body is most objectionable.

Size and Symmetry—The most desirable weight in show condition is 27 pounds for the dog and 25 pounds for the bitch. The height at the shoulder should be approximately 18 inches. This terrier must be active, lithe and wiry in movement, with great animation; sturdy and strong in substance and bone structure, but at the same time free from clumsiness, for speed, power and endurance are most essential. The Irish Terrier must be neither "cobby" nor "cloddy," but should be built on lines of speed, with a graceful, racing outline.

The weights herein mentioned are ideal and serve as a guide to both breeder and judge. In the show ring, however, the informed judge readily identifies the oversized or undersized Irish Terrier by its conformation and general appearance. The weights named should be regarded as limit weights, as a rule, but it must be considered that a comparatively small, heavily built and "cloddy" dog—which is most undesirable, and not at all typical—may easily be of standard weight, or over it; whereas another Terrier which is long in leg, lacking in substance and built somewhat upon the lines of a Whippet—also undesirable and not at all typical—may be of the exact weight, or under it; therefore, although the standard weights must be borne well in mind, weight is not the last word in judgment. It is of the greatest importance to select, in so far as possible, terriers of moderate and generally accepted size, possessing the other various necessary characteristics.

Temperament—The Irish Terrier is game and asks no quarter. He is of good temper, most affectionate, and absolutely loyal to mankind. Tender and forbearing with those he loves, this rugged, stout-hearted terrier will guard his master, his mistress, children in his charge, or their possessions, with unflinching courage and with utter contempt of danger or hurt. His life is one continuous and eager offering of loyal and faithful companionship, and devoted, loving service. He is ever on guard, and stands between his house and all that threatens.

POSITIVE POINTS

Head, ears and expression ...	20	Hindquarters and stern	10
Legs and feet	15	Coat	15
Neck	5	Color	10
Shoulders and chest	10	Size and symmetry	10
Back and loin	5	Total	100

NEGATIVE POINTS

White nails, toes and feet, minus	10	Coat shaggy, curly or soft	10
Much white on chest	10	Uneven in color	5
Dark shadings on face	5	Total	50
Mouth undershot or cankered	10		

DISQUALIFICATIONS

Nose—Any other color than black. Mouth—Much undershot or overshot. Ears—Cropped ears. Color—Any other color than red, golden red, or red wheaten. A small patch of white on the chest is permissible; otherwise parti-colored coats disqualify.

Approved July, 1929

Head—Long, but not exaggerated and in good proportion to the rest of the body. Well balanced, with little apparent difference between the length of the skull and foreface. (20 points) *Skull*—Flat, with very slight stop, of but moderate breadth between the ears, and narrowing very slightly to the eyes. *Cheeks*—Clean and level, free from bumpiness. *Ears*—V-shaped, small but not out of proportion to the size of the dog, of moderate thickness, carried forward close to the cheeks with the top of the folded ear slightly above the level of the skull. A "dead" ear houndlike in appearance is very undesirable. *Foreface*—Jaws deep, strong and muscular. Foreface full and well made up, not falling away appreciably below the eyes but moderately chiseled out to relieve the foreface from wedginess. *Nose*—Black, nostrils large and wide. *Teeth*—Strong, white and either level or with the upper (incisors) teeth slightly overlapping the lower teeth. An undershot mouth should be strictly penalized. *Eyes*—Dark, small, not prominent, well placed and with a keen terrier expression. Anything approaching a yellow eye is very undesirable.

Neck—Clean and moderately long, gradually widening to the shoulders upon which it should be well set and carried proudly. (5 points) *Shoulders and Chest*—Shoulders fine, long and sloping, well laid back and well knit. Chest deep and of but moderate breadth. (10 points) *Legs and Feet*—Legs moderately long with plenty of bone and muscle. The forelegs should be straight from both front and side .view, with the elbows hanging perpendicularly to the body and working clear of the sides in movement, the pasterns short, straight and hardly noticeable. Both forelegs and hind legs should move straight forward when traveling, the stifles turning neither in nor out. (10 points) Feet should be strong, compact, fairly round and moderately small, with good depth of pad free from cracks, the toes arched, turned neither in nor out, with black toenails.

Body—Back short, strong and straight (*i.e.* level), with no appearance of slackness. Loin short and powerful with a slight tuck-up, the ribs fairly well sprung, deep rather than round. (10 points) *Hindquarters and Stern*— Hindquarters strong and muscular with full freedom of action, free from droop or crouch, the thighs long and powerful, stifles well bent and turned neither in nor out, hocks near the ground and, when viewed from behind, upright and parallel with each other, the dog standing well up on them. Tail should be set on high, of moderate length and carried gaily erect, the straighter the tail the better. (10 points)

Color—The correct mature color is any shade of blue gray or gray blue from deep slate to light blue gray, of a fairly uniform color throughout except that distinctly darker to black parts may appear on the muzzle, head, ears, tail and feet. (10 points) Kerry color, in its process of "clearing" from an apparent black at birth to the mature gray blue or blue gray, passes through one or more transitions—involving a very dark blue (darker than deep slate), shades or tinges of brown, and mixtures of these, together with a progressive infiltration of the correct mature color. Up to 18 months such deviations from the correct mature color are permissible without preference and without regard for uniformity. Thereafter, deviation from it to any significant extent must be severely penalized. Solid black is never permissible in the show ring. Up to 18 months any doubt as to whether a dog is black or a very dark blue should be resolved in favor of the dog, particularly in the case of a puppy. Black on the muzzle, head, ears, tail and feet is permissible at any age. *Coat*—Soft, dense and wavy. A harsh, wire or bristle coat should be severely penalized. In show trim the body should be well covered but tidy, with the head (except for the whiskers) and the ears and cheeks clear. (15 points)

General Conformation and Character—The typical Kerry Blue Terrier should be upstanding, well knit and in good balance, showing a well developed and muscular body with definite Terrier style and character throughout. A low-slung Kerry is not typical. (10 points)

Height—The ideal Kerry should be 18½ inches at the withers for a dog, slightly less for a bitch. In judging Kerries, a height of 18–19½ inches for a dog, and 17½–19 inches for a bitch should be given primary preference. Only where the comparative superiority of a specimen outside of the ranges noted clearly justifies it, should greater latitude be taken. In no case should it extend to a dog over 20 inches or under 17½ inches, or to a bitch over 19½ inches or under 17 inches. The minimum limits do not apply to puppies. *Weight*—The most desirable weight for a fully developed dog is from 33–40 pounds, bitches weighing proportionately less.

DISQUALIFICATIONS

Solid black. Dewclaws on hind legs.

Approved September 15, 1959

Lakeland Terrier

General Appearance—The Lakeland Terrier is a small, workmanlike dog of square, sturdy build and gay, friendly, self-confident demeanor. He stands on his toes as if ready to go, and he moves, lithe and gracefully, with a straight-ahead, free stride of good length. His head is rectangular in contour, ears v-shaped, and wiry coat finished off with fairly long furnishings on muzzle and legs.

Head—Well balanced; rectangular, the length of skull equalling the length of the muzzle when measured from occiput to stop, and from stop to nose-tip. The *skull* is flat on top and moderately broad, the cheeks almost straight-sided, and the stop barely perceptible. The *muzzle* is broad with straight nose-bridge and good fill-in beneath the eyes. The *nose* is black, except that liver-colored noses shall be permissible on liver-coated dogs. *Jaws* are powerful. The *teeth*, which are comparatively large, may meet in either a level, edge-to-edge bite, or a slightly overlapping scissors bite. Specimens with teeth overshot or undershot are to be disqualified. The *ears* are small, v-shaped, their fold just above the top of the skull, the inner edge close to the cheeks, and the flap pointed down. The *eyes*, moderately small and somewhat oval in outline, are set squarely in the skull, fairly wide apart. Their normally dark color may be a warm brown or black. The *expression* depends upon the dog's mood of the moment; although typically alert, it may be intense and determined, or gay and even impish.

Neck—Reachy and of good length; refined but strong; clean at the throat, slightly arched and widening gradually into the shoulders. The withers, that point at the back of the neck where neck and body meet, are noticeably higher than the level of the back.

Body—In overall length-to-height proportion, the dog is approximately square. The moderately narrow *chest* is deep; it extends to elbows which are held close to the body. Shoulder blades are sloping, that is, well laid back, their musculature lean and almost flat in outline. The *ribs* are well sprung and moderately rounded. The *back* is short and level in topline. *Loins* are taut and short, although they may be a trifle longer in bitches than in dogs. *Quarters* are strong, broad and muscular.

Legs and Feet—*Forelegs* are strongly boned, clean and absolutely straight as viewed from the front or side, and devoid of appreciable bend at the pasterns. *Hind legs* too are strong and sturdy, the second thighs long and nicely angulated at the stifles and the hocks. *Hocks* are well let down, with the bone from hock to toes straight and parallel to each other. The small *feet* are round, the toes compact and well padded, the nails strong. Dewclaws, if any, are to be removed.

Tail—Set high on the body, the tail is customarily docked so that when the dog is set up in show position, the tip of the docked tail is on an approximate level with the skull. In carriage it is gay or upright, although a slight curve in the direction of the head is considered desirable. The tail curled over the back is faulty.

Coat and Color—Two-ply or double, the outer coat is hard and wiry in texture, the undercoat soft. Furnishings on muzzle and legs are plentiful as opposed to profuse. The *color* may be blue, black, liver, black and tan, blue and tan, red, red grizzle, grizzle and tan, or wheaten. Tan, as desirable in the Lakeland Terrier, is a light wheaten or straw color, with rich red or mahogany tan to be penalized. Otherwise, colors, as specified, are equally acceptable. Dark-saddled specimens (whether black grizzle or blue) are nearly solid black at birth, with tan points on muzzle and feet. The black recedes and usually turns grayish or grizzle at maturity, while the tan also lightens.

Size—The ideal *height* of the mature dog is 14½ inches from the withers to the ground, with up to a one-half-inch deviation either way permissible. Bitches may measure as much as one inch less than dogs. The *weight* of the well balanced, mature specimen in hard, show condition, averages approximately 17 pounds, those of other heights proportionately more or less.

Size is to be considered of lesser importance than other qualities, that is, when judging dogs of equal merit, the one nearest the ideal size is to be preferred. Symmetry and proportion, however, are paramount in the appraisal, since all qualities together must be considered in visualizing the ideal.

Movement—Straight and free, with good length of stride. Paddling, moving close and toeing-in are faulty.

Temperament—The typical Lakeland Terrier is bold, gay and friendly, with a self-confident, cock-of-the-walk attitude. Shyness, especially shy-sharpness, in the mature specimen is to be heavily penalized.

SCALE OF POINTS

Head	15
Eyes, ears, expression	15
Neck	5
Body	10
Coat	15
Legs and Feet	10
Size and Symmetry	10
Movement	10
Temperament	10
	100

DISQUALIFICATION

The front teeth overshot or undershot.

Approved June 1963

Head—Long, narrow, tight skinned, almost flat, with a slight indentation up the forehead; slightly wedge shaped, tapering to the nose, with no visible cheek muscles, and well filled up under the eyes: tight lipped jaws, level in mouth and functionally level teeth or the incisors of the upper jaw may make a close slightly over lapping contact with the incisors of the lower jaw. *Nose*—black.

Ears (Toy Variety)—Of moderate size; set well up on the skull and rather close together; thin, moderately narrow at base; with pointed tips; naturally erect carriage. Wide, flaring, blunt-tipped or "bell" ears are a serious fault; cropped or cut ears shall disqualify.

Ears (Standard Variety)—Erect, or button, small and thin; smaller at the root and set as close together as possible at the top of the head. If cropped, to a point, long and carried erect.

Neck and Shoulders—The neck should be a moderate length, slim and graceful; gradually becoming larger as it approaches, and blend smoothly with the sloping shoulders; free from throatiness; slightly arched from the occiput.

Chest—Narrow between the legs; deep in the Brisket.

Body—Moderately short, with robust loins; ribs well sprung out behind the shoulders; back slightly arched at the loin, and falling again to the tail to the same height as the shoulder. *Legs*—Forelegs straight, of proportionate length, and well under body. Hind legs should not turn in or out as viewed from the rear; carried back; hocks well let down. *Feet*—Compact, well arched, with jet black nails; the two middle toes in the front feet rather longer than the others; the hind feet shaped like those of a cat. *Tail*—Moderately short, and set on where the arch of the back ends; thick where it joins the body, tapering to a point, not carried higher than the back.

Coat—Smooth, short, thick, dense, close and glossy; not soft.

Color—Jet black and rich mahogany tan, which should not run or blend into each other but abruptly forming clear, well-defined lines of color division. A small tan spot over each eye; a very small tan spot on each cheek; the lips of the upper and lower jaws should be tanned, extending under the throat, ending in the shape of the letter V; the inside of the ears partly tanned. Tan spots, called rosettes, on each side of the chest above the front legs, more pronounced in puppies than in adults. There should be a black "thumb mark" patch on the front of each foreleg between the pastern and the knee. There should be a distinct black "pencil mark" line running lengthwise on the top of each toe on all four feet. The remainder of the forelegs to be tan to the knee. Tan on the hind legs should continue from the penciling on the feet up the inside of the legs to a little below the stifle joint; the outside of the hind legs to be black. There should be tan under the tail, and on the vent, but only of such size as to be covered by the tail. White in any part of the coat is a serious fault, and shall disqualify whenever the white shall form a patch or stripe measuring as much as one-half inch in its longest dimension.

Weight (Toy Variety)—Not exceeding 12 pounds. It is suggested that clubs consider dividing the American-bred and Open Classes by weight as follows: 7 pounds and under, over 7 pounds and not exceeding 12 pounds.

Weight (Standard Variety)—Over 12 pounds and not exceeding 22 pounds. Dogs weighing over 22 pounds shall be disqualified. It is suggested that clubs consider dividing the American-bred and Open Classes by weight as follows: over 12 pounds and not exceeding 16 pounds, over 16 pounds and not exceeding 22 pounds.

DISQUALIFICATIONS

Color—*White in any part of the coat, forming a patch or stripe measuring as much as one-half inch in its longest dimension.*
Weight (Standard Variety): Over 22 pounds.
Ears—*(Toy Variety): Cropped or cut ears.*

Approved July 1962

Norwich Terrier

Head—Skull wide, slightly rounded with good width between the ears. Muzzle strong but not long or heavy, with slightly "foxy" appearance. Length about one third less than the measurement from the occiput to the bottom of the stop, which should be well defined. *Faults*—A long narrow head; over square muzzle; highly rounded dome. *Ears*—Prick or drop. If pricked, small, pointed, erect and set well apart. If dropped, neat, small, with break just above the skull line, front edge close to cheek, and not falling lower than the outer corner of the eye. *Faults*—Oversize; poor carriage. *Eyes*—Very bright, dark and keen. Full of expression. *Faults*—Light or protruding eyes. *Jaw*—Clean, strong, tight lipped, with strong, large, closely-fitting teeth; scissors bite. *Faults*—A mouth badly over- or undershot. *Neck*—Short and strong, well set on clean shoulders.

Body—Moderately short, compact and deep with level top line, ribs well sprung. *Faults*—Long weak back, loaded shoulders. *Legs*—Short and powerful and as straight as is consistent with the short legs for which we aim. Sound bone, round feet, thick pads. *Faults*—Out at elbow, badly bowed, knuckled over. Too light in bone. *Quarters*—Strong, rounded, with great powers of propulsion. *Faults*—Cowhocks. *Tail*—Medium docked, carriage not excessively gay.

211

Color—Red (including red-wheaten), black and tan or grizzle. White markings on the chest, though allowable, are not desirable. *Faults*—White markings elsewhere or to any great extent on the chest. *Coat*—As hard and wiry as possible, lying close to the body, with a definite undercoat. Top coat absolutely straight; in full coat longer and rougher forming almost a mane on shoulders and neck. Hair on head, ears and muzzle, except for slight eyebrows and slight whiskers, is absolutely short and smooth. These dogs should be shown with as nearly a natural coat as possible. A minimum amount of tidying is permissible but excessive trimming, shaping and clipping shall be heavily penalized by the judge. *Faults*—Silky or curly coat.

Weight—Ideal 11 to 12 pounds.

Height—Ideal, 10 inches at the withers.

General Appearance—A small, low rugged terrier, tremendously active. A perfect demon yet not quarrelsome and of a lovable disposition, and a very hardy constitution. Honorable scars from fair wear and tear shall not count against.

DISQUALIFICATION

Cropped ears shall disqualify.

Approved June 1961

Schnauzer, Miniature

General Appearance—The Miniature Schnauzer is a robust, active dog of terrier type, resembling his larger cousin, the Standard Schnauzer, in general appearance, and of an alert, active disposition. He is sturdily built, nearly square in proportion of body length to height, with plenty of bone, and without any suggestion of toyishness.

Head—Strong and rectangular, its width diminishing slightly from ears to eyes, and again to the tip of the nose. The forehead is unwrinkled. The topskull is flat and fairly long. The foreface is parallel to the topskull, with a slight stop, and is at least as long as the topskull. The muzzle is strong in proportion to the skull; it ends in a moderately blunt manner, with thick whiskers which accentuate the rectangular shape of the head. *Teeth*—The teeth meet in a scissors bite. That is, the upper front teeth overlap the lower front teeth in such a manner that the inner surface of the upper incisors barely touches the outer surface of the lower incisors when the mouth is closed. *Eyes*—Small, dark brown and deep-set. They are oval in appearance and keen in expression. *Ears*—When cropped the ears are identical

212

in shape and length, with pointed tips. They are in balance with the head and not exaggerated in length. They are set high on the skull and carried perpendicularly at the inner edges, with as little bell as possible along the outer edges. When uncropped, the ears are small and V-shaped, folding close to the skull.

Neck—Strong and well arched, blending into the shoulders, and with the skin fitting tightly at the throat.

Body—Short and deep, with the brisket extending at least to the elbows. Ribs are well sprung and deep, extending well back to a short loin. The underbody does not present a tucked-up appearance at the flank. The topline is straight; it declines slightly from the withers to the base of the tail. The over-all length from chest to stern bone equals the height at the withers.

Forequarters—The forequarters have flat, somewhat sloping shoulders and high withers. Forelegs are straight and parallel when viewed from all sides. They have strong pasterns and good bone. They are separated by a fairly deep brisket which precludes a pinched front. The elbows are close, and the ribs spread gradually from the first rib so as to allow space for the elbows to move close to the body. *Hindquarters*—The hindquarters have strong-muscled, slating thighs: they are well bent at the stifles and straight from hock to so-called heel. There is sufficient angulation so that, in stance, the hocks extend beyond the tail. The hindquarters never appear overbuilt or higher than the shoulders. *Feet*—Short and round (cat-feet) with thick, black pads. The toes are arched and compact.

Action—The trot is the gait at which movement is judged. The dog must gait in a straight line. Coming on, the forelegs are parallel, with the elbows close to the body. The feet turn neither inward nor outward. Going away, the hind legs are parallel from the hocks down, and travel wide. Viewed from the side, the forelegs have a good reach, while the hind legs have a strong drive with good pick-up of hocks.

Tail—Set high and carried erect. It is docked only long enough to be clearly visible over the topline of the body when the dog is in proper length of coat.

Coat—Double, with a hard, wiry outer coat and a close undercoat. The body coat should be plucked. When in show condition, the proper length is not less than three-quarters of an inch except on neck, ears and skull. Furnishings are fairly thick but not silky.

Size—From 12 to 14 inches. Ideal size 13½ inches. (*See disqualifications.*)

Color—The recognized colors are salt and pepper, black and silver, and solid black. The typical color is salt and pepper in shades of gray; tan shading is permissible. The salt and pepper mixture fades out to light gray or silver white in the eyebrows, whiskers, cheeks, under throat, across chest, under tail, leg furnishings under body, and inside legs. The light under-body hair is not to rise higher on the sides of the body than the front elbows.

213

The black and silvers follow the same pattern as the salt and peppers. The entire salt-and-pepper section must be black.

Black is the only solid color allowed. It must be a true black with no gray hairs and no brown tinge except where the whiskers may have become discolored. A small white spot on the chest is permitted.

Type—Toyishness, raciness, or coarseness. *Structure*—Head coarse and cheeky. Chest too broad or shallow in brisket. Tail set low. Sway or roach back. Bowed or cowhocked hindquarters. Loose elbows. *Action*—Sidegaiting. Paddling in front, or high hackney knee action. Weak hind action. *Coat* —Too soft or too smooth and slick in appearance. *Temperament*—Shyness or viciousness. *Bite*—Undershot or overshot jaw. Level bite. *Eyes*—Light and/or large and prominent in appearance.

Dogs or bitches under 12 inches or over 14 inches. Color solid white or white patches on the body.

Approved May 13, 1958

Scottish Terrier

Skull (5 points)—Long, of medium width, slightly domed and covered with short, hard hair. It should not be quite flat, as there should be a slight stop or drop between the eyes. *Muzzle* (5 points)—In proportion to the length of skull, with not too much taper toward the nose. Nose should be black and of good size. The jaws should be level and square. The nose projects somewhat over the mouth, giving the impression that the upper jaw is longer than the lower. The teeth should be evenly placed, having a scissors or level bite, with the former being preferable. *Eyes* (5 points)—Set wide apart, small and of almond shape, not round. Color to be dark brown or nearly black. To be bright, piercing and set well under the brow. *Ears* (10 points)—Small, prick, set well up on the skull, rather pointed but not cut. The hair on them should be short and velvety.

Neck (5 points)—Moderately short, thick and muscular, strongly set on sloping shoulders, but not so short as to appear clumsy. *Chest* (5 points)— Broad and very deep, well let down between the forelegs.

Body (15 points)—Moderately short and well ribbed up with strong loin, deep flanks and very muscular hindquarters. *Legs and Feet* (10 points)— Both forelegs and hind legs should be short and very heavy in bone in pro-

214

portion to the size of the dog. Forelegs straight or slightly bent with elbows close to the body. Scottish Terriers should not be out at the elbows. Stifles should be well bent and legs straight from hock to heel. Thighs very muscular. Feet round and thick with strong nails, forefeet larger than the hind feet. *Note:* The gait of the Scottish Terrier is peculiarly its own and is very characteristic of the breed. It is not the square trot or walk that is desirable in the long-legged breeds. The forelegs do not move in exact parallel planes— rather in reaching out incline slightly inward. This is due to the shortness of leg and width of chest. The action of the rear legs should be square and true and at the trot both the hocks and stifles should be flexed with a vigorous motion. *Tail* (2½ points)—Never cut and about 7 inches long, carried with a slight curve but not over the back.

Coat (15 points)—Rather short, about 2 inches, dense undercoat with outer coat intensely hard and wiry.

Size and Weight (10 points)—Equal consideration must be given to height, length of back and weight. Height at shoulder for either sex should be about 10 inches. Generally, a well-balanced Scottish Terrier dog of correct size should weigh from 19 to 22 pounds and a bitch, from 18 to 21 pounds. The principal objective must be symmetry and balance.

Color (2½ points)—Steel or iron gray, brindled or grizzled, black, sandy or wheaten. White markings are objectionable and can be allowed only on the chest and that to a slight extent only.

General Appearance (10 points)—The face should wear a keen, sharp and active expression. Both head and tail should be carried well up. The dog should look very compact, well muscled and powerful, giving the impression of immense power in a small size.

Penalties: Soft coat, round or very light eye, overshot or undershot jaw, obviously oversize or undersize, shyness, timidity or failure to show with head and tail up are faults to be penalized. No judge should put to Winners or Best of Breed any Scottish Terrier not showing real terrier character in the ring.

SCALE OF POINTS

Skull	5	Legs and feet	10
Muzzle	5	Tail	2½
Eyes	5	Coat	15
Ears	10	Size	10
Neck	5	Color	2½
Chest	5	General appearance	10
Body	15	Total	100

Approved June 10, 1947

Sealyham Terrier

The Sealyham should be the embodiment of power and determination, ever keen and alert, of extraordinary substance, yet free from clumsiness. *Height*—At withers about 10½ inches. *Weight:* 21 pounds for dogs, and 20 pounds for bitches. It should be borne in mind that size is more important than weight.

Head—Long, broad and powerful, without coarseness. It should, however, be in perfect balance with the body, joining neck smoothly. Length of head roughly, three-quarters height at withers, or about an inch longer than neck. Breadth between ears a little less than one-half length of head. *Skull*— Very slightly domed, with a shallow indentation running down between the brows, and joining the muzzle with a moderate stop. *Cheeks*—Smoothly formed and flat, without heavy jowls. *Jaws*—Level, powerful and square. Overshot or undershot bad faults. *Teeth*—Sound, strong and white, with canines fitting closely together. *Nose*—Black, with large nostrils. White, cherry or butterfly bad faults. *Eyes*—Very dark, deeply set and fairly wide apart, of medium size, oval in shape with keen terrier expression. Light, large or protruding eye bad faults. *Ears*—Folded level with top of head, with forward edge close to cheek. Well rounded at tip, and of length to reach outer corner of eye. Thin, not leathery, and of sufficient thickness to avoid creases. Prick, tulip, rose or hound ears bad faults.

Neck—Length slightly less than two-thirds of height of dog at withers. Muscular without coarseness, with good reach, refinement at throat, and set firmly on shoulders. *Shoulders*—Well laid back and powerful, but not over-muscled. Sufficiently wide to permit freedom of action. Upright or straight shoulder placement highly undesirable.

Legs—Forelegs strong, with good bone; and as straight as is consistent with chest being well let down between them. Down on pasterns, knuckled over, bound, and out at elbow, bad faults. Hind legs longer than forelegs and not so heavily boned. *Feet*—Large but compact, round with thick pads, strong nails. Toes well arched and pointing straight ahead. Forefeet larger, though not quite so long as hind feet. Thin, spread or flat feet bad faults.

Body—Strong, short-coupled and substantial, so as to permit great flexibility. Brisket deep and well let down between forelegs. Ribs well sprung.

Back—Length from withers to set on of tail should approximate height at withers, or 10½ inches. Topline level, neither roached nor swayed. Any deviations from these measurements undesirable. *Hindquarters*—Very powerful, and protruding well behind the set on of tail. Strong second thighs, stifles well bent, and hocks well let down. Capped or cowhocks bad faults.

Tail—Docked and carried upright. Set on far enough forward so that spine does not slope down to it.

Coat—Weather-resisting, comprised of soft, dense undercoat and hard, wiry top coat. Silky or curly coat bad fault. *Color*—All white; or with lemon, tan or badger markings on head and ears. Heavy body markings and excessive ticking should be discouraged. *Action*—Sound, strong, quick, free, true and level.

Note—The measurements were taken with calipers.

Approved March 12, 1935

Skye Terrier

General Appearance—The Skye Terrier is a dog of style, elegance and dignity; agile and strong with sturdy bone and hard muscle. Long, low and lank—he is twice as long as he is high—he is covered with a profuse coat that falls straight down either side of the body over oval-shaped ribs. The hair well feathered on the head veils forehead and eyes to serve as protection from brush and briar as well as amid serious encounters with other animals. He stands with head high and long tail hanging, and moves with a seemingly effortless gait. Of suitable size for his hunting work, strong in body, quarters and jaw.

Temperament—That of the typical working terrier capable of overtaking game and going to ground, displaying stamina, courage, strength and agility. Fearless, good-tempered, loyal and canny, he is friendly and gay with those he knows and reserved and cautious with strangers.

Head—Long and powerful, strength being deemed more important than extreme length. Moderate width at the back of the skull tapers gradually to a strong muzzle. The stop is slight. The dark muzzle is just moderately full as opposed to snipy, and the nose is always black. Powerful and absolutely true jaws and mouth with the incisor teeth closing level, or with the upper teeth slightly overlapping the lower. *Eyes*—Brown, preferably dark brown, medium in size, close-set and alight with life and intelligence. *Ears*—Sym-

217

metrical and gracefully feathered. They may be carried prick or drop. When prick, they are medium in size, placed high on the skull, erect at their outer edges and slightly wider at the peak than at the skull. Drop ears, somewhat larger in size and set lower, hang flat against the skull.

Neck—Long and gracefully arched, carried high and proudly.

Body—Pre-eminently long and low. The backline is level, the chest deep, with oval-shaped ribs. The sides appear flattish due to the straight falling and profuse coat.

Legs and Feet. Forequarters—Legs short, muscular and straight as possible. "Straight as possible" means straight as soundness and chest will permit; it does not mean "terrier straight." Shoulders well laid back, with tight placement of shoulder blades at the withers, and elbows should fit closely to the sides and be neither loose nor tied. Forearm should curve slightly around the chest. *Hindquarters*—Strong, full, well developed and well angulated. Legs short, muscular and straight when viewed from behind. *Feet*—Large hare-feet preferably pointing forward, the pads thick and nails strong and preferably black.

Movement—The legs proceed straight forward when traveling. When approaching, the forelegs form a continuation of the straight line of the front, the feet being the same distance apart as the elbows. The principal propelling power is furnished by the hind legs which travel straight forward. Forelegs should move well forward, without too much lift. The whole movement may be termed free, active and effortless and give a more or less fluid picture.

Tail—Long and well feathered. When hanging, its upper section is pendulous, following the line of the rump, its lower section thrown back in a moderate arc without twist or curl. When raised, its height makes it appear a prolongation of the backline. Though not to be preferred, the tail is sometimes carried high when the dog is excited or angry. When such carriage arises from emotion only, it is permissible. But the tail should not be constantly carried above the level of the back nor hang limp.

Coat—Double. Undercoat short, close, soft and woolly. Outer coat hard, straight and flat, 5½ inches long without extra credit granted for greater length. The body coat hangs straight down each side, parting from head to tail. The head hair, which may be shorter and softer, veils forehead and eyes and forms a moderate beard and apron. The long feathering on the ears falls straight down from the tips and outer edges, surrounding the ears like a fringe and outlining their shape. The ends of the hair should mingle with the coat at the sides of the neck.

Color—The coat must be of one over-all color at the skin but may be of varying shades of the same color in the full coat, which may be black, blue, dark or light gray, silver, platinum, fawn or cream. The dog must have no distinctive markings except for the desirable black points of ears, muzzle and tip of tail, all of which points are preferably dark even to black. The shade of head and legs should approximate that of the body. There must be no trace of pattern, design or clear-cut color variations, with the exception of the breed's only permissible white which occasionally exists on the chest not exceeding 2 inches in diameter.

The puppy coat may be very different in color from the adult coat. As it is growing and clearing, wide variations of color may occur; consequently this is permissible in dogs under 18 months of age. However, even in puppies there must be no trace of pattern, design or clear-cut variations with the exception of the black band of varying width frequently seen encircling the body coat of the cream-colored dog, and the only permissible white which, as in the adult dog, occasionally exists on the chest not exceeding 2 inches in diameter.

Size—Dogs: Shoulder height 10 inches. Length, chest bone over tail at rump, 20 inches. Head 8½ inches. Tail 9 inches. Bitches: Shoulder height 9½ inches. Length, chest bone over tail at rump, 19 inches. Head 8 inches. Tail 8½ inches. A slightly higher or lower dog of either sex is acceptable providing body, head and tail dimensions are proportionately longer or shorter. The ideal ratio of body length to shoulder height is 2 to 1, which is considered the correct proportion.

Measurements are taken with the Skye standing in natural position with feet well under. A box caliper is used vertically and horizontally. For the height, the top bar should rest on the withers. The head is measured from the tip of the nose to the back of the occipital bone, and the tail from the root to tip. Dogs 8 inches or less at the withers and bitches 7½ inches or less at the withers are to be penalized.

Approved March 1964

Staffordshire Terrier

General Impression—The Staffordshire Terrier should give the impression of great strength for his size, a well put-together dog, muscular, but agile and graceful, keenly alive to his surroundings. He should be stocky, not long-legged or racy in outline. His courage is proverbial.

Head—Medium length, deep through, broad skull, very pronounced cheek muscles, distinct stop; and ears are set high. *Ears*—Cropped or uncropped, the latter preferred. Uncropped ears should be short and held half rose or prick. Full drop to be penalized. *Eyes*—Dark and round, low down in skull and set far apart. No pink eyelids. *Muzzle*—Medium length, rounded on upper side to fall away abruptly below eyes. Jaws well defined. Underjaw to be strong and have biting power. Lips close and even, no looseness. Upper teeth to meet tightly outside lower teeth in front. Nose definitely black.

Neck—Heavy, slightly arched, tapering from shoulders to back of skull. No looseness of skin. Medium length. *Shoulders*—Strong and muscular with blades wide and sloping. *Back*—Fairly short. Slight sloping from withers to rump with gentle short slope at rump to base of tail. Loins slightly tucked. *Body*—Well-sprung ribs, deep in rear. All ribs close together. Forelegs set rather wide apart to permit of chest development. Chest deep and broad. *Tail*—Short in comparison to size, low-set, tapering to a fine point; not curled or held over back. Not docked. *Legs*—The front legs should be straight, large or round bones, pastern upright. No resemblance of bend in front. Hindquarters well-muscled, let down at hocks, turning neither in nor out. Feet of moderate size, well-arched and compact. Gait must be springy but without roll or pace.

Coat—Short, close, stiff to the touch, and glossy. *Color*—Any color, solid, parti, or patched is permissible, but all white, more than 80 per cent white, black and tan, and liver not to be encouraged.

Size—Height and weight should be in proportion. A height of about 18 to 19 inches at shoulders for the male and 17 to 18 inches for the female is to be considered preferable.

Faults—Faults to be penalized are Dudley nose, light or pink eyes, tail too long or badly carried, undershot or overshot mouths.

Approved June 10, 1936

Welsh Terrier

Head—The skull should be flat, and rather wider between the ears than the Wirehaired Fox Terrier. The jaw should be powerful, clean-cut, rather deeper, and more punishing—giving the head a more masculine appearance than that usually seen on a Fox Terrier. Stop not too defined, fair length from stop to end of nose, the latter being of a black color. *Ears*—The ear should be V-shaped, small, not too thin, set on fairly high, carried forward and close to the cheek. *Eyes*—The eye should be small, not being too deeply set in or protruding out of skull, of a dark hazel color, expressive and indicating abundant pluck. *Neck*—The neck should be of moderate length and thickness, slightly arched and sloping gracefully into the shoulders.

Body—The back should be short, and well-ribbed up, the loin strong, good depth, and moderate width of chest. The shoulders should be long, sloping, and well set back. The hindquarters should be strong, thighs muscular and of good length, with the hocks moderately straight, well let down, and fair amount of bone. The stern should be set on moderately high, but not too gaily carried. *Legs and Feet*—The legs should be straight and muscular, possessing fair amount of bone, with upright and powerful pasterns. The feet should be small, round and catlike.

Coat—The coat should be wiry, hard, very close and abundant. *Color*—The color should be black and tan, or black grizzle and tan, free from black penciling on toes.

Size—The height at shoulder should be 15 inches for dogs, bitches proportionately less. Twenty pounds shall be considered a fair average weight in working condition, but this may vary a pound or so either way.

SCALE OF POINTS

Head and jaws	10	Legs and feet	10
Ears	5	Coat	15
Eyes	5	Color	5
Neck and shoulders	10	Stern	5
Body	10	General appearance	15
Loins and hindquarters	10	Total	100

DISQUALIFICATIONS

(1) *Nose: white, cherry or spotted to a considerable extent with either of these colors.* (2) *Ears: prick, tulip or rose.* (3) *Undershot jaw or pig-jawed mouth.* (4) *Black below hocks or white to an appreciable extent.*

West Highland White Terrier

General Appearance of the West Highland White Terrier is that of a small, game, hardy-looking terrier exhibiting good showmanship, possessed with no small amount of self-esteem, with varminty appearance strongly built, deep in chest and back ribs, straight back and powerful hindquarters on muscular legs, and exhibiting in a marked degree a great combination of strength and activity. The coat should be about 2 inches long, white in color, hard, with plenty of soft undercoat, and no tendency to wave or curl. The tail should be as straight as possible and carried not too gaily, and covered with hard hair, but not bushy. The skull should be not too broad, being in proportion to the terribly powerful jaws. The ears shall be as small and sharp-pointed as possible and carried tightly up, and must be absolutely erect. The eyes of moderate size, as dark as possible, widely placed with a sharp, bright, intelligent expression. The muzzle should not be too long, powerful and gradually tapering toward the nose; the roof of mouth and pads of feet are usually black in color. The dog should be tidied up. Considerable hair should be left around the head to act as a frame for the face to yield a typical Westie expression.

221

Color—Pure white; any other color objectionable.

Coat—Very important, and seldom seen to perfection; must be double-coated. The outer coat consists of hard hair, about 2 inches long, and free from any curl. The undercoat, which resembles fur, is short, soft and close. Open coats are objectionable.

Size—Dogs should measure about 11 inches at the withers, bitches, about one inch less.

Skull—Should not be too narrow, being in proportion to his powerful jaw, not too long, slightly domed, and gradually tapering to the eyes, between which there should be a slight indentation or stop, eyebrows heavy. There should be little apparent difference in length between the muzzle and the skull. *Eyes*—Widely set apart, medium in size, as dark as possible in color, slightly sunk in the head, sharp and intelligent, which, looking from under the heavy eyebrows give a piercing look. Full eyes and also light-colored eyes are very objectionable. *Muzzle*—Should be nearly equal in length to the rest of the skull, powerful and gradually tapering toward the nose, which should be fairly wide. The nose itself should be black in color. The jaws level and powerful, the teeth square or evenly met, well set and large for the size of the dog. Teeth much overshot or much undershot should be heavily penalized. Muzzles longer than the skull and not in proportion thereto are objectionable. *Ears*—Small, carried tightly erect and never dropped, set wide apart and terminating in a sharp point. The hair on them should be short, smooth and velvety and they should never be cut. The ears should be free from fringe at the top. Round-pointed, broad and large ears are very objectionable as are ears set too closely together or heavily covered with hair.

Neck—Muscular and nicely set on sloping shoulders. *Chest*—Very deep, with breadth in proportion to the size of the dog. *Body*—Compact, straight back, ribs deep and well arched in the upper half of rib, presenting a flattish side appearance, loins broad and strong, hindquarters strong, muscular and wide across the top.

Legs and Feet—Both fore and hind legs should be short and muscular. The shoulder blades should be comparatively broad, and well sloped backwards. The points of the shoulder blades should be closely knitted into the back-bone, so that very little movement of them should be noticeable when the dog is walking. The elbow should be close into the body both when moving or standing, thus causing the foreleg to be well placed in under the shoulder. The forelegs should be straight and thickly covered with short hard hair. The hind legs should be short and sinewy. The thighs very muscular and not too wide apart. The hocks bent and well set in under the body, so as to be fairly close to each other either when standing, walking, or trotting. The forefeet are larger than the hind feet; are round, proportionate in size, strong, thickly padded, and covered with short hard hair. The hind feet are smaller and thickly padded. Cowhocks detract from the general appearance.

Straight or weak hocks, both kinds, are undesirable, and should be guarded against.

Tail—Five or 6 inches long, covered with hard hairs, no feather, as straight as possible, carried gaily but not curled over back. Tails longer than 6 inches are objectionable.

Movement—Should be free, straight and easy all round. In front the leg should be freely extended forward by the shoulder. The hind movement should be free, strong and close. The hocks should be freely flexed and drawn close in under the body, so that when moving off on the foot the body is thrown or pushed forward with some force. Stiff, stilty movement behind is very objectionable.

ATTENTION OF JUDGES

Under no consideration should a West Highland White Terrier be judged or trimmed as a Scottish Terrier. They are a distinct breed differing in head, body, hindquarters, movement and general over-all type. They are *not* white Scottish Terriers.

SCALE OF POINTS

Value

General appearance	15	Neck	5
Color	7½	Chest	5
Coat	10	Body	10
Size	7½	Legs and feet	7½
Skull	5	Tail	5
Eyes	5	Movement	7½
Muzzle	5	Total value	100
Ears	5		

FAULTS

Coat—Any silkiness, wave or tendency to curl is a serious blemish as is an open coat, single coat or one having black, gray or wheaten hairs therein. *Size*—Any specimens under the minimum or over the maximum weight or height limits are objectionable. *Eyes*—Full or light-colored. *Ears*—Round-pointed, poorly placed, drop, semierect or overly large. *Muzzle*—Overly long forefaces, teeth too much overshot or too much undershot or defective teeth.

Approved September 15, 1959

33

Bibliography

Books of general interest dealing with dogs of all breeds.

Ash, E. C.—*Dogs and All About Them*, 1925. *Dogs, Their History and Development*, 1927, 2 vols. *The Practical Dog Book*, 1931, Derrydale Press. *This Doggie Business*, 1934

Ashmont—*Kennel Secrets*, 1893 and subsequent editions

Barton, F. T.—*The Kennel Encyclopedia*, (no date). *Dogs, Their Selection, Breeding and Keeping*, (no date); Our Dogs and All About Them, (no date). *The Dog in Health, Accident and Disease*, 1907

Beilby, Walter—*The Dog in Australasia*, 1897

Bell—*British Quadrupeds*, 1837

Brown, Thomas—*Biographical Sketches and Authentic Anecdotes of Dogs*, 1829

Bruette, Dr. W. A.—*The Complete Dog Book*, 1921

Burges, Arnold—*The American Kennel and Sporting Field*, 1876 and 1883

Bylandt, Comte Henri De—*Les Racs De Chiens*, many editions, 2 vols.

Caius, Dr. Johannes—*De Canibus Britannicis*, 1570

Compton, Herbert—*The Twentieth Century Dog*, 1904, 2 vols.

Dalziel, Hugh—*British Dogs*, 1881 and 1897, 3 vols.

Davis, Henry—*The Modern Kennel Encyclopedia*, 1949

Dickie, James—*The Dog*, 1933

Dogs, *Melbourne's Sporting Library*, 1907

Drury, W. D.—*British Dogs*, 1903

Edwards, Sydenham—*Cynographia Britannica*, 1800

Fleming, Abraham—*Of Englishe Dogges*, 1576

Herbert, W. H.—*Dinks, Mayhew and Hutchinson on the Dog*, 1857

Hochwalt, A. F.—*Dogcraft*, 1907 and 1912

Hubbard, C. L. B.—*The Observer's Book of the Dog*, 1945

Hutchinson, Walter—*Hutchinson's Dog Encyclopedia*, 1932, 3 vols.

Jardine, William—*The Naturalist's Library*, circa 1842, 2 vols.

Jesse, George R.—*Researches Into the History of the British Dog*, 1866, 2 vols.

Jones, A. F.—*Care and Training of Dogs*, 1949

Lee, Rawdon—*Modern Dogs*, 1893–94 and 1897–99, 4 vols.

Leighton, Robert—*The New Book of the Dog*, 1907, 4 vols. *The Complete Dog Book*, 1922

Little, Dr. George W.—*Dr. Little's Dog Book*, 1925

Lucas, Capt. Jocelyn—*Pedigree Dog Breeding*, 1925

Marples, Theo.—*Show Dogs*, (no date)

Mason, Charles H.—*Our Prize Dogs*, 1888

Mayhew, Edward—*Dogs, Their Management*, 1897

Mills, Wesley—*The Dog*, 1895

Pearce, Rev. T. (Idstone)—*The Dog*, 1872

Rine, Josephine Z.—*The Dog Owner's Manual*, 1936

Sanderson, C. C.—*Pedigree Dogs as Recognized by the Kennel Club*, 1927

Shaw, Vero—*The Illustrated Book of the Dog*, 1881. *Encyclopedia of the Kennel*, 1913

Shields, G. O.—*The American Book of the Dog*, 1891

Smith, A. Croxton—*The Power of the Dog*, circa 1903. *British Dogs at Work*, 1906. *Everyman's Book of the Dog*, 1909. *About Our Dogs*, 1931

Smith, C. H.—*Natural History of Dogs*, 1839–40, 2 vols.

Smith and Harrison—*British and Foreign Dogs* (unfinished) 1835–36

Stables, Dr. Gordon—*Our Friend the Dog*, 1885

Taylor, Major J. M.—*Bench Show and Field Trial Records and Standards of Dogs in America*, 1892

Taynton, Mark—*Successful Kennel Management*, 1951

Turner, J. Sidney—*The Kennel Encyclopedia*, 1911, 4 vols.

Vesey-Fitzgerald, Brian—*The Book of the Dog*, 1948

Vyner, Robert T.—*Notitia Venatica*, 1841

Walsh, J. H. (Stonehenge)—*The Dog in Health and Disease*, 1859–87, 4 editions. *The Dogs of the British Islands*, 1867–86, 5 editions

Watson, James—*The Dog Book*, 1906, 2 vols.

Webb, Henry—*Dogs, Their Points, Whims* etc., 1872–74, 4 editions

West, Stanley—*The Book of Dogs*, 1936

Youatt, W.—*The Dog*, 1845 and many subsequent editions

Hundreds of other general dog books are available in addition to those listed; there can be no complete listing here because of space limitations. The books noted are all considered useful either because of knowledge of the author and/or the thoroughness of the work.

In addition, the following books deal in detail with the standards of perfection for the several Terrier breeds: *Standards of the Breeds*, Field and Fancy Publishing Co. (1922); *Pure Bred Dogs* (1929) and subsequent editions entitled *The Complete Dog Book*, all published by the American Kennel Club, and the English Kennel Club standards (1955) and other editions.

Books about Books Relating to Dogs including Works of Art

Arrianus, Flavius—*The Cynegeticus of the Younger Xenophon*, 1831

Baege, Bruno—*Kynologische Bibliographie*, 1934 (scientific subjects)

Baillie-Grohman, W. A.—*Sport in Art, circa* 1919

Bejeau, Ph. C.—*The Book of Dogs,* 1865

Burton, Richard—*Dogs and Dog Literature,* 1902

Chapin—*The Peter Chapin Collection of Books on Dogs* (catalog) 1938

Derrydale Press—*Tenth Anniversary Catalog,* 1937

Higginson, A. Henry—*British and American Sporting Authors,* 1951

Hubbard, C. L. B.—*An Introduction to the Literature of British Dogs,* 1949

Gee, Ernest R.—*Early American Sporting Books,* 1928. *The Sportsman's Library* (Derrydale Press), 1940

Mason, Marcus M.—*Bibliography of the Dog,* 1959 (scientific subjects)

Massey, Gerald—*The Kennel Gazette* (Eng.)—The First Printed Dog Book, May 1949 pp 381–383. The First Dog Book Printed in English, June 1949 pp 503–505. The First Illustrated English Dog Book, July 1949 pp 603–605; Aug. 1949 pp 723–725. The Sportsman's Cabinet, Sept. 1949 pp 837–840. The Dog Fancier's Companion and Other English Dog Books of the Early Nineteenth Century, Dec. 1949 pp 1190–1192.

Monkhouse, W. Cosmo—*The Works of Sir Edwin Landseer,* 1875

National Sports of Great Britain (Alken prints) 1903

Nevill, Ralph—*Old English Sporting Prints,* 1908. *Old English Sporting Prints* (Limited Edition), 1923

Phillips—*Bibliography of Sporting Books,* 1930

Roe, F. Gordon—*Sporting Prints of the 18th and 19th Centuries,* 1927

Siltzer, Capt. Frank—*The Story of British Sporting Prints,* 1925, 1929

Slater, J. Herbert—*Illustrated Sporting Books,* 1899

Sparrow, W. Shaw—*British Sporting Artists From Barlow to Herring,* 1922. *A Book of Sporting Painters,* 1931

Tooley, R. V.—*Some English Books With Coloured Plates,* (no date).

Zoeller, Marcus M.—A Jewell For Gentrie. *Country Life in America,* Oct. 1936 pp. 37–40, 82, 90, 95–96

Sporting Books

Beckford, Peter—*Thoughts Upon Hunting,* 1781 and subsequent editions

Berners, Dame Juliana—*The Boke of St. Albans,* 1486

Blome, Richard—*The Gentleman's Recreation,* 1686

Blaine, D. P.—*An Encyclopedia of Rural Sport,* 1840

Brown, Thomas—*Biographical Sketches and Authentic Anecdotes of Dogs,* 1829

Cox, Nicholas—*The Gentleman's Recreation,* 1674 and subsequent editions

Cuming, E. D.—*British Sport, Past and Present,* 1909

Daniel, Rev. W. B.—*Rural Sports,* 1801, 4 vols.

Day, J. W.—*The Dog in Sport,* 1938

du Fouilloux, Jacques—*La Venerie, circa* 1560

Egan, Pierce—*Annals of Sporting,* 1822

Johnson, T. B.—*The Complete Sportsman,* 1817

La Chace du Cerf, circa 1250

Lawrence, John—*The Sportsman's Repository,* 1820

Mills, John—*Mills' Sportman's Library,* 1846

Markham, Gervase—*The Gentleman's Acadamie, circa* 1625
Scott, William Henry—*British Field Sports,* 1818
Skinner, John S.—*The Dog and the Sportsman,* 1845
The Sportsman's Companion, 1791
The Sportsman's Dictionary or the Country Gentleman's Companion, 1735
St. Johns, Charles—*Highland Sports,* 1846
Strutt, Joseph—*The Sports and Pastimes of the British People,* 1801
Surflet, Richard—*Maison Rustique,* 1600
Taplin, W.—*The Sportsman's Cabinet,* 1803, 2 vols.
Thornhill, Richard—*The Shooting Directory,* 1804
Turbeville, George—*The Noble Arte of Venerie or Hunting,* 1575
Twici, G.—*Art de Venerie, circa* 1320
Walsh, J. H. (Stonehenge)—*Manual of Rural Sports,* 1856 and subsequent editions
Wilson, Effingham—*The Field Book,* 1833

Working Terriers

Ackerman, Irving—A Sporting Parson and His Dogs, *American Kennel Gazette,* March 1927 pp 14–18, 102

Bristow-Noble, J. C.—*Working Terriers, Their Management and Training,* 1925

Cameron, L. C. R.—*Otters and Otter Hunting,* 1908

Clapham, Richard—*Fox Hunting on the Lakeland Fells,* 1920. *Foxes, Foxhounds and Fox Hunting,* 1923

Davies, E. W. L.—*Memoir of the Rev. John Russell,* 1878 and 1902

Day, J. W.—*The Dog In Sport,* 1938

de Broke, W.—*Hunting the Fox,* 1921

Free, Roger—*Beagle and Terrier,* 1946

King, H. H.—*Working Terriers, Badgers and Badger Digging,* (no date)

Lloyd, Freeman—*American Kennel Gazette:* Some Dogs I Knew In My Youth, June 1929 pp 20–24, 127–128. What Terriers Are Used For, Nov. 1930 pp 28–31, 131; Dec. 1930 pp 47–49, 164

Lucas, Capt. Jocelyn—*Hunt and Working Terriers,* 1931. *The Spectator* (Eng.) March 18, 1949 p 354

Miller, Warren—*Airedale, Setter and Hound,* 1916

O'Conor, Pierce—*Sporting Terriers,* 1925

Oorang Comments—Catalogue of Oorang Kennels, *circa* 1920–1922

Popular North Country Terriers, *Country Life* (London) 1916 pp 389 *et seq.*

Russell, Dan—*Working Terriers,* 1948

Serrell, Alys F.—*With Hound and Terrier in the Field,* 1904

Smith, A. Croxton—*Hounds and Dogs,* Lonsdale Library, 1932

Webb, J. Watson—The Shelburne Terrier, *The Sportsman,* July 1927. A vignette on the life and activities of Mr. Webb will be found in *Country Life in America,* Nov. 1934 pp 69–71, 96

227

General Terrier

Barton, F. T.—*Terriers, Their Points and Management,* 1907

Bristow-Noble, J. C.—*Working Terriers, Their Management and Training,* 1925

Cox, Harding—*Dogs,* by Well Known Authorities, 1906

De Zutter, Micheline—How To Keep Terriers Fit, *American Kennel Gazette,* April 1932 pp 19, 122

Gray, D. J. Thomson—*The Dogs of Scotland,* 1887 and 1891

James, Ed.—*Terrier Dogs,* 1873

Lee, Rawdon—*Modern Dogs,* Terrier Volume, 1894 and 1896: History and Description of Modern Dogs of Great Britain and Ireland, 1896

Lloyd, Freeman—*American Kennel Gazette:* Some Terriers of Other Times, Nov. 1926 pp 33–37, 134; Scottish Dogs in Song and Story, June 1928 pp 14–18; May 1928 pp 21–24, 59; April 1928 pp 23–26, 114; The Bonnie Terriers of Scotland, Nov. 1932 pp 22, 26, 73; Jan. 1933 pp 24–28; Mar. 1933 pp 12–16; Dog Breeds of The World, Mar. 1939 pp 12–16, 108; Nov. 1938 pp 10–14, 192; July 1939 pp 10–14, 187. *National Geographic Magazine,* Feb. 1936 pp 459–480, Man's Oldest Ally.

Lucas, Capt. Jocelyn—*Hunt and Working Terrier,* 1931

Matheson, Darley—*Terriers,* 1922

Maxtee, J.—*British Terriers,* 1909, 2 vols.

O'Conor, Pierce—*Sporting Terriers,* 1925

Russell, Dan—*Working Terriers,* 1948

Smith, A. Croxton—*Terriers, Their Training, Working and Management,* 1937. *Hounds and Dogs,* Lonsdale Library, 1932

Terriers, The Breeds and Standards as Recognized by *The American Kennel Club,* 1935.

Genetics, Anatomy and Movement

Burns, Marca—*The Genetics of the Dog,* 1952

Gray, James—*How Animals Move,* 1953

Lyon, McDowell—*The Dog In Action,* 1950, 1964

Meyer, Enno—Your Dog Has Many Gaits, *American Kennel Gazette,* Sept. 1932 pp 12–14

Paramoure, Anne F.—*Breeding and Genetics of the Dog,* 1959

Whitney, Dr. L. F.—*The Basis of Breeding,* 1928. *How To Breed Dogs,* Rev. ed. 1948

Airedale Terriers

Aspinall, J. L. E.—*The Airedale Terrier,* (no date)

Baker, W. E.—*The Airedale Terrier Standard Simplified,* 1921

Bowen, Aylwin—*Airedales,* (no date)

Bruette, Dr. W. A.—*The Airedale,* (no date)

Buckley, Holland—Chapter on Airedales in *Dogs by Well Known Authorities*, 1906. *The Airedale Terrier*, 1913

Edwards, Gladys—*The Complete Airedale*, 1962

Haynes, William—*The Airedale*, 1911

Hayes, I. E.—*The Airedale Terrier*, 1960

Hockwalt, A. F.—*The Airedale for Work and Show*, 1921

Johns, Rowland—*Our Friend the Airedale*, 1933

Jones, A. F.—*American Kennel Gazette:* A Long Trail to Airedales (Kennels of Fred H. Hoe), June 1933 pp 7–11, 127; An Airedale Loyalty Founded Shelterock's Fame, Jan. 1934 pp 5–9, 120; An Airedale Made Stanric, Dec. 1939 pp 41–45, 201

Jowett, F. M.—*The Complete Airedale*, 1913

Lingo and Lytle—*Your Airedale*, 1917

Lloyd, Freeman—*American Kennel Gazette:* Dog Breeds of the World, Nov. 1937 pp 16–20, 180; Jan. 1938 pp 14–18, 174; Feb. 1938 pp 18–22; Mar. 1938 pp 22–26, 115; April 1938 pp 14–18, 125

Miller, Warren—*Airedale, Setter and Hound*, 1916

Oorang Comments—Various catalogues *circa* 1920–1922

Palmer, R. M.—*All About the Airedale*, 1911

Phillips, W. J.—*The Modern Airedale*, 1921

Saunders, James—*The Modern Airedale*, 1929

Smith, A. Croxton—The Old Waterside Terrier, *Country Life* (London), Oct 21, 1922 pp 502–503

Strebeigh, Barbara—*The Pet Airedale Terrier*, 1963

Australian Terriers

Australian Terrier (The Show), pamphlet of 21 pages, 1945

Australian Terrier Club of America pamphlet *circa* 1960

Beilby, Walter—*The Dog in Australasia*, 1897

Daly, McDonald—*Odd Dogs*, 1955

Davies, Idris—Chapter in *The Book of the Dog*, Vesey-Fitzgerald, 1948

Smith, A. Croxton—*About Our Dogs*, 1931

Bedlington Terriers

Hutchinson, Walter—*Hutchinson's Dog Encyclopedia*, Vol. 1 pp 114–124, 1932

Jones, A. F.—How a Bedlington Started It All, *American Kennel Gazette*, June 1927 pp 9–13, 118

Lee, Rawdon—*Modern Dogs*, Terrier Vol. pp 173–194, 1894

The Natural Bedlington, *Country Life* (London) 1916 p 492 *et seq*

Noble, Eugene—Bedlington Terriers Once Known As Gypsy Dogs, *American Kennel Gazette*, June 1936 pp 22–24, 163

Redmarshall—*A List of Leading Bedlington Terriers*, 1932 and 1935

Warnes, Harold—Chapter on Bedlingtons in *Dogs by Well Known Authorities*, 1906

Border Terriers

Border Terrier Club of America Breed Booklets, 1954, 1958, 1962

Horn, Montagu H.—*The Border Terrier,* (no date)

Juteopolis—The Border Terrier, *Our Dogs* (Eng.) Dec. 10, 1909

Lazonby, T.—*Border Lines,* 1948

Lee, Rawdon—*Modern Dogs,* Terrier Vol. pp 395–401, 1894

Lucas, Capt. Jocelyn—*Pedigree Dog Breeding,* pp 86–91, 1925. Hunt and Working Terriers, pp 137–143, 173–177, 1931

Marples, Theo.—*Show Dogs,* 3rd ed. pp 143–145, (no date)

Morris—The Border Terrier, *Our Dogs* (Eng.) Dec. 1916

Russell, Dan—*Working Terriers,* 1948

Smith, A. Croxton—Hounds and Dogs, pp 139–143, 1932. Terriers, Their Training, Working and Management, pp 34–38, 1937; The Little Warrior from the Border Country, *Country Life* (London) Nov. 18, 1922 pp 636–638

Bull Terriers

Adlam, Gladys M.—*Forty Years of Bull Terriers,* 1952

Armitage, George—*Thirty Years With Fighting Dogs,* 1935

Ash, Edward—The Modern Bull Terrier Is One of the Most Remarkable of All Pure-Bred Dogs, *American Kennel Gazette,* Feb. 1937 pp 23–26, 96

Briggs, L. Cabot—*Bull Terriers, The Biography of the Breed,* 1940

Brown, Dr. John—*Rab and His Friends,* 1862

Bull Terrier Club of America Yearbooks, various years

Bull Terriers of Today, Bull Terrier Club of America, 1951

Butler—*Dogography,* 1856

Colby, Joseph—*The American Pit Bull Terrier,* (no date)

Davis, Richard Harding—*The Bar Sinister,* 1903

de Fonblanque, Robert—Chapter on Bull Terriers in *Dogs by Well Known Authorities,* 1906

Eberhart, Ernest—*The Complete Bull Terrier,* 1959

Ewart and Decies—The Miniature Bull Terrier, chapter on variety in *Dogs by Well Known Authorities,* 1906

Ford, Fred W.—The White 'Un Is a Good 'Un, *American Kennel Gazette,* May 1928 pp 26–27

Fox, R. K.—*The Dog Pit,* 1890

Haynes, William—*The Bull Terrier,* 1912

Heaney, Rev. Frank—Give a Dog a Bad Name, *American Kennel Gazette,* June 1925 pp 30–32, 89

Hogarth, T. W.—*The Bull Terrier,* (no date)

Hollander, V. C.—*Bull Terriers,* 1951

Johns, Rowland—*Our Friend The Bull Terrier,* 1934

Jones, A. F.—White Cavaliers of Coolyn Hill Help Lead Breed Again to Fame, *American Kennel Gazette,* March 1934 pp 7–12, 106

Meyer, Enno—Here Is The Normal Bull Terrier, *American Kennel Gazette,* Jan. 1932 pp 17–19

Montgomery, Dr. E. S.—*The Bull Terrier*, 1946

Smith, A. Croxton—A Prince Among Dogs, *Country Life* (London) March 11, 1939 pp 262–263

Cairn Terriers

Beynon, J. W. H.—*The Popular Cairn, circa* 1947

The Cairn Terrier, *Dog Lover's Library,* (no date)

Cairn Terrier Club (Eng.) Yearbook, various editions

Gabriel, Dorothy—*The Scottish Terrier,* includes chapter on Cairn Terriers by Kate L. Stephens, (no date)

Gray, D. J. Thomson—*The Dogs of Scotland,* 1887 and 1893

Johns, Rowland—*Our Friend The Cairn,* 1932

Jones, A. F.—*American Kennel Gazette:* How a Sky-Line Kennel Makes Good (Tapscot), Aug. 1928 pp 9–13, 94; How Cairmore Blazed a Trail, April 1929 pp 9–14, 104; Tapscot Moves To An Ideal Home, June 1930 pp 9–14, 55; Cairndania Wants Its Finest Dogs of the Show Ring to be True Pals, Nov. 1936 pp 18–22, 175; Pinefair Believes That Its Cockers and Cairns Should Create Happiness, May 1938 pp 24–28, 179; Noted Cairndania Danes and Cairns Have New Home, May 1939 pp 17–21, 179.

Macpherson, C. Brewster—Cairns Are Working Terriers, *American Kennel Gazette,* June 1933 pp 24–27, 123

Official Book of the Cairn Terrier Club of America (Yearbook), various years

Rogers, Alice and Corrine S. W. Ward—Why We Needed a New Standard For The Cairn, *American Kennel Gazette,* Oct. 1934 pp 17–21, 152

Rogers, Mrs. Byron—*Cairn and Sealyham Terriers,* 1922

Ross, Florence M.—*The Cairn Terrier, circa* 1925

Whitehead, H. F.—*Cairn Terriers,* 1959

Dandie Dinmont Terriers

Blagg, E. W. H.—Chapter on the Dandie in *Dogs by Well Known Authorities,* 1906

Cook, Charles—*The Dandie Dinmont Terrier,* 1885

Dandie Doings, various issues published by the Dandie Dinmont Terrier Club of America

Gordon, John F.—*The Dandie Dinmont Terrier,* 1959

Jones, A. F.—Gay Lea Sees the Dandie Dinmont Terrier Gaining a Justified Popularity, *American Kennel Gazette,* May 1937 pp 14–18, 169

Lee, Rawdon—*Modern Dogs* (Terrier Vol.) pp 269–300, 1894

Popular Dogs, The Dandie Dinmont Club of America, 30 Years of Progress, Sept. 1962

Smith, A. Croxton—*Terriers, Their Training, Working and Management,* 1937

Williams—*The Dandie Dinmont Terrier,* (no date)

Fox Terriers

Ackerman, Irving—*The Wire-Haired Fox Terrier*, 1927. *The Complete Fox Terrier*, 1938. *American Kennel Gazette:* One More of the Old Guard Goes (On the death of Francis Redmond), Sept. 1927 pp 14–18, 114; Oct. 1927 pp 32–35, 129; The Meersbrook Dynasty, Mar. 1928 pp 29–32; Apr. 1928 pp 15–17, 84; It Was Never Decided, Sept. 1928 pp 27–28, 70; Old Tip, The "Adam" of his Breed, Nov. 1928 pp 14–16, 124; Dog Battles Outside Ring, Dec. 1928 pp 38–40, 177; From Old Tip To Simon, Aug. 1929 pp 29–31, 98; Builders of the Wire Fox Terrier, Oct. 1929 pp 24–27, 135; Carrying Coals to Newcastle, Nov. 1929 pp 31–32, 63; The Story of Ch. Short Circuit, Nov. 1930 pp 22–23, 124; The Story of Talavera Simon, Aug. 1930 pp 14–16, 60; Skeleton of Belgrave Joe Exhibited at Kennel Club, Apr. 1939 pp 10–12

American Fox Terrier Club Yearbooks, various years, particularly 1934

Beak, L. G.—*Wire Fox Terriers*, 1960

Baker, M.—The Last Word in Practicality (Lewspen Kennels), *American Kennel Gazette*, Jan. 1925 pp 18–21, 141

Breese, Vinton—Two Kennels (Catawba and Wissaboo), *Country Life in America*, Sept. 1939 pp 32, 76–77

Bruce, Rev. Rosslyn—*Fox Terrier Breeding*, 1931; *The Popular Fox Terrier*, 1950

Castle, Sidney—*Monograph on the Fox Terrier*, with Astley and Dalziel, 1907. Same with Marples and Hughes, (no date). *Breeding Fox Terriers*, 1927

Country Life (London), 1910, p 852 and following; 1913 p 810 and following. Show Terriers at Work, 1911 pp 152–153; 538–540

Dalziel, Hugh—The Fox Terrier, 1889; The Fox Terrier Stud Book, 1889 and four following volumes

Dalziel with J. Maxtee—The Fox Terrier, 1899

The Fox Terrier Club Jubilee Yearbook, 1926

Johns, Rowland—*Our Friend the Fox Terrier*, 1933

Jones, A. F.—*American Kennel Gazette:* How Cleanliness is a Kennel God (Wildoaks Kennels) Nov. 1925 pp 33–37, 230; Tanglewold Has Proved a Theory (Smooths) Apr. 1926 pp 7–11, 112; Whence Came Such Fame (Welwire Kennels) Dec. 1926 pp 9–13, 155; Where Terriers Are Glorified (Annadale Kennels) July 1927 pp 9–13, 52; Roughwood Aims For Personality, March 1928 pp 9–13, 78; Why Croydon Produces Such Wires, Feb. 1929 pp 9–13; White Eagle Is Soaring High, Aug. 1931 pp 9–12, 112; How Wildoaks Earns Such Fame, Oct. 1931 pp 9–13, 117; Show Honors an Incident in Blarney's Breeding Plans, Dec. 1933 pp 9–14, 162; Glynhir Breeds Fox Terriers, Nov. 1937 pp 26–30; Why Smooths Rule Wissaboo, Dec. 1937 pp 28–32, 217; Foxspan Sporting Atmosphere Fosters Worthiest Breeding, Feb. 1942 pp 30–33; Andelys Finds Best Quality Follows Long Planning, March 1942 pp 32–36, also see Nov. 1938 *Gazette* pp 23–27, 194 for further information on this kennel

Haynes, William—*The Fox Terrier*, 1927

Harrison, T. H.—*Breeding Show Fox Terriers*, 1897

Holdsworth, M. J.—*The Smooth Fox Terrier*, 1950

Lee, Rawdon—*The Fox Terrier*, 4 editions 1889–1902

McComb, Dr. R. Payne—The Wire Haired Fox Terrier, 1933 (manuscript only)

Naylor, L. E.—*The Modern Fox Terrier*, 1933

Pardoe, J. H.—*Fox Terriers*, 1949

Popular Dogs—Special Fox Terrier Issue, December 1946

Reynolds, Don—*Champion of Champions*, 1950 (A biography of Nornay Saddler)

Rolf, A. F.—Fox Terrier Pedigree Lines (Smooths) Larro Research study, manuscript only

Silvernail, Evelyn—*The Complete Fox Terrier*, 1961

Skelly, George—*All About Fox Terriers*, 1948, 1962

Skinner, Rev. A. J.—*The Popular Fox Terrier*, 1925

Spring, James W.—A Fox Terrier 142 Years Ago, *Country Life In America*, March 1939 pp 38–39, 86–87, 106

Wood, E. Lindley—*Smooth Fox Terriers*, 1960

Irish Terriers

Denby, Mrs. Garvin—That Loyal Irish Gentleman, *American Kennel Gazette*, May 1927 pp 22–25

Green, James E.—*The Scottish and The Irish Terrier*, 1894

Haynes, William—*Scottish and Irish Terriers*, 1925

Johns, Rowland—*Our Friends the Irish and Kerry Blue Terriers*, 1935

Jones, A. F.—*American Kennel Gazette:* Where Terriers Are Glorified (Annadale Kennels) July 1927 pp 9–12, 52; Wawapek Aids Nature's Work, July 1928 pp 9–13; Experience (re John Mulcahy) Sept. 1936 pp 8–12

Jones, E. Howard—*Irish Terriers*, 1959

Jowett, F. M.—*The Irish Terrier*, 1912

Lee, Rawdon—*Modern Dogs* (Terrier Vol.) pp 195–230, 1894

Maxtee, J.—*Scotch and Irish Terriers*, 1923

Montgomery, Dr. E. S.—*The Complete Irish Terrier*, 1958

Ramsay-Ramsay, T.—Chapter on Irish Terriers in *Dogs by Well Known Authorities*, 1906

Thorndike, J. R.—*The Irish Terrier Standard Simplified*, 1925

Kerry Blue Terriers

Clarke, Egerton—*The Popular Kerry Blue Terrier*, 1927

Green, James E.—*The Scottish and the Irish Terrier*, 1894

Handy, Violet E.—*The Modern Kerry Blue Terrier*, *circa* 1931

Johns, Rowland—*Our Friends The Irish and Kerry Blue Terriers*, 1935

Jones, A. F.—*American Kennel Gazette:* Oakcrest Kennels Are True Blue, Sept. 1930 pp 9–13, 108; Why Blue Leader Sets The Pace, May 1931 pp 9–14, 115

Maxtee, J.—*Scotch and Irish Terriers*, 1923

Popular Dogs, Features the Kerry Blue in the June 1952 issue pp 16–30

Montgomery, Dr. E. S.—*The Complete Kerry Blue Terrier*, 1950

Rathborne—*The Kerry Blue*, 1927

United States Kerry Blue Terrier Club Yearbooks, various issues

Lakeland Terriers

Ash, E. C.—Lakeland Terrier, *American Kennel Gazette*, Aug. 1936

Clapham, Richard—*Fox Hunting on the Lakeland Fells*, 1920. *Foxes, Foxhounds and Fox Hunting*, 1923

Hutchinson, Walter—*Hutchinson's Dog Encyclopedia* pp 1121–1132, 1935
Lloyd, Freeman—Dog Breeds of the World, *American Kennel Gazette,* July 1938 pp 14–18, 202
Lucas, Capt. Jocelyn—*Hunt and Working Terriers,* 1931
Smith, A. Croxton—*Terriers, Their Training, Working and Management,* 1937
Vesey-Fitzgerald, Brian—*The Book of the Dog,* 1948

Manchester Terriers

Dean, C. S.—The Black and Tan Terrier, chapter in *Dogs by Well Known Authorities,* 1906
Dempsey, Dixie—*The Complete Manchester Terrier (Toy),* 1950
Lee, Rawdon—*Modern Dogs* (Terrier Vol.) pp 69–90, 1894
Lloyd, Freeman—Manchester Terriers, *American Kennel Gazette,* May 1933 pp 14–18; June 1933 pp 12–16, 123
Mack, Janet—*Pet Manchester,* 1956
Meyer, Enno—*Toy Manchester Terriers, Ideals and Faults,* 1939

Norwich Terriers

Harkness, John Ross—Undergraduates at Cambridge Made the Norwich Terrier a Fad More Than a Half a Century Ago, *American Kennel Gazette,* March 1936 pp 8–9, 92
Hutchinson, Walter—*Hutchinson's Dog Encyclopedia,* Vol. 2 pp 1256–1258, 1932
Lloyd, J. Ivester—The Ears of An Earth Dog, *The Field,* June 26, 1958
Lucas, Capt. Jocelyn—*Hunt and Working Terriers,* 1931
Monckton, Sheila—*The Norwich Terrier,* 1962
Norwich Terrier News, various issues, published by the Norwich Terrier Club of America
Popular Dogs, Sept. 1962 issue features the breed

Miniature Schnauzers

Fitzgerald, Anne—*The Schnauzer Book,* 1932. *The Miniature Schnauzer,* 1935
Jones, A. F.—*American Kennel Gazette,* How Mardale Became Important, April 1931 pp 9–13, 120; How Marienhof Shaped An Ideal, June 1934 pp 7–12, 153–157
Paramoure, A. F.—*The Complete Miniature Schnauzer,* 1959
Scwabacher, Joseph—*History of the Schnauzer and Miniature Schnauzer,* 1930
Slattery, Marie—*Pet Miniature Schnauzer*

Scottish Terriers

Ash, E. C.—*The Scottish Terrier,* 1936
Bruette, Dr. William—*The Scottish Terrier,* 1934

Barrie, Caswell—The New Scottish Terrier Standard, *American Kennel Gazette* March 1925 pp 22, 151

Buckley, Holland—*The Scottish Terrier*, 1913

Caspersz, D. S.—*Scottish Terrier Pedigrees*, 1930 with supplements. What the Scottie Will Become, *American Kennel Gazette*, July 1931 pp 25–27, 119. *The Scottish Terrier*, 1938; *The Scottish Terrier* (Foyles) 1958; *The Popular Scottish Terrier*, 1962

Davies, C. J.—*The Scottish Terrier*, 1906

Deu, Edna et al—Stars In the Doghouse (Deephaven Kennels) *Country Life in America*, April 1939 pp 55, 109–110

Ewing, Dr. Fayette—*The Book of the Scottish Terrier*, 1932 and subsequent editions

Gabriel, Dorothy—*The Scottish Terrier*, (no date)

Gray, D. J. Thomson (Whinstone)—*The Dogs of Scotland*, 1887 and 1891

Green, James E.—*The Scottish Terrier and the Irish Terrier*, 1894

Haynes, William—*Scottish and Irish Terriers*, 1925

Johns, Rowland—*Our Friend The Scottish Terrier*, 1933

Jones, A. F.—*American Kennel Gazette:* Ballantrae's Reasons For Success, March 1927 pp 13–17, 71; Hillwood Turns To The Scottie, Feb. 1932 pp 9–13; Bred By Science and Humanity (Sporran Kennels) July 1932 pp 7–11, 124; Vigal Is Building Slowly, Dec. 1932 pp 24–28, 157; A Kennel Without a Fault (Relgalf Kennels) July 1934 pp 7–11, 173; Why Braw Bricht's Aim Is To Breed Scotties of Highest Quality, Feb. 1936 pp 12–15, 99; Companionship, The Standard For Scotties of Miss Hull (Glenafton) March 1936 pp 11–14, 79; Raising Scotties That Win Is Greatest Enjoyment to Owners of Barberry Knowe, July 1936 pp 13–16, 152; Scotties Started Relgalf on Its Way to Fame, Aug. 1938 pp 27–31

Kirk, Dr. Alan—*American Scottish Terrier Champions' Pedigrees*, 1962

Maxtee, J.—*Scotch and Irish Terriers*, 1923

McCandlish, W. L.—Chapter on Scotties in *Dogs by Well Known Authorities*, 1906. *The Scottish Terrier*, 1909

Megargee, Edwin S.—The Ideal Scottish Terrier, *American Kennel Gazette*, Jan. 1933 pp 17–20, 136

Robertson, James—*Historical Sketches of the Scottish Terrier*, 1899

Van Dine, S. S. Crashing the Dog Breeding Gate, *American Kennel Gazette*, Dec. 1930 pp 29–32, 166

Sealyham Terriers

Chenuz, F. J.—*Sealyhams*, 1956; *Sealyham Terriers*, 1960

Davies, Frank E.—What One Pro Did For the Sealyham, *American Kennel Gazette*, June 1927 pp 44–45, 114

Johns, Rowland—*Our Friend the Sealyham Terrier*, 1934

Jones, A. F.—*American Kennel Gazette:* Perfection All The Name Implies (Pinegrade Kennels) May 1927 pp 9–13, 114; How Ideas Have Made Shelterfield, May 1928 pp 9–13, 119; Why Rensal's Sealys Bear Renown, Dec. 1928 pp 33–37, 158; Earnestness Is Elkat's Secret, Nov. 1930 pp 9–13, 120; A British Breed Goes American (Cresheim Kennels) May 1932 pp 9–13, 118; Why Croglin Scores With Sealyhams, March 1938 pp 10–14, 118

Lloyd Freeman—Dog Breeds of the World, *American Kennel Gazette,* July 1934 pp 14–18, 86; Aug. 1934 pp 20–24, 157; Oct. 1934 pp 12–13, 163; Nov. 1934 pp 24–28, 175

Lucas, Capt. Jocelyn—*The Sealyham Terrier, circa* 1922. *The New Book of The Sealyham,* 1929

Morgan, W. R. V.—Chapter on the Sealyham in *The Fox Terrier* by Dalziel, (no date)

Rogers, Mrs. Byron—*Cairn and Sealyham Terriers,* 1922

Yearbooks of the American Sealyham Terrier Club, various editions

Skye Terriers

Alexander, Sir Claude—Chapter on Skyes in *Dogs by Well Known Authorities,* 1906

Country Life (London), The Skye Terrier, March 20, 1909 pp 412–413

Jones, A. F.—Iradell Brings Back the Skye, *American Kennel Gazette,* Oct. 1938 pp 24–28, 147

Miles, Lady Marcia—*The Skye Terrier, circa* 1951

Montgomery, Dr. E. S.—*The Complete Skye Terrier,* 1962

Nicholas, Anna K.—*The Skye Terrier,* 1960

Wilmer, Agnes—*The Skye Terrier,* (no date)

Staffordshire Terriers

Armitage, George C.—*Thirty Years With Fighting Dogs,* 1935

Betts, Allan W.—*Meet the Staffordshire Terrier, Dogdom,* May 1940

Colby, Joseph L.—*The American Pit Bull Terrier,* (no date)

Denlinger, Milo G.—*The Complete Pit Bull or Staffordshire Terrier,* 1948

The Dog Fancier, Battle Creek, Mich., all issues

Dunn, Joseph—*The Staffordshire Bull Terrier,* 1951

Gordon, John F.—*The Staffordshire Bull Terrier,* 1951

Hollander, V. C.—*Staffordshire Bull Terriers,* 1952

James, Ed.—*Terrier Dogs,* 1873

Orsmby, Clifford A.—*The Staffordshire Terrier,* 1956

The Pit Bull Fancier, Caldwell, Kansas, all issues

Pit News, Tulsa, Okla., all issues

Welsh Terriers

Glynn, Walter S.—Chapter on the Welsh in *Dogs by Well Known Authorities,* 1906

Jones, A. F.—Where Terriers Are Glorified (Annadale Kennels), *American Kennel Gazette,* July 1927 pp 9–13, 155

Lloyd, Freeman—Dog Breeds of the World, *American Kennel Gazette*, Aug. 1927, pp 12–16, 150; Sept. 1937 pp 20–24, 127; Oct. 1937 pp 16–20, 138

Maxtee, J.—*English and Welsh Terriers*, (no date)

Thomas, I. M.—*The Welsh Terrier Handbook*, 1959

Welsh Terrier Club of America Yearbooks, all issues

West Highland White Terriers

Benyon, J. W. H.—*The Popular Cairn Terrier*, 1930

Blochin, Elizabeth—White Earth Dogges, *Kennel and Bench* (Canada) Sept. 1938 pp 16–17

Buckley, Holland—*The West Highland White Terrier*, 1911

Cameron, L. C. R.—*Otters and Otter Hunting*, 1908 pp 42–43

Country Life (London)—The Terriers of Poltalloch, May 11, 1901 pp 588–590; West Highland White Terriers, Aug. 14, 1909 p 242; Cairn Terriers, Sept. 23, 1911 pp 454–456; The Poltalloch White Terriers, Nov. 5, 1921 pp 570–572; The Terriers of Scotland, Sept. 2, 1922 pp 267–268; The Ever-Ready West Highland White Terrier, Nov. 5, 1959 p 753

Gabriel, Dorothy—*Scotch Terriers* pp 61–63, (no date)

Gray, D. J. Thomson (Whinstone)—*The Dogs of Scotland*, 1887 and 1891

Johns, Rowland—*Our Friend the West Highland*, 1935

Jones, A. F.—*American Kennel Gazette:* Whom Glory Cannot Well Forget (Nishkenon Kennels) Nov. 1926 pp 28–32; Rosstor, Rolling Stone of Dogdom, Feb. 1927 pp 9–13, 84–85; Bonnie Bairns of Edgerstoune, Nov. 1931 pp 9–13, 122–124; Why Edgerstoune Succeeds, Dec. 1934 pp 25–29, 196

Lloyd, Freeman—Dogs and Sport In Scotland, *American Kennel Gazette*, Feb. 1939 pp 12–15

Malcolm, Col. E. D.—Chapter on the Westie in *Dogs by Well Known Authorities*, 1906

Marvin, John T.—*The Complete West Highland White Terrier*, 1961

Pacey, May—*West Highland White Terriers*, 1963

Popular Dogs, September 1952 issue features the Westie

Powlett, B. W.—Chapter on the Westie in *McCandlish's Scottish and West Highland White Terriers*, 1909

Ross, Florence M.—*The Cairn Terrier* pp 39–48, 1925

Appendix

Aberdeen Terrier—See Scottish Terrier
Airedale Terrier—See chapter on breed
American Pit Bull Terrier—See Staffordshire Terrier
Aussie—See Australian Terrier
Australian Terrier—See chapter on breed
Australian Rough Terrier—See Australian Terrier
Bedlington Terrier—See chapter on breed
Bingley Terrier—See Airedale Terrier
Black and Tan Terrier—See Manchester Terrier
Blue Paul Terrier—See Bull Terrier
Blue Poll Terrier—See Bull Terrier
Blue Tan Terrier—See Halifax and Yorkshire
Border Terrier—See chapter on breed
Bull and Terrier Dog—See Bull Terrier
Bull Terrier—See chapter on breed
Cairn Terrier—See chapter on breed
Catcleugh Terrier—See Dandie Dinmont Terrier
Charlie's Hope Terrier—See Dandie Dinmont Terrier
Cheshire Terrier—Fox Terriers from the once famous Cheshire Kennels. See also
    Working Terriers
Clydesdale Terrier—See Skye Terrier
Dandie Dinmont Terrier—See chapter on breed
Daredevil—See Irish Terrier
Dartmoor Terrier—See Fox Terrier, also Working Terriers
Deutsche Jagdeterrier—See chapter on Working Terriers
Die-Hard—See Scottish Terrier
Elterwater Terrier—See Working Terriers; also Border Terrier
English Terrier—See early history of English breeds (Generic name)
Fancy Skye Terrier—See Skye Terrier

238

Fell Terrier—See Lakeland Terrier
Fox Terrier—See chapter on breed
Glasgow Terrier—See Skye Terrier
Glen of Imaal Terrier—See Working Terriers
Halifax Blue Tan—Now known as Yorkshire Terrier classed as Toy
Haute-Agooue Terrier—See Niam Niam
Highland Terrier—Generic name for Cairn, Skye, Scottish and West Highland
    White
Hindlee Terrier—See Dandie Dinmont Terrier
Isle of Skye Terrier—See Skye Terrier
Irish Blue Terrier—See Kerry Blue Terrier
Jack Russell Terrier—See Working Terriers
Jones Terrier—See Norwich Terrier, also Working Terriers
Kerry Blue Terrier—See chapter on breed
Lakeland Terrier—See chapter on breed
Manchester Terrier—See chapter on breed
Mick—See Irish Terrier
Miniature Schnauzer—See chapter on breed
Mustard and Pepper Terrier—See Dandie Dinmont Terrier
Niam Niam—See Working Terriers
Northern Counties Fox Terrier—See Bedlington Terrier
Norfolk Terrier—See Norwich Terrier, also Working Terriers
Norwich Terrier—See chapter on breed
Nyam Nyam—See Niam Niam
Old English Wire-Haired Black and Tan Terrier—See Welsh Terrier
Otter Terrier—See Dandie Dinmont Terrier
Paisley Terrier—See Skye Terrier
Patterdale Terrier—See Lakeland Terrier
Pembrokeshire Terrier—See Sealyham Terrier
Pit Bull Terrier—See Staffordshire Terrier
Pittenweem Terrier—See Working Terriers, also West Highland White Terrier
Poltalloch Terrier—See West Highland White Terrier
Red Smut Terrier—See Working Terriers, also Bull Terrier
Reedwater Terrier—See Border Terrier
Rodberry Terrier—See Bedlington Terrier
Roseneath Terrier—See West Highland White Terrier
Rothburry Terrier—See Bedlington Terrier
Rothbury Terrier—See Bedlington Terrier
Scotch Terrier—Early generic name for Cairn, Westie, Skye, Dandie and Scottish
    Terriers
Scottish Terrier—See chapter on breed
Sealydale Terrier—See Working Terriers
Sealyham Terrier—See chapter on breed
Shelburne Terrier—See Working Terriers
Silky Coated Skye Terrier—See Skye Terrier
Short-Coated Working Skye—See Scottish Terrier
Short-Haired Skye—See Cairn Terrier
Skye Otter Terrier—See Cairn Terrier
Skye Terrier—See chapter on breed
Staffordshire Terrier—See chapter on breed
Tod-Hunter—See Cairn Terrier
Trumpington Terrier—See Norwich Terrier

Ullswater Terrier—See Border Terrier
Waterside Terrier—See Airedale Terrier
Welsh Terrier—See chapter on breed
Westie—See West Highland White Terrier
West Highland White Terrier—See chapter on breed
Wharfedale Terrier—See Airedale Terrier
White English Terrier—now extinct, see early Terriers
Yankee Terrier—See Staffordshire Terrier
Yorkshire Blue Tan—Now known as Yorkshire Terrier; classed as Toy
Yorkshire Terrier—Now a Toy breed
Yorkshire Waterside Terrier—See Airedale Terrier

AKC Recognized Breeds Frequently Known by Alternate Names

Airedale Terrier
  See chapter on breed
  Bingley Terrier
  Waterside Terrier
  Wharfedale Terrier
  Yorkshire Waterside Terrier

Australian Terrier
  See chapter on breed
  Aussie
  Australian Rough Terrier

Bedlington Terrier
  See chapter on breed
  Northern Counties Fox Terrier
  Rodberry Terrier
  Rothburry Terrier
  Rothbury Terrier

Border Terrier
  See chapter on breed
  Elterwater Terrier
  Reedwater Terrier
  Ullswater Terrier

Bull Terrier
  White and Colored Varieties, See chapter on breed
  Blue Paul Terrier
  Blue Poll Terrier
  Bull and Terrier dog
  Redsmut Terrier

Cairn Terrier
  See chapter on breed
  Highland Terrier (early generic name)
  Scotch Terrier (early generic name)
  Short-haired Skye Terrier
  Skye Otter Terrier
  Tod-Hunter

Dandie Dinmont Terrier
  See chapter on breed
  Catcleugh Terrier
  Charlie's Hope Terrier
  Hindlee Terrier

Mustard and Pepper Terrier
Otter Terrier
Scotch Terrier (early generic name)
Fox Terrier
  Wire Haired and Smooth Varieties, See chapter on breed
  Cheshire Terrier
  Dartmoor Terrier
  English Terrier (early generic name)
Irish Terrier
  See chapter on breed
  Daredevil
  Mick
Kerry Blue Terrier
  See chapter on breed
  Irish Blue Terrier
Lakeland Terrier
  See chapter on breed
  Fell Terrier
  Patterdale Terrier
Manchester Terrier
  See chapter on breed
  Black and Tan Terrier
  English Terrier (early generic name)

Miniature Schnauzer
  See chapter on breed
Norwich Terrier
  See chapter on breed
  Jones Terrier
  Norfolk Terrier
  Trumpington Terrier
Scottish Terrier
  See chapter on breed
  Aberdeen Terrier
  Die-hard
  Highland Terrier (early generic name)
  Scotch Terrier (early generic name)
Sealyham Terrier
  See chapter on breed
  Pembrokeshire Terrier
Skye Terrier
  See chapter on breed
  Clydesdale Terrier
  Fancy Skye Terrier
  Glasgow Terrier
  Highland Terrier (early generic name)
  Isle of Skye Terrier
  Paisley Terrier
  Scotch Terrier (early generic name)
  Silky Skye Terrier
Staffordshire Terrier
  See chapter on breed
  American Pit Bull Terrier
  Pit Bull Terrier
  Yankee Terrier

Welsh Terrier
    See chapter on breed
    Old English Wire Haired Black and Tan Terrier
West Highland White Terrier
    See chapter on breed
    Highlander
    Highland Terrier (early generic name)
    Pittenweem Terrier
    Poltalloch Terrier
    Roseneath Terrier
    Scotch Terrier (early generic name)
    Westie
Yorkshire Terrier
    (Now in Toy Group)
    Halifax Blue Tan
    Yorkshire Blue Tan

Pseudonyms

Nineteenth and early twentieth century writers frequently wrote under assumed or fictitious names. The practice was so widespread that it is frequently difficult to determine the authorship of many older works on the subject of dogs and sports. In order to aid in this determination there is listed below the proper name and the pseudonym of many of the better known writers, many of whom have been mentioned and/or quoted in this book.

G. O. Shields	Coquina
Hugh Dalziel	Corsicon
William Henry Herbert	Frank Forester
Dr. T. Pearce	Idestone
Dr. N. Rowe	Mohawk
W. C. Kennerly	Old Dominion
James Watson	Porcupine
Henry H. Soule	Seneca
Dr. E. C. Franklyn	Senex
Arnold Burges	Setter
John Henry Walsh	Stonehenge
T. G. Tucker	T. G. T.
D. J. Thomson Gray	Whinstone